UP AMONG THE PANDIES.

"UP AMONG THE PANDIES."
THE IRON BRIDGE—LUCKNOW.

UP AMONG THE PANDIES:

OR,

A Year's Service in India.

BY

LIEUT. VIVIAN DERING MAJENDIE,

The Naval & Military Press Ltd

Published jointly by

The Naval & Military Press Ltd

In reprinting in facsimile from the original, any imperfections are inevitably reproduced and the quality may fall short of modern type and cartographic standards.

PREFACE.

THE greater part of the following narrative of my personal adventures in India was penned during my sojourn in that country, and the occupation served to pass away very pleasantly some weary hours in camp, when other amusements were impracticable, or unattainable.

When scorching in my tent before Lucknow, and in Oude—in solitary dâk bungalows ; while travelling along the Grand Trunk Road—amid the romantic scenery of the Himalayas—or, in my little cabin on board ship, when rolling homewards across the Atlantic and Indian Oceans, these pages have been my companions. If they only do for my reader what they have done for me, and shorten a long hour or two which might otherwise hang heavy on his hands ; or if they should serve to recal to such of my comrades as may take the trouble to read them some of the scenes mentioned herein, the fatigues or the pleasures of which we shared together, and induce them to carry their thoughts back to some hours spent on picket and on the march, not altogether unhappy ones—spite of their many discomforts—I shall be satisfied, and my main object in publishing these reminiscences will be accomplished.

Some portion of this narrative has already appeared in the pages of "Bentley's Miscellany," and I hope that in this, its more complete and extended form, it may meet with as favourable a reception as it did when figuring in the pages of that magazine.

V. D. M.

BARTONFIELDS, CANTERBURY,
July, 1859.

CONTENTS.

CHAPTER I.

First Tidings of the Mutiny—Preparations for stemming the Storm—"Eastward ho!"—The Voyage—The Cape—Ceylon—Madras . . . . pp. 1—11

CHAPTER II.

The Sunderbunds—Diamond Harbour—Our last Revel aboard —The Hooghly . . . . 12—22

CHAPTER III.

Arrival at Calcutta—Letters from Home—The Chowringhee —The City of Palaces . . . . 23—33

CHAPTER IV.

Mosquitoes—The Disembarkation—Harpies—Sore Trial of Temper—"Puggree" to the Rescue!—A Brief Retrospective review of Puggree's career in my Service—Coolies —Some Reflections incidental to arriving in India,
34—46

CHAPTER V.

Town of Calcutta—Tour of Inspection in a Palkee—Palkee-bearers—A Comparison between them and the genus "Cabby"—"Burning ghât"—Native bazaar—Calcutta Post Office—The heavy, murmuring swell succeeding the Great Storm—Cast-aways saved from the wreck, and thrown up upon the High Shore of Human Charity and Sympathy—A few words about the Sepoys—Indian servants . . . . pp. 47—61

CONTENTS.

CHAPTER VI.

"*Malbrook s'en va-t-en guerre*"—Pursuit of packing under difficulties—Howrah—East Indian Railway—Raneegunge,
pp. 62—70

CHAPTER VII.

Journey by "Bullock-train"—The Fashion of it—A Night in a Cart—Grand Trunk Road—Moving Accidents, 71—86

CHAPTER VIII.

Sasseram—Traces of the Mutineers—Benares—Fort of Allahabad—A Pen-and-ink Sketch from its Walls at Sunset,
87—97

CHAPTER IX.

Allahabad—the native town—Country ride near Allahabad—Perilous railway journey—Railway officials—Kharga,
98—107

CHAPTER X.

First impressions of Cawnpore—"Wheeler's entrenchment"—An every-day scene at Cawnpore—Camp-followers——The remains of the "Slaughter House" and the "Well"—The Assembly Rooms, as they were and as they are—A backward glance at Cawnpore in happier days gone by,
108—120

CHAPTER XI.

A Ride through the Bazaar at Cawnpore—We cross into Oude—The March—Oonao—Morose Remarks about Camels . . . . 121—134

CHAPTER XII.

The Advance upon Lucknow—Scenery and Incidents on the March . . . . 135—139

CHAPTER XIII.

The March to Lucknow (continued)—Nawabgunge—Busserat-gunge—Bunterah—An Alarm—"Stand to your arms"—The Dilkoosha—The First Glimpse of Lucknow,
pp. 140—150

CHAPTER XIV.

Commencement of the Siege of Lucknow—Night March of the Trans-Goomtee column—A pleasant morning scene—The halt for breakfast—Sir James Outram . 151—160

CHAPTER XV.

Pandy's Tactics—Outline of the Plan of Attack on Lucknow—Cavalry Skirmish on the Race-course—Charge of the Bays—Death of Major Percy Smith—A Touch of Roughing it—The Night of March 6th . . 161—172

CHAPTER XVI.

Attack on our Camp—Repulse of the Enemy—Outlying Picket—Advance of March 9th—Jungle Fighting——*Horrida Bella*—Another glimpse of Lucknow,
173—182

CHAPTER XVII.

Fight at the "Yellow Bungalow"—Captain St. George—Sharp Work—A Frightful Scene of Cruelty—Capture of the "Badshah Bagh"—The Ghoorkas—Engagement of March 11th—More Jungle-fighting . . . . 183—196

CHAPTER XVIII.

The Musjid—*En Avant!*—A Large "Bag"—Capture of the Stone Bridge—Loot—Capture of the Iron Bridge—Should Officers be Executioners? . . . . 197—206

CONTENTS.

CHAPTER XIX.

On Picket at the Iron Bridge—"Loot"—"The Kaiserbagh" captured—The Fight in the "Engine House"—Horrors of War—The Little Drummer Boy . . pp. 207—219

CHAPTER XX.

Our Sojourn at the Iron Bridge—Extracts from Journal—A hasty Trial, and a rough Execution—Reflections—Further Successes—Capture of the "Muchee Bhowun" and Stone Bridge—The 16th March . . . . 220—228

CHAPTER XXI.

Scenes in the Streets and about the City—Tragedy and Comedy—A Sketch at Eventide from the Iron Bridge—The Residency—Lucknow is Ours at last—A Legend of the Iron Bridge—Remarks on the Siege of Lucknow, with some criticisms which it is hoped may not be considered presumptuous . . . . 229—241

CHAPTER XXII.

Rides about the Captured City—The "Kaiserbagh"—A Scene of Destruction—The Residency—Alterations and Improvements in the City—The "Great Emanbarra"—A View from its Minarets—Lucknow after the Siege—A stroll up the Choke—Return of its Inhabitants, 242—252

CHAPTER XXIII.

Reaction—Great Heat—Job's Comforters—Cool Contrivances—Languor—Up and Doing again—The Summer Campaign in Oude—The March . . . . . 253—260

CONTENTS. xi

CHAPTER XXIV.

A Day in Camp during the Hot Weather Campaign—The heat—Morning—Noon—Night—A Weary Time—Our Meals—A few Words about Beer—Dress and Appearance of the Troops—I give Vent to my Feelings in a Growl,
pp. 261—276

CHAPTER XXV.

Doondiakera—Night March to Nugger—May 12th—Ravages of Sunstroke and Apoplexy—The Fight at Simaree—Serious Night Alarm and Panic . . . . . 277—287

CHAPTER XXVI.

Great Sickness—The Return March to Lucknow—Sick sent into Hospital at Lucknow—Brutal Conduct of some Sepoys—A Digression on a Subject which has been much discussed—Battle of Nawab-gunge—Summary of the State of Affairs at the beginning of July, 1858 . . . 288—301

CHAPTER XXVII.

Commencement of the Rains—The Camp at Nawab-gunge—Away to Fyzabad—The History of Rajah Maun Singh of Shah-gunge . . . . 302—311

CHAPTER XXVIII.

The March to Fyzabad—The Kupoorthulla Rajah's Troops—Sketches on the March—Derriabad—Outskirts of Fyzabad—We encamp—Maun Singh's Visit to Sir Hope Grant—Maun Singh's Breakfast, and a Few Words about the *Siege* of Shah-gunge—Operations of Brigadier Horsford's Column, and Fight at Sultanpore—Conclusion of Summer Campaign. . . . . 312—324

CONTENTS.

CHAPTER XXIX.

How we spent the Time at Fyzabad—A Day in Camp during the Rains—A Dreary Picture—I start on Sick Leave to the Hills—Horse-carriage Dâk—Cawnpore to Delhi—Visit Futteygurh *en route* . . . . . pp. 325—335

CHAPTER XXX.

Arrival at Delhi: The "City of the Great Mogul"—The "Delhi Hotel"—Scene in the "Chandney Choke"—The "Jumma Musjid"—A Bird's-eye View of Delhi—The Palace—The "Cashmere Gate"—Scene of the Assault,
336—348

CHAPTER XXXI.

Delhi to Umballa—Kalka—Travelling by "Jampan"—The Himalayas—Hurreepore—Scenery by the Way—Simla—How time is passed there—I leave Simla to return to England—Cessation of the Company's Rule in India—The Queen's Proclamation—Farewell to India, and to the Reader . . . . 349—360

UP AMONG THE PANDIES.

CHAPTER I.

First tidings of the Mutiny—Preparations for stemming the Storm—" Eastward ho !"—The voyage out—The Cape—Ceylon—Madras.

Any one who was in England during the summer of 1857 will recollect how, one morning, on taking up the newspaper, and looking carelessly through its closely printed sheets—scanning the leading articles, glancing at the play-bills, or getting muddled over the Money Market and City Intelligence—our eyes were arrested by the announcement of the mutiny of a native regiment in India. At first, in our ignorance of, perhaps inattention to, the affairs of that country, we put the paper down, munched our muffin unconcernedly, continued our breakfast, and thought but little of the matter. Another mail, another mutiny! Mail succeeded mail, and still the weary burden was the same, until we awoke with a start from our dream of fancied security, examined the map of Hindostan very attentively, and came to the dreadful conclusion that the native army of Bengal had risen *en masse*, and that India was in flames! From home to home, from town to village, the grievous tidings flew throughout the land. Newspapers teemed with the dreadful news;

telegraph-offices were beset with eager, breathless crowds, anxious to gain further information; the funds fell; the ministers shook their heads (in the vain hope of finding something in them); while by night in London did the news-criers ply a busy trade, as in street, and square, and squalid lane they shrieked the sought-after accounts, and disposed of the eagerly-bought second editions.

Then followed those frightful and heart-rending details which struck all Europe with horror, blanched every lip, and made the blood of England to run cold. Awe-stricken, we read in each succeeding paper how darling friends whom we had parted from, it might be, a few short months before, or whom we had hoped ere long to greet and welcome back to their native land, had fallen victims to Sepoy cruelty. Mail after mail in sickening confirmation of the truth of the sad story—mail after mail told how some "nearer one still, and a dearer one yet than all other," had been immolated on the shrine of black-hearted treachery and Asiatic cruelty, till one by one the bereaved and heart-broken mourner found that all he ever loved or cared for had been snatched from him, and had passed away for ever. It was a bitter occupation for the weeping mother, that attempt to realize that her darling boy, who but last year had left England in all the pride and excitement of the commencement of a soldier's career, was now no more; it was strange and horrible to read over that last letter—now so cherished,—and to see the absence of suspicion expressed therein, or how, hoping against hope, he had proudly vaunted the staunchness and fidelity of those very men who, perchance, ere the ink was dry, had lopped off the hand that wrote it. It was hard to believe, and harder still to realize, the dreadful indignities and sufferings to which tender women and innocent children had been exposed. It was a dreary, dreary task that waiting for the next mail, in the fond expectation that it would point out some bright spot in this dark horizon. But no! there was no pause, no respite; thick as hail did the blows fall, and the eagerly looked-for next mail brought but a repetition and extension of those horrors, so frightful that in many cases the narrators dared not describe them—those cruelties and savage outrages which threw all past atrocities far back into the shade, and compared with which the hitherto unequalled "*noyades*" and "*mitraillades*" of the Reign of Terror, or the inhuman tortures practised by a Marat or a Robespierre, were as nothing; till one rose from the perusal scared and terrified, and cried involuntarily, "Is not this all a dream?" But it was no dream; it was a stern and awful reality, a crisis to meet which England must brace every nerve, strain every energy, and put out the right arm of her strength; her power was trembling in the balance, her Indian empire hung upon a thread, which one false move might sever. The occasion, indeed, was awful, but England was equal to it. Expeditiously were the measures for the defence of her Eastern empire commenced, steadily were those measures continued; nor can one ever forget the sensation of relief with which one read day after day how regiment after regiment left her shores, and with what delight one hailed each announcement of fresh departures—a long stream of war which poured continuously from England's bleeding side—a stream which was destined to wash out the cruel stain, to palsy and arrest the dark and blood-stained hand in the reeking triumph of its treachery, and to revenge, as all hearts prompted, the base indignities and savage ill-treatment of our murdered countrywomen and children.

Reader, it was with this avenging stream that I left old England, and here will I commence my narrative.

Suppose me, then, aboard one of those magnificent transports which, about the time above mentioned, sailed or steamed day after day from England's well-loved shores; suppose aboard a living freight of some seven hundred men; suppose that the white handkerchiefs on the pier have waved their last adieux, and are now wiping the tears from glistening eyes; suppose that throbbing hearts ashore, ay, and aboard too, are beating quick and heavily; suppose that we are looking over the vessel's side at the fast receding shores, which somehow or other seem to have a thick mist hanging over them (how is this? for it is a bright, fine, sunny day!)—suppose the engines to be rattling out their never-varying song, and suppose, in fact, that we at last are fairly under weigh. Don't be afraid, reader, I am not going to bore you with a description of a voyage which was like all others, neither more interesting nor less monotonous: there was that chaotic confusion on first going aboard so characteristic of and inseparable from occasions of this sort; there was the old sensation of stifling and suffocation on entering one's small dark cabin, with a smell of paint, tar, horsehair cushions, ropes, wood, bottled beer, and bilge water; there was the old necessity for physical exertion to effect an entry into one's narrow berth; there was the old up-and-down, up-and-down business on getting out to sea, with the old result, that misanthropical tendency to lean silent and pensive over the vessel's side apart from one's fellow man; those sudden and surprising departures from the dinner-table; those guttural and mysterious noises issuing from the surrounding cabins, and all those numerous ills that flesh (at sea) is heir to. Let us then draw a veil, as novel-writers say, over this period of suffering and misery, and behold us, ere many days are over, emerging from our cabins radiant in the proud consciousness of having come into possession of our sea-legs, and of having passed through the ordeal, after paying the usual tribute of wretchedness and—ahem! et cætera—at Neptune's watery shrine. I will not detain you at St. Vincent (Cape Verde), that aridest and barrenest of isles, of which all that can be said is that it is hot, rocky, and uninteresting; nor is any very long description of the tropics necessary; we found them much the same as usual—hot, calm, and flying-fishy.

We saw several ships, and shot at porpoises, and ate, and drank, and slept a great deal, and examined the compass and the chart very attentively, and looked over the vessel's side at the glittering waves, and up aloft at the tapering masts, and yawned, and read books, and wrote letters, and got up a newspaper, which died a natural death after a few weeks, owing to the contributors, from confinement, want of exercise, indigestion, and general bad humour, becoming splenetic and personally abusive. And so the days passed by, and we speeded on, on, on, upon our outward way.

Then by degrees we got into lower latitudes, where we saw whales disporting themselves, and Cape pigeons, and albatrosses, and we were very nearly frightened into not firing at the latter birds by a perusal of the *Ancient Mariner;* and then we wearied, and yawned again, and slept, and ate, and looked at the chart again, and on the whole felt more bored than ever we had done in our life. Oh, and then the bad jokes we made! *faute de mieux;* they were quite miraculous in their short-comings. I distinctly recollect our being so hard up on one occasion that we actually accepted as a *bon mot* a paltry attempt to obtain notoriety by talking of getting into other latitudes by *degrees!!* And the extent to which we played ship-quoits and " bull," and tried every means from champagne to chaff to make the days slip quickly by, as we sped on, still on upon our outward way.

Our voyage as above described continued, with but little to break its weary monotony, until our arrival at the Cape, when we heard, and some anxious hearts were soothed and comforted by the news, that Havelock's force had effected a junction with that small body of English men and English women, on whom, as they held those few square yards in Lucknow against all rebel Oude, opposing with calm heroism the desperate attacks of

VOYAGE OUT.

fanatics or the wily devices of traitors, the eyes of all Europe had been fixed with an earnest, anxious gaze, a gaze which was but withdrawn, from time to time, to glance hurriedly and nervously at the progress made by the advancing succours, which, we now had the pleasure of hearing, had at last reached them. Here, too, we heard of the fall of Delhi, so long hoped for and so long expected; and, in fact, affairs in India generally had apparently assumed so favourable a hue, that many of us thought, not without a pang, that we should be too late to have "a crack at the niggers" after all; and anxious to get on, impatient of delay, we were not sorry when we once more felt the heavy trembling motion of the revolving screw, and found ourselves steaming merrily away into the Indian Ocean. Again long days of sea and sky, and nothing more; again tossing up and down upon the wide open sea, the steady beat of the engines seeming, as it were, slowly to mark the weary time which lazily slipped by.

It was all very well for Mr. Dibdin to make songs about the sea and the freedom of a sailor's life, and the pleasures of a tar's existence, and for people in snug drawing-rooms to roar out "a life on the o-o-o-ocean wave!" and other such naval ditties, but, speaking from personal experience, I am compelled to state that these enthusiastic descriptions of the ocean, and this fanatical love of the sea, is but a pleasing fiction, encouraged by poets from the scope which it gives to their fancy, and indulged in by popular singers from the ditto afforded their voices by ballads of a nautical tendency. But just place one of these gentlemen, who is so very earnest on the subject of being afloat, and who is stating at the top of his voice that "the ocean's his home and the bark is his bride," in close juxtaposition with this bride for three or four months, and he will find, like some other better halves that I could name, that she palls on one after a time; place him, I say, aboard the good troop-ship *Hydaspes*, very many degrees of latitude south of the Cape, on a gusty day, wind dead in one's teeth, drenching rain, or, between the showers, a sort of drizzling atmosphere, between a Scotch mist and a shower-bath; ship making little or no way, but tossing impatiently up and down over thick, dark, cold, cruel-looking waves; drops of wet from the dripping rigging falling playfully down one's neck; a sort of permanent damp pervading everything, and making even the tumblers and knives and forks in the saloon look as if they were breaking out into a cold perspiration; every one seen through a medium of waterproof, and everything through an unpleasant veil of drizzle, damp, and cold, and then I'll trouble the enthusiastic singer aforesaid to chant "I'm afloat! I'm afloat!" with the same cheery feelings and jaunty air that he indulged in last time he gave tongue to this piratical ditty, before numerous and admiring friends at home.

But stay!—the scene shifts. Ceylon, with its scented breezes and its shady groves is reached at last. Beautiful Ceylon! with your tropical scenery and rich and varied vegetation, almost realizing a dream of fairy-land, and justifying the enthusiasm of that traveller whose fancy tempted him to fix on you as the Garden of Eden of old, worthy a

ASPECT OF CEYLON.

Byron to sing sweet praises of thy charms, worthy the pencil of a Claude to immortalize on canvas thy fair and blooming landscapes!

Oh! island *fait à peindre*, fain would I tell of the pleasant stroll which we enjoyed that warm summer evening beneath thy graceful cocoa-nut-trees, whose tall heads waved lightly to and fro, fanned by a gentle breeze; fain would I tell how enraptured we were by thy beauties, and how we revelled in the luxuriance of thy charms; of thy cottages, half-hidden behind budding banks, o'er-hung by thick and fruitful foliage, of thy woodland walks and shady dells, &c. &c., until I speak with a grateful reminiscence of the delightfully Oriental sensation of sitting, for the first time, at dinner beneath the cooling influence of a punkah, of the epicurean pleasure we derived from that never-to-be-forgotten *bonne bouche* a prawn curry, and how, as we looked around and saw black servants waiting on us, Indian chairs with elongated and luxurious arms, provoking to a sweet after-dinner *dolce far niente*, and a general Indian indolence prevailing, we thought to ourselves, as we complacently reclined in the chairs aforesaid, puffing white wreaths of smoke from our delicate Manillas, and sipping our iced brandy-and-water, that now indeed did we feel purely and thoroughly Oriental, unconsciously striving the while to give an Eastern tone to our conversation, and talking of tiffin, and calling for more *brandy pawnee* with an air a rajah might have envied.

Hoist the blue-peter, weigh anchor, and once more away nine knots an hour through the blue waters, the land momentarily growing dimmer in the distance till the fair isle is out of sight, and we think of it but as a past and pleasant dream, as we gaze once more on sea and sky, tossing up and down upon the wide ocean, and speeding on, still on, upon our outward way.

A few days, and "Land, ahoy!" calls our attention to the flat, low outline of the Madras coast, towards which we are proceeding for the purpose of landing a portion of our living freight. Steadily we steam onward, till at last, plain and distinct, Madras is before us: not as we had expected, a noble town, Eastern-looking and magnificent, surrounded by fine trees, or backed up by high and rugged hills, but a comparatively insignificant-looking city—with some fine buildings, of course—a large proportion of "black town," and a strong fort, all situated on an arid, open coast, with not a bay, or creek, or curve to break its monotonous outline, the whole place looking dull and hot in the extreme, and scarcely like the capital of a flourishing and extensive presidency.

A high surf is breaking angrily upon the open beach, and around us crowd a noisy fleet of those very extraordinary Mussoola boats in vogue on this Coromandel coast, the thin planks of which are not nailed but sewn together, and built light and pliable as leather, to carry them safely over the foaming waves that come rolling in across the Bay of Bengal, and in which no English boat could live when the swell runs high.

Natives in dresses forcibly reminding one of night-shirts by their scantiness and simplicity, and others in no dresses at all, flock on board. What they all want Heaven knows! The dark crews of the Mussoola boats talk all at once, waving their black, skinny arms, and gesticulating inelegantly with their dusky, naked forms, and quite realizing one's *beau idéal* of imps and others the inhabitants of "another place" (as they say in Parliament), to which, in point of heat, even India must yield the palm; and a shudder involuntarily comes over one as you reflect that to the merciless cruelty and savage devices of fiends of this form and dye were our poor countrymen and women exposed; and, perchance, the same idea flashed across the minds of the soldiers, for they exhibited an unjust, though somewhat natural desire to throw every nigger as he came on board over the vessel's side, while a John Bullish longing on the part of muscular individuals to measure their strength and enter into a single combat, then and there, with a "round dozen of 'em" became apparent, and seemed, at one time, if not checked by the strong arm of discipline, to be on the point of being indulged.

CHAPTER II.

The Sunderbunds—Diamond Harbour—Our last revel aboard—The Hooghly.

PRESTO! away once more! and, like a shifting scene in a dissolving view, the Coromandel coast, with its fringe of white foam, fades swiftly from our sight, and once more we see the blue sea gliding rippling by our vessel's sides, till on the succeeding slide of this the ever-varying magic lantern of nature, appears painted, in dull reddish colours, the low muddy outline of the Sunderbunds, those deadly swamps where the sway of the royal Bengal tiger is divided with King Death who here holds high court, with all his obsequious myrmidons, Messrs. Fever, Malaria, and Co.; and that he asserts his supremacy and power to the utmost in these dreary marshes may be seen by the emaciated faces and tottering forms of those adventurous sportsmen who, considering the skin of a tiger to be cheaply purchased at the price of a ruined constitution, have dared to beard the cruel monarch in this his securest stronghold, and have paid—how heavily judge by those pallid cheeks—for their temerity and love of sport

Steadily beat the engines, and swiftly do we approach this fatal tract, and at last enter one of the hundred mouths of the celebrated Ganges; and as we watch the banks narrowing and closing in on either side, as the landscape assumes less

MOUTHS OF THE GANGES.

the appearance of an archipelago, and more that of a river, we listen with gaping mouths to blood-chilling legends anent the deeds of rapacious and peckish tigers, who are wont—so runs the tale—to swim off from the shores, board ships and boats, and gobble up the unsuspecting and unhappy crews; and then horrible whispers are circulated about the "man who trims the lamp in the lighthouse" (what lamp or what lighthouse I do not know), and who was obliged "once upon a time," as the old story-tellers say, to live in an iron cage to avoid the attacks of the rapacious tigers aforesaid, who—oh, horror!—grinned through the iron bars at him in ghastly derision as he sat within, possibly occupied in calculating nervously the strength of the various materials composing his little fortress; and there is something so indescribably unpleasant and awful in the idea of the relative positions of man and beast being thus reversed, added to a certain guilty consciousness of having, but shortly before leaving England, paid a visit to the Royal Zoological Gardens, and then and there having chuckled, exulted over, and taunted the Royal Bengal tiger as he lay in bondage and captivity, that our fevered imaginations originated wild fallacies of vision, and so distorted our powers of observation as to cause us to mistake trees and bushes on shore (diminished as they appeared by distance) for these dreaded beasts taking a constitutional previous to swimming off to obtain their wonted meal, or to imagine that large logs of wood floating down the stream represented the advance-guard of a large force of these terrible quadrupeds, who, goaded by hunger and cannibal-*ic* tastes, were boldly swimming off to claim us as their prey. See, reader, what it is to have a guilty conscience, and take this timely warning: never chaff a Royal Bengal Tiger!

The river narrows as we go steaming up it, guided and directed along our tortuous and difficult course by the experienced hand and eye of one of the numerous pilots in the service of the Hon. East India Company, and cheered on our way by traditions redolent of shipwreck and disaster connected with those hidden shoals and sneaking banks which we are passing so rapidly, related to us by the pilot with a sort of professional gusto which is peculiarly charming, but traditions, nevertheless, sufficiently awful to make one begin fervently to wish one was well out of it.

That night we anchored at Diamond Harbour, about forty or fifty miles from Calcutta; on the morrow our voyage would be completed!—for one hundred days had it been dragging its weary length along. One hundred days at sea!—an age! a lifetime! and yet, long and dreary as this time may have been, there is a peculiar feeling, almost that of parting with an old friend, in the knowledge that to-morrow your voyage will have ended; you hate the sea, you detest being aboard ship, you are not the least bit nautical in word, thought, or deed, but still it seems hard to realize that this life, to which you have resigned yourself with a passive reluctance for three long months and a half, shall to-morrow be at an end; and you begin to look more kindly on the old ship now you are going to leave her; and the tanned and weather-beaten faces of the tarry, dirty, hard-working sailors, assume a more friendly aspect; while you find that you have imperceptibly contracted friendships, the strength of which you were ignorant of until it comes to the time for dissolving them. That bluff old boatswain, too, becomes transformed into a "right good fellow," as you remember how for a hundred days he has borne with your landsman's infirmities, and how "many a time and oft" he has witnessed you ruthlessly disturbing those neatly rolled coils of rope, or cruelly sullying the—would-be—unspotted whiteness of the deck, by carelessly dropping upon it the extremely dirty ashes of your pipe, or letting fall, and then treading into it, the caps of your rifle when improving your ball-practice, during some of those weary hundred days, by firing at sharks, cape-pigeons, boobies, or bottles, and you reflect, with a warm and grateful swelling of the heart, how to all these numerous injuries, though they cut him to the quick, he submitted without a murmur, except when an involuntary "Well, I *am* blowed," crawled unsolicited from the gruff depths of his broad chest; the compass, too, which has so often been the object of your anxious inspection when storm-racks have been driving overhead, though it can tell you nothing *now*, still you must go and have one more look at it for old acquaintance sake; while an observant passenger cannot but notice that about this time the stewards brighten up wonderfully, bustling about with the most unusual alacrity, almost knocking one another down in their unwonted eagerness to get you the liver-wing of the chicken at dinner, or the hot toast at tea; the soldiers on board are unusually jolly, they all seem suddenly endowed with the power of singing, and they *do* sing; fiddles which have squeaked in discordant rivalry throughout the voyage, now join one another on the most friendly terms, occasionally in their excitement losing one another for a few bars, but what of that? The "ear-piercing fife," which has hitherto contented itself with jigs, hornpipes, and other equally minor and contemptible effusions, now shrilly gives vent to its feelings in the more sublime strain of "Rule Britannia," or becoming maudlin, squeaks out an air which bears a certain melancholy resemblance, however slight, to "Auld Lang Syne."

"Clear the decks for a dance." "Hear, hear!" At it they go—pell-mell; soldiers heated and excited, foot it featly with sailors tarry and impetuous; stokers, so black that all their other characteristics, moral as well as physical, appear to be hidden behind the sooty veil which enshrouds them, and firemen not less begrimed, thread the mazy dance with an energy worthy of a better cause; mates, stewards, carpenters, all suffering equally from heat and emotion, danced wildly, as though their very lives were at stake, the only disputes that arise being those consequent on some slight difficulty in discerning which is the lady of each couple. "Old 'ard there, Bill, you ain't the lady." "I tell yer I am, Joe." "Now then, ma'arm, *if* you please!" "What a 'urry you're in, yer won't give a poor woman time to get a bit of a quid into 'er mouth," &c. &c. &c. Never mind, keep it up! hands across, and down the middle! one more round!—excitement momentarily becoming more tremendous, while the man in the moon looks down from his placid, silvery home upon this noisy scene with wonder and astonishment depicted in his usually unmeaning face, until at last a lusty "God save the Queen," in which the "whole strength of the company" (as the play-bills have it) took part, almost shakes the old ship's timbers, and—by Heavens! they *do* shake (can it be with emotion?) at those three deafening cheers in her honour which burst forth loud and clear, breaking the calm silence of the still night-air, and sending the affrighted jackals scampering with wild yells from their foul midnight meal on the rotting carcase of a Hindoo, which lies in the soft clammy mud of the neighbouring bank.

Our last night at sea! a farewell to our sea home—*voilà tout!* I answer to any reader "with soul so dead" that he cannot enter into those feelings of mingled pleasure and regret, or who would not, on a similar occasion, have acted in a similar manner; while if he should happen to think with the poet, that

> An adieu should in utterance die,
> Or, if written, but faintly appear;
> Only heard through the burst of a sigh,
> Only read through the blot of a tear,

I have only to remark that opinions differ, and to express my regret that his feelings should have been so far outraged by the above unseemly revelry.

The decks are cleared, the excitement has subsided, friends linger still with friends, and, in not a few instances, that "touch of nature which makes the whole world kin" having been roused by the hearty good humour of the above scene, the generous feelings come tumbling up in wild but glad confusion to the surface of the rough, blithe heart, bursting through the flimsy covering of pride which alone had kept them down, and causing many a pair of horny hands which had long been estranged to clasp in friendly unity, and many a pair of muscular arms to entwine amicably with one another, as the *entente cordiale* which some slight circumstance had disturbed was thus pleasantly renewed—and so in little knots of twos and threes, old friends and old foes together, the merry group dispersed, and all is still and quiet.

We weigh anchor for the last time! Beat away merrily, ye engines, for to-night shall ye be at rest! Rumble away, old screw, to your heart's content, and show to us this Calcutta, of which we have heard, and read, and thought so much!

A pretty river is the Hooghly, though somewhat muddy, twisting and meandering about between pleasant banks, covered with the most luxuriant vegetation; the cocoa and the palm trees proudly rearing their stately heads above the thick tangled jungle, which crouches in dense masses round their feet, clothed in all the varied hues of Nature's sylvan livery, from the dull green of the thick rank grass, growing tall and high in the rich shiny soil, to the bright reddish yellow of the falling, fading leaf, or the yet more cheerful colours of those glowing flowers which appear to have wandered by mistake into this dark labyrinth of vegetation, and to be now peeping out their gaudy heads in an endeavour to discover a means of escape to some more genial spot where their bright faces will no longer be shaded from the sun's burnished rays, nor their "sweetness wasted" —as it now is—"upon the desert air;" prickly pears, too, hug in a close embrace the scarce less prickly brier, and many another plant, whose name is unknown to me, grows in that closely-packed group of botanic marvels—plants with broad flat leaves, plants with long thin leaves, plants with short stumpy leaves, bearing now berries—now fruit—now flowers, and mixed up in prodigal and bewildered confusion, as though Nature wished to make up for the flatness of the scenery, and to give to the stranger, as he passes these thickly-clad banks, samples of all the various materials with which she has adorned this same country of Hindostan, and to acquaint him by this lavish display of her charms with the diversified and extensive nature of the wardrobe wherefrom she clothes alike the snow-capt mountains of the Himalaya and the burnt, wide-spreading plains of the ever-summery South.

Sly creeks which try hard to look like rivers, and wind about under this delusion in the most self-important manner, stroll away independently from the main course of the stream, but, apparently becoming alarmed at the idea of losing their way in that dark-wooded shore, stop short abruptly, after feebly swaggering a short distance, and remain shy and embarrassed, trying *not* to look like elongated duck-ponds, or vainly endeavouring to hide their shame and confusion by getting under the black shadow of friendly

trees, or, in some cases, brazening it out by
taking up a position near a village, and assuming the most ridiculous airs, as if those clumsy,
old broken-down native boats were huge and prosperous East Indiamen, freighted with rich merchandise, and the slimy mud in which they lie,
quietly rotting away, was the clear water of some
vast and navigable stream. This village, too, upon
thy banks, oh! little vain-glorious creek! is as
unlike a vast mercantile capital as can be!—such
quaint, unassuming, tropical-looking little places,
reader, affording no display of Gothic, Elizabethan,
or other architecture, save that which may possibly have existed in the rudest periods of the
antediluvian era; not clean and pleasant cottages
as in " merry England," with the goodwife washing the rosy little imps before the flower-covered
porch, and bidding them " run and give old *feyther*
a kiss," as he returns, with the sweat of honest
labour on his brow, from the fields wherein he
gains the wherewithal to make that home so
happy and so bright—no merry laughs from
the " boisterous urchins on the village green"
here ring through the air, but a strange, dull
stillness (so unbroken that you can hear the
subdued hum of a million summer insects, rendering it yet more palpable) hangs like a pall
over these mud-built cottages, against the low,
brown walls of which, or against the dark trunks
of the surrounding trees, white-clad forms stand
out in strong relief as they flit to and fro—a somewhat ghostly reminder that these Indian villages
really are the habitations of men. Here and there
a few naked children, more black than rosy, are

rolling about in the hot-baked ground, as though making a desperate effort to amalgamate themselves with their original element, to which sooner or later we must all return, and which, as regards colour, they so nearly resemble.

A diversion is here effected; we run to the vessel's side to have a look at a few corpses which are floating leisurely down the stream, large, unclean birds calmly seated upon them, with outstretched wings, glutting their obscene maws, and disputing savagely with one another the pieces of flesh which they tear off the black carcase, the spirit of which has long since fled.

"Hullo! 'ere's a stout un a-coming, Bill!" cries out an observant soldier to his comrade, as the huge carcase of a dead elephant floats towards us, saluting our olfactory nerves with *triple extrait* of the "essence of mortality," and looking more like an immense black India-rubber figure inflated to an unusual size, and quaintly distorted, than anything else I can think of.

More cocoa and palm trees on the banks; more tangled jungle; more mud villages; more sly creeks; more white spectral forms; more naked children; till the ever-twisting river discloses to our view scenery of a somewhat more civilized description: a house! actually and literally a habitable house! with a nice little garden, then a bit more jungle, then another house!—two!—three! opening upon us in quick succession as we enter "Garden Reach," till the banks present one long vista of pretty villas, with their green verandahs, looking bright and pleasant in the warm sun, while the fast narrowing river enables us to dispense with glasses, as our eyes roam delighted over the fair scene. English faces peep from the windows, ayahs (native nurses) carrying English children stroll about the beautiful gardens which stretch down to the water's edge, and so rapid has been the transition from barbarous wilds to civilized scenes, that one can hardly credit that the eye, which now runs over the fair proportions of these villa-palaces, and the blooming gardens laid out with English taste and neatness, was but five minutes since gazing on rude mud villages, surrounded by nought save the dense and savage jungle.

CHAPTER III.

Arrival at Calcutta—Letters from home—The "Chowringhee"—
The City of Palaces.

SHIPS and boats of various sorts, shapes, and sizes, momentarily becoming more numerous, floated by us, and the cry of "Half speed !" " Quarter speed !" and the more frequent ejaculations, " Hard a port !" " Steady !" " Starboard !" informed us of the pleasing fact that we were fast approaching our journey's end. As we round a point a forest of masts breaks upon us, and, as our good ship completes the curve, hundreds upon hundreds of vessels become visible, and, at last, behold Calcutta !

At first a mass of magnificent buildings, half hidden, in the most tantalizing manner, by the shipping, then becoming more confused in its grandeur, and more bewildering in its stately beauty, as we go on——on——on, passing all sorts of vessels, from the little, long, low river steamers (formed by a number of narrow flats, fastened astern of one another, thus becoming, as it were, a pliable ship, peculiarly well adapted to the narrow, winding rivers they have to navigate), to the small craft, gun-boats, fishing-boats, beautiful clipper ships, huge merchantmen, still larger transports, noble Peninsular and Oriental steamers, and stately men-of-war, which compose the vast and motley fleet ; still steaming on, at the lowest possible speed, dexterously and almost miraculously threading our way in and out, escaping fatal collisions by hairs'-breadths, and running through friendly openings which hardly appeared wide enough to admit a small boat, much less an immense steamer of some two thousand tons.

On every side something new and interesting. Everybody talking at once, nobody listening to any one else, and everything seen through a mist of excitement. "Hallo! there's the ship we came home from the Crimea in;" or, "My dear fellow, come and have a look at the *So-and-so*, the old tub we used to buy beer and fowls from in the Crimea, when we were so confoundedly hard up for grub;" or, "By George! there's the ——— arrived before us; she must have made a quick passage!" And so on, *ad infinitum*. But you pay no attention whatever to these remarks, though perchance you give a vacant assent, as your strained eyes are eagerly looking, through the network of rigging which surrounds you, at the fine, neatly-trimmed parapets of Fort William, with its many embrasures, from which peep ominously the dark muzzles of the guns, while English soldiers, on sentry, pace up and down its vast ramparts.

The noise and confusion aboard have been gradually working themselves up to the culminating point of discord, which they have now attained; your legs become entangled with hawsers, which appear to be wriggling about the deck in a state of imbecile excitement, and you bark your shins cruelly against great chain cables, which are exhibiting strong symptoms of temporary insanity;

ARRIVAL AT CALCUTTA.

you are elbowed to and fro in the most discourteous manner, and wherever you take up your position you find that somehow or another it materially interferes with the working of the ship; the pilot, too, *will* insist on hailing neighbouring vessels, his eloquence, though loudly told forth, assuming a muffled and slightly obscure character on issuing from the speaking-trumpet, as if all the words were having a good romp, and doing their best to smother one another with bolsters. Nobody thinks of making the commonest remark except at the very top of his voice; the engine is whistling, puffing, and hoarsely shouting, in an attempt to attract the attention of other engines of its acquaintance, and the chaotic nature of the confusion is something beyond description. And what is all this? Simply our good ship getting into its place; *nearly* as great a fuss, reader, as a modern lady makes, in these crinoline days, about sitting down, or getting into *her* place, is it not?

"Stop her!" and the trembling beat of the screw ceases, the engine gives a great cry of relief, and for a few moments there is a strange stillness, as if the drum of your ear had been broken by the accumulation of noises which assailed it, and in this brief instant of quiet you have time to collect your scattered thoughts sufficiently to realize the fact that you have arrived.

Arrived!—the desideratum is attained at last, and a sort of mental vacuum, consequent on the sudden achievement of that object which has riveted one's attention and engrossed one's thoughts for so many a long day, is the consequence.

Presently, the noise recommences as badly as ever; in fact, I think the engine becomes, if possible, more disagreeable than before, pretending he is letting off steam, or making some other equally frivolous excuse; while as for the shouting, it is augmented triple-fold by the numerous greetings from Damons aboard to Pythiases in small boats, which are crowding alongside; greetings consisting for the most part in stentorian "How—are—you,—old—fellows?" issuing from hoarse and agitated throats, and saluting the ear of him for whom they are intended long before the boat that bears him has reached our vessel's side; then a welcome arrival—not at all calculated to allay the excitement—takes place, in the shape of a bag of letters, when those who get any, wildly dash through their contents, and those who do not, look grumpy and—go without.

To a close observer of human nature there could be few moments more interesting than such a one as this: to watch the varied emotions flitting over the faces of the readers, brightening some and shading others; to see the married man tearing open the thick budget, which tells him of home, of wife, of little ones; the would-be Benedict fondly scanning those crossed and recrossed pages of beloved writing, and feeding, with bee-like avidity, on honeyed extracts from its fervid pages; the boyish recruit, seated, insensible alike to noise, hurry, confusion, to all—save the cramped, ill-spelt words, and rude, unlettered sentences, which express—oh, how eloquently!—the yearning fondness of his mother's widowed heart, which tell of that love, so great that it would fain hide from her darling the lonely anguish which rends her inmost soul—fain hide her fears, her despondency, her heart-sinkings—fain avoid making *him* a sharer of her woe. Ah! vain deceit! ah! foolish, weeping mother! when that one little tear comes trickling down thy aged cheek, and, placing its soft seal upon the paper which lies below, unsays all that forced cheerfulness, unsays all that laboured joyousness, and remains a mute witness of the would-be hidden grief, till kissed from the page by a son's fond lips, and placed with a gentle, holy care in a son's warm heart, there to remain for ever. See here the smile which the huge, shaky pot-hooks of a little sister's first attempt at caligraphy call forth; see there the tear which the black-bordered envelope causes to flow—watch these, and you will see more of human nature, and learn more of human hearts, in this one passing moment, than in long years of study and observation amid the cold formalities of society, when so many a generous impulse is hidden behind that thick veil, the fabric of which is humbug, and the showy trimmings, embroideries, and fringes of which are woven with tawdry threads of fashion and etiquette.

Calcutta! How hard it is to remember all I thought, and all I saw when first I gazed upon thee—how difficult to dissect and analyze the confused and ambiguous mass of feelings which flashed upon me as I gazed, and to give in cold detail what are commonly called "my ideas upon the subject!"

Ask the man whose eyes ache with a recent

inspection of the beauties of the kaleidoscope, to describe one by one the endless forms and varieties of the figures therein, and you do not set him a harder task than mine would be, had I to describe all that first greeted my delighted eyes on arriving at Calcutta; so, shunning a laborious, nay, an impossible task, I must try some other mode of conveying to you my impressions. Let me see! How would the Murray-Handbook-and-Useful-Knowledge style do? Thus:

"CALCUTTA.—This beautiful and flourishing city, situated on the left bank of the Hooghly, is the capital of Bengal Proper, and the seat of British Government in India; contains three or four Protestant churches, a cathedral, a Scotch, Portuguese, Greek, and Armenian church, several mosques, many Hindoo temples, and a college; also a large fort. Chief exports—salt, sugar, rice, opium, and silks. Lat. 88° 28′ E. Long. 22° 23′ N. Population, &c. &c."

That is the instructive style; but, as it is just within the bounds of possibility that this style might fail to give you any very lucid idea of the appearance of Calcutta, I must effect a sort of compromise between the detailed and the dry, and endeavour to hit off the golden mean between the two.

As I before observed, one's eye is forcibly arrested by the vast parapets of Fort William, its noble outline, its scientifically traced ditches, and its long white row of barracks, but half visible above the green fortifications. Stretching away from this, along the banks of the river, and fringed with houses, is the "Chowringhee," or immense Maidän, which forms the Hyde Park, the Rotten-row of Calcutta; and here, as evening approaches, the dusty, parched-up plain, which during the day has been the resort of a few heat-braving crows, a few gasping dogs, or some sun-proof Hindoos, now presents an appearance at once pretty, animated, and novel. Here rolls along the luxurious London-made landau, but a black Jehu sits perched on its lofty box, and on the little footboard, where erst the pride of London flunkeys displayed his noble calves, stands an Asiatic lacquey, with strikingly undeveloped legs; there the Calcutta exquisite tools his neat buggy through the gathering crowd; now the Oriental palanquin, with its four black and grunting bearers, passes swiftly by; now the equestrian complacently urges his prancing steed along—

> While his off heel, insidiously applied,
> Provokes the caper which he feigns to chide;

here the creaking, bullock-drawn hackery (something like a rickety double-post-and-rail on wheels) wends its slow and painful way; there the chariot which bears the sleek and homage-loving rajah, with his jewelled turban, his turned-up slippers, and his fat and indolent form; and on every side such a variety of coaches, carriages, and vehicles, as at once to baffle and defy description.

Ever changing, too, are the hues which pervade this heterogeneous assemblage. The snow-white garments of the natives act as a fluttering foil to the gay rustling silks and many-coloured toilettes of England's charming daughters; the *séduisante* Parisian bonnet coquettishly flirts about among the more head-protecting turbans; here and there the English hat proudly displays its black and funnel-shaped form to the wonder-stricken Hindoo; the scarce less awe-inspiring crinoline strangely contrasts with the lank, close-fitting garments of the Asiatic; uniforms of every colour, form, and make vary the bright scene with their presence. Bheesties (water-carriers) run along hither and thither, sprinkling the dusty thoroughfares with water from the skin, or *mussuk*, in vogue in India for the purpose; syces (grooms) flit before you as they run alongside the horse or buggy of their masters, ever ready, when he stops, to seize the relinquished rein, or to brush away the flies with that little fan of horsehair, or chowrie, which is a sort of conventional badge of their profession.

Every tint of

> The shadowed livery of the burnish'd sun

may here be seen in great perfection; the dark, shiny skin of the *coolie* (labouring class); the less burnt, and hence less sepia-dyed rajah; the half-caste, with that peculiar complexion, neither white nor black, but a sort of sallow compromise between the two; the blooming English girl; the sickly, yellow face of the old Anglo-Indian, whom thirty years of hard service in this country, thirty years of liver-enlarging grilling beneath its burning sun, have dried up into a mummy; the sleek, vain Bengalee baboo, with his well oiled hair, his sly, pliable features, so cringing to superiors, so arrogant to inferiors, and his assumed English air and bearing; the tall, dusky Punjabee; the fair Cashmerian; Russians, Turks, French, Germans, Spanish, Armenians, even the black tribes of Africa, all have their representatives among this motley mass, and all contribute their quota to this strange *bizarre* assemblage.

Nor are the gentler scenes of English life wanting, for a band is playing, and stirred by its swelling notes, beaux, bolder grown, whisper soft nothings into willing ears, " soft eyes looked love to eyes which spake again," and, to complete the sketch, in Byron's own musical words—

> All went merry as a marriage bell.

The setting sun is just shedding a thousand rays on the golden glittering points of a gilded and fantastical Hindoo temple or monument, just diffusing a mellowed light over the picture which this poor pen has feebly attempted to depict; so, before the fiery orb quite disappears behind that belt of palm trees in the red-blushing distance of the West, let us turn from this parti-coloured scene, this human rainbow, and view the fair and far extent of palaces and buildings which compose Calcutta itself.

First, by its position, beauty, and size, stands the noble structure of Government House, while around it and beyond it, as though paying it homage, gather those hundreds of smaller buildings—the clubs, the residences of the rich merchants, the public offices, the palatial hotels, the magnificent shops, the extensive warehouses, the churches and the temples, which have earned for Calcutta the hackneyed, but well merited title " The City of Palaces." Far away does this prospect of architectural beauties extend—far away, till it dwindles imperceptibly into the dirty native town, where the tapering minarets, and the carved domes of temples rise high above the confined and squalid streets, till the eye, lost in the misty distance, is satiated and glutted by this *embarras de richesses*. Along the crowded banks of the river are the various *ghauts* (or landing-places), the scenes of a busy trade; at some, passengers are landing or embarking, at others, merchant ships are disgorging their freights into the greedy jaws of huge warehouses, receiving in return a rich cargo of silks or indigo, or other of that valuable merchandize which has made British India what it is; huge bales of costly fabrics swing in mid-air from colossal cranes, or lie in tempting profusion on the heavily-laden wharfs.

All is active, bright, and interesting, and as one's eye wanders again and again over the scenes above described, you become conscious of the absence of a something to which you have generally been accustomed, you miss some familiar object which you fancy should be here — what is it? Look attentively up at that blue sky, down at those snow-white houses, along the gay Chowringhee, and say what that "something" is! Ah! *Eureka!* SMOKE! Citizen of London, think of that! Citizen of Birmingham, think of that! Citizens of Manchester and Liverpool, think of that, and realize it if you can! No smoke! And herein lies the secret—added to the brightness of the sun—of that astoundingly new, clean, fresh, cheerful *coup d'œil* which Calcutta presents. No murky vapours, in dark conspiracy with fogs and mists, hang black or gloomy, to shade by their presence the clear outlines of the buildings, and to give that indefinable air of *tristesse* for which our own London is so justly celebrated; no curling wreaths of smoke to blacken freshly painted houses, and stain the unsullied purity of white glittering walls or bright green verandahs and venetians. And it is the absence of these dim and dulling vapours which gives to Calcutta something of the dazzling appearance of a town reflected in a highly polished mirror, or in the clear surface of some unruffled lake, as the stranger views it through that sun-glint, which is ever dancing and sparkling before it. Such is Calcutta; such did it appear to me when I first beheld it—a bright, fairy city, unlike any place I had ever seen before; such, reader, will you probably find it when you honour it with your presence; such, perchance, you may have already found it, oh! Anglo-Bengalee, in years gone by, when you sojourned in the land!

CHAPTER IV.

Mosquitoes—The disembarkation—Harpies—Sore trial of temper—"Puggree" to the rescue!—A brief retrospective review of Puggree's career in my service—Coolies—Some reflections incidental to arriving in India.

"GOODNESS gracious! my dear fellow, where have you been?" Such was the salutation which greeted me as I appeared at breakfast on the following morning, after a night, the recollection of which will never, never be effaced, spent among the mosquitoes. Oh! that night—that night! the tossing and the tumbling, and the rolling to and fro; the single combats that I fought, the general actions with large bodies of the enemy that I engaged in, the scratching, and the tearing, and the groaning—ye gods! what words can tell?

I anointed wound after wound, as I received them, with Eau de Cologne, salad-oil, lime-juice, mustard, and a hundred other "infallible cures;" but, alas! 'twas of no avail. I groaned,—I walked about my cabin,—I went up on deck,—I drank gallons of cold water,—I buffeted wildly in the air with bolsters,—I tore myself with my nails,—seizing the most bristly clothes-brush procurable, I groomed myself, after the manner of a steed, I—ah! what did I not do during that awful night?

On rising in the morning and looking in the glass, behold! hands, neck, face, one mass of mosquito-empoisoned flesh. As far as I could ascertain by inquiry and private interviews with my looking-glass, it appeared to me that I had four cheeks on the left side of my face and three on the right; two and a-half upper lips, five eyelids, one nose and three-quarters, and a large proportion of ears, particularly on the right side of my head. In fact, how I found room for all these additional organs, I am at a loss to discover; but there they were, rather in the way than otherwise, for my lips kept getting into my mouth, my eyelids were in a chronic state of wink, almost entirely obscuring my sight, the enlarged state of my ears materially interfered with brushing my hair; while, as for getting my hat on to my head —ha, ha!—why, it would have been suicide to think of it!

Nor was I the only sufferer. A dear friend came to breakfast with one side of his face apparently under the influence of Joe Miller, while the other side was dressed as though about to attend a funeral, if one might judge from the lugubrious and gloomy appearance that it presented. Even the soldiers' and sailors' tough hides failed to protect them from these little buzzing, winged demons, and many a gallant warrior in her Britannic Majesty's pay bore unmistakeable signs that morning of having been among the "musquitties."

A ship is not a pleasant place while the process of disembarkation is going on. There is a creaking of blocks and tackle, a perpetual chorus of "Walk away with it, lads!" and "Lower 'andsomely!" and a chafing of ropes, and a great many solo performances on a shrill metallic whistle by the boatswain—not to speak of the imminent risk one runs of unexpectedly and gracefully strolling (without the aid of steps or ladder) into the lower hold, *viâ* one of the many hatchways which are conveniently yawning open, or the scarcely less agreeable possibility of receiving on the top of one's head one of the many descending bales of goods, varying in weight from one hundredweight to a couple of tons. All sorts of people on all sorts of business, and some on no business at all, flock aboard. There are coolies, black and shiny, and innocent of garments as of any attempt or intention to over-fatigue themselves by physical exertion; there are Asiatic tailors, who talk the most extraordinary English, and dispose of inferior articles at fine full-grown prices; there are men who insist on following you all round the ship, and thrusting into your face dirty pieces of paper, containing the information that the bearer, Bohwahl Sing, or Pultoo Bux, served Ensign X Y Z in the capacity of khitmutghar for three days, during which lengthened period he gave unprecedented satisfaction! There are various officers of high standing in certain military departments who are busily performing that arduous duty entitled "superintending the disembarkation of troops," which means —Well, well, never mind what it means; but they have nice gold-lace caps, and "staff peaks," and faultless coats, and well-cut trousers, and altogether look so smart and spruce that it really is a pleasure to see them even when they are doing nothing. Then there are gentlemen unctuous

THE DISEMBARKATION. 37

both in manner and speech, who converse with you affably on any subject you may desire, answering all your questions with a playful urbanity, and oiling the wheels of conversation with a fluent lubricity, positively charming, and finally putting into your hands the creamiest of cream-laid notes, on perusing which you have the satisfaction of discovering that " Messrs. Varnish, Tact, and Co., having for many years been honoured with the agency, &c. &c. &c., of a very large number of officers belonging to her Majesty's and the Honourable East India Company's services, respectfully beg to solicit the favour," &c. &c. &c. Then there are friends, visitors, relations, and acquaintances, to whom, of course, you extend your hospitality, and invite down to the saloon to have something to eat and drink, to which they all respond with one stereotyped phrase " Well—I—d'you know—I—thank you—I think—ar—aw—I *should* like a glass of beer." And down you go, and very soon find out that they are not only good for a glass, but a bottle, to say nothing of a plate or two of sandwiches. Yes; all these people—all these sayings, doings, noises, and nuisances are inseparable from occasions of this sort; but this period of purgatory, like everything else, must have an end, and the moment arrives at last when, having seen the last round of ammunition, the last knapsack, the last gun carriage, and the last man stowed into a boat, you descend the companion-ladder, bid farewell to the ship, and steer towards the shore.

Oh, for the pen of a Boz! oh, for the pencil of a Leech! to describe as they deserve the humours of this landing! Oh, lover of the ridiculous, where are you now? Caricaturist, bring hither thy sketch-book, and portray to the western world the scenes we here beheld. Ah! I fear that its copious leaves will scarcely suffice to show all we then endured—the haggling with rapacious boatmen; how they eventually consented to be satisfied with about five times their legitimate fare; the pushing through the dense crowd of noisy idlers who surrounded us, who blocked up the way, who hung upon our footsteps, who wanted to bear us perforce to their palanquins, who shouted to us, who thrust their goods into our faces, who fought with one another, who volunteered their services, and who, by their importunity, succeeded at last in ruffling the serenity of our ordinarily placid tempers, and causing expressions more pithy than parliamentary to issue from our lips. In vain one grew angry, in vain one implored, in vain one stamped, and pushed, and fought; like bees gathering at the mouth of the hive, did these human birds of prey—these black and naked tormentors—crowd round us and cling to us; the confusion of tongues was worthy of Babel's palmiest days; and, indeed, it was in this, our ignorance of the language, that our chiefest misfortune lay. So desperate did I become, that my mind temporarily wandered, and a wild hallucination predominated, that, in the absence of any intimate acquaintance with the Hindostanee tongue, maybe I might employ French with a mollifying effect, with which language I therefore plentifully interlarded my conversation, not unfrequently throwing in a round German phrase, which I thought must be decisive; but my *mille tonnerres* and most guttural *der Teufel* alike fell harmless and ineffectual upon my foes: till, in despair, I resorted to the usually infallible physical force. As well might I have attempted to empty the Hooghly with a teaspoon as to disperse this vilest and most tenacious of mobs.

What was to be done? I tried to humour them; with a sickly smile I examined the articles they had for sale. Good Heavens! what should I, who had peg-top unmentionables of the most immaculate Bond-street and Conduit-street cuts, in the originating of which a hundred master minds had thrown a loose rein upon the necks of their imagination, and in the execution of which the edges of a thousand pairs of skilful shears had grown blunt and dull—who had coats which knew not a wrinkle, and waistcoats which clung to me like wax—what should I, I say, who possessed such garments as these, want with the inferior straight-cut, Calcutta-made, imitation "Sydenhams," with which these harpies strove to tempt me? The ghost of the great Stultz seemed to rise before me at the thought; while shadowy shapes, with the faces of Poole and Sandilands, Morgan and Matheson, and many another immortal, seemed to group themselves around, with looks more of sorrow than of anger, as they bent their eyes upon me. Why, again, should I fritter away my money on paste jewellery, on bad cutlery, or worthless imitations of English goods? What could I possibly do with a bottle purporting to contain Harvey's Sauce, at that time in the morning? Why, when I was carrying a pith helmet in my hand, should

I want another? Why should I now yield to the seductions of bad Parisian knick-knacks, when the most glittering baubles that the Palais Royal could produce had hitherto failed to tempt me? and why, oh! why should it be necessary for me to invest a rupee in a live tortoise, which one of these Hindoo pedlers pressed upon me as indispensable to a stranger arriving in India?

These considerations rapidly flitted through my mind, and I turned from the unsightly goods, once more pressing on, through the thronging mass, towards the barrack accommodation which had been set apart for my comrades and myself; but still my train followed and pressed upon me: "Sahib, me ver good ting to sale!"—" Palanquin, sahib—dis way!"—" Me ver good Khitmudgar, sahib!" &c. &c. &c., till I cursed the very title wherewith they honoured me, and, sighing, thought of home.

At last, a bright idea flashed across my bewildered mind, as a dirty bit of paper (stating the excellent behaviour and unimpeachable honesty of the owner—by name "Puggree"—during his periods of former service) was waved before my eyes. I snatched it from his hand, I cried (in that peculiar and fanciful English, wherewith John Bull loves to address and mystify a foreigner), "You name Puggree?" "Yes, sahib." "You be my *sarevant?*" "Yes, sahib." "All right—come long." Thus, by a subtle stroke of policy, I engaged at once a servant, an interpreter, and an ally, and its good effects were immediately apparent, as with this reinforcement I set to work to accomplish the herculean task of dispersing my enemies. How they disappeared before Puggree's fluent Hindostanee!—how they fled like chaff before his threatening gestures!—how all-powerful was Puggree, my ally and my friend.

Good Puggree!—best of menials!—dearest and most invaluable of men! — the recollection of thy signal services on this occasion, as I look back on them through the dim vista of time and space, almost effaces the bitterness of that fatal moment when I discovered —alas! too late, that, in engaging thee, I had taken a viper to my bosom. Oh, Puggree! Puggree! I could have forgotten thee when thou toldest me that thou spakest English, though "Yes, sahib," was all you knew—I could have forgiven thee that stupidity and ignorance of our language, which caused thee one evening after dinner, when coffee was on the table, and I sent thee for my pipe, to bring me a flannel shirt instead—I could have forgiven thee that love of money which prompted thee to charge me six rupees for a chillum-chee (or brass basin), when the retail price was three!—I could have borne the mysterious disappearance of those socks and handkerchiefs without taunting thee with peculation—I could have submitted with gentle patience, as became a griff, to the purloining from time to time of small sums of money from my purse, and stray coins from my table—I think—I think, Puggree, I could have borne all this; but oh! it was cruel of thee to forsake me, and to leave me when I was about to proceed up country; it was cruel, not to say dishonest, of thee to elope with those five rupees, which I had paid thee in advance, to give, as thou toldest me with trembling voice, thy accents and thy English alike broken, to the weeping wife and family that thou wert leaving behind!—it was cruel, this desertion, and it wrung my aching heart, oh, my friend, and more than brother! And yet, who knows? Puggree, thou mayest have intended it as a kindness! Might it not have been that, as thy babes clung to thy knees, and sobbing, sought to delay thy departure, that at the sight of these innocents thou thoughtest of me, and, revolving in thy mind what charity thou couldst do me, or kindness show me, in gratitude for past favours, thou resolvedst to give the sincerest proof of thy affection, and—and thou didst leave me! Who knows, I say, that it may not have been so? Who knows what it may not have cost thee (literally, as well as metaphorically), thus tearing thyself from me? for, since that time, Puggree, I have heard caustic and bitter tongues "damn thee with faint praise"—I have seen fists clench and lips compress at mention of thy name; I have e'en known pens to splutter with emotion as they wrote accounts defamatory of thy subsequent services; and I fear, Puggree, that in the regard I entertained for thee, I "loved not wisely, but too well."

Arrived at the barracks, we found our men revelling in all the luxury of being ashore again, bed *vice* hammocks, bread *vice* biscuit, and all the hundred other little comforts which, to the private soldier, at least, are unattainable on board ship: there was another source of intense wonder and

INDIAN MILITARY HABITS. 43

amusement in the shape of some score of dusky attendants, who, having been "entertained" (as hiring a servant is called in India) by grateful "John Company" for the service of our men, were bustling about with officious activity, grinning and greeting their future masters. It is at first difficult for the English soldier to realize that he, who has hitherto cooked his own dinner, drawn his own water, swept, cleaned, and garnished his own room, and performed each and every domestic duty, by himself and for himself, has now cooks, bheesties, mhaters, and other menials at his " nod and beck ;" and it is charming to see the contempt with which Gunner Thomas Smith, large of limb, and colossal of mould, and just landed in India, elbows off half a dozen puny, gasping, grunting coolies, who are vainly endeavouring to shoulder a—to them—ponderous package, and with a " Be off with you, niggers !" trudges away unassisted with the bundle, to the astonishment and no small gratification of Messrs. Coolie and Co.; and there was much truth in the remark made by a certain gallant sergeant on one occasion to some fifty of this genus coolie, who, in the attempt to move a heavy piece of baggage from the boat to the shore, were grunting, yelling, jabbering, talking all at once, and making a wild noise, as is their wont. Impatiently surveying them for some time, the worthy sergeant could resist no longer, and at last addressed them with an unmistakeable Hibernian brogue : " Silence ! silence there, boys ! Don't have so much *tarl*king wid ye. Bedad ! when a man opens his mouth, sure half his strength just pops out of it." It is needless to add that this apophthegm (an old piece of barrack-yard chaff, by the way, which had doubtless sunk deep into the heart of many a recruit in the drill-ground at home), uttered as it was in the vernacular, fell unappreciated upon the ears of his present audience.

Well, well, Gunner Thomas Smith, like privates Brown, Jones, and Robinson who have gone before him, drops imperceptibly into Indian ways; and ere many weeks have sped he finds out that it is better fun confining himself to the operation of eating his dinner than having to eat and cook it too; he learns with wonderful promptness the value of a bheestie, and he acquires a taste for the pleasures of repose in a shorter time than could possibly have been expected; but, spite this aptitude for falling into Indian customs, it is a very long time before T. Smith aforesaid will succumb entirely and thoroughly to Oriental indolence, or learn to do nothing with that easy dignity beseeming the Anglo-Bengalee; and the longer time the better, for it is pitiable to see the state of helplessness to which some soldiers—"old stagers" in India, arrive—a helplessness fostered by traditional fallacies, and founded on erroneous and ruinous precedents. Doubtless there are many things that the English soldier has been accustomed to do at home which become impossibilities in India, and for the performance of which he must depend greatly on natives; doubtless a large, and to the eye of a European, an overwhelming staff of natives must, from the very peculiar character of Indian warfare, from the exigencies of the climate, and many another minor cause, be constantly in attendance on every English regiment; doubtless it is not only prudent but necessary to protect our friend Thomas Smith as much as possible from the fatal effects of the sun, unless you wish a week after his arrival in the country to accompany him with " arms reversed," and a band wailing forth the sad music of the " Dead March in Saul," to his last resting-place on earth; but it is not—it cannot be necessary or judicious to pamper him as though he were some indolent rajah, and to " wink at " his procuring natives to clean his boots or appointments, or to brush him for parade.

Possibly the large influx of English troops into this country during the last year will upset much of this ridiculous and injurious custom, this overgrown, though to a certain extent necessary, evil, as it already has done some others; for what old Indian would not have smiled if, in the year 1855, you had told him that in 1858 he would be sweltering in a tent throughout an Indian summer, or marching about Oude, and fighting battles in the " leafy month of June?" Who would not have sneered at, perchance pitied, the prophet of these events, with " Poor fellow!—head, you know, little touched. Mad as—yes—March-hare!" If we reform one thing, why not another? If we overturn one fallacy, why not two? And why, when we are cleansing and burnishing up anew our Eastern empire, should we not carefully remove every speck of rust which corrodes its bright surface, and eats slowly perhaps, but surely into the very core? Oh! how well I can see the contemptuous face of the old Indian as he lights upon this passage! How distinctly do I hear the sneering remark which disposes of it as the "Aw—confound the fellow!—impertinent ignorance of a 'griff'—aw." Now do, like a dear, good, old, yellow-faced gentleman that you are, go on with your mulligatawney and your curry, and don't, please don't, spoil your dinner by getting into a bad humour.

CHAPTER V.

Town of Calcutta—Tour of inspection in a Palkee—Palkee bearers—A comparison between them and the genus "Cabby"—Burning ghât—Native bazaar—Calcutta Post Office—The heavy, murmuring swell succeeding the great storm—Castaways saved from the wreck, and thrown up upon the high shore of human charity and sympathy—A few words about the Sepoys—Indian servants.

Suppose we get into a palanquin, and in this very peculiar and Oriental conveyance enter the " City of Palaces," and form an opinion of its interior. Away we go, our two palanquins abreast —jog, jog, jog,—grunt, grunt, grunt, from the bearers, across the Chowringhee; jog, jog, jog —and in a very few minutes, as the clowns say at Christmas, " Here we are !" It is hardly necessary to go twenty yards to discover that the City of Palaces is likewise a City of Incongruities, and it would be rather a nice question to decide as to whether it looks most like Belgravia, with a few palaces hired for the occasion, and dropped down into the middle of an inferior Irish village, while some inquisitive mosques and minarets have strolled up to assist at the ceremony, or whether Constantinople has not wandered by mistake to Wapping, picking up the principal faubourgs of Paris, together with the London Docks, *en route*. Stately houses are jostled in the most discourteous manner by insignificant little hovels, which look as much out of place as a pickpocket would in the House of Lords, but which, nevertheless, elbow their gigantic neighbours with a free-and-easy, self-possessed air charming to behold; and it would warm a Frenchman's heart to see the *liberté, égalité, et fraternité* existing among these vagabondish cabins, who appear to glory impudently in their democratic and republican propensities.

Owing to the nature of the climate and the baneful effects of the sun, goods are not here exposed in the shop-windows as in England, hence the streets bear more the appearance of rows of large private houses than immense "Emporiums of wealth and commerce," and this, though perhaps improving the town by giving it a more Westendish look, quite does away with that gay and variegated aspect, that play of colours, which so greatly adds to the attractiveness of French and English cities; and I think, on the whole, what with the indiscriminate mixture of splendour and indigence—the absence of those flower-beds of merchandise which to us as a "nation of shopkeepers" should have a peculiar charm—the pre-Adamite nature of the oil-lamps wherewith a portion of the town is lighted, and the general obsolete, out-of-date appearance of many objects which greet the eye in a drive through its streets, that Calcutta is painfully disappointing to the eager stranger, who, having surveyed from shipboard, with charmed gaze, its fair and promising outline, finds himself brought at last face to face with the less pleasing details. There is a sort of new-cloth-in-an-old-garment look about it, and there are spots where the enamel and paint have been rubbed off or never applied—spots where the pruning-knife of progress and civilization is sadly wanted.

There is an old story told of an Irishman who was playing cards, and on counting the pool, cried out, " Here's a shilling short; who put it in?" And on beholding Calcutta, and becoming alive to the fact of how much there is "short" in the way of modern improvements and refinement, one feels tempted to echo the remark of the son of Erin aforesaid, and cry with him, "Who put it in?" or, to drop the somewhat obscure metaphor of Hibernian phraseology, to whom are these shortcomings attributable—to want of energy on our parts, or to the remnant of the old leaven of native barbarism, which clings with such unconquerable tenacity, more or less, to all our Indian institutions, and which in many cases we have scarcely troubled ourselves to shake off?

Faugh! how crowded, dirty, and noisy are the streets of the native portion of the town, as one drives on a tour of inspection through the bazaars, while one's palanquin is beset by a host of panting, shouting vendors of all descriptions of commodities, from the delicately carved curiosities of China, to inferior editions of English books, and bad imitations of English sauces and pickles; and it is no uncommon sight to have a box of French plums, or some other sweetmeat, offered for sale at one door of your palanquin, and a *Walker's Pronouncing Dictionary* at the other, and as all commercial transactions of this nature are carried on without stopping, or even slackening the rapid jog, jog, jog of your palkee, a great facility is afforded the buyer, by keeping the seller, who is running alongside, in conversation until he is completely "blown," and then offering him half the price demanded; when, being at his last gasp, he generally closes the bargain, and you jog on exulting in your victory, though the odds are ten to one that even then you have paid more than double the proper value.

While I am on the subject of palanquins, I must devote a few words to the bearers of the same, and relate a little stratagem lately resorted to by them which is worthy of notice. Like a certain class of public servants at home, these bearers have been frequently brought to task for attempting to extort from unwary strangers a fare considerably above what they are entitled to, and for grumblingly indulging in Hindostanee figures of speech answering to the " Wha-a-at's this?—*this* ain't my fare!—you call *your*self a gemman indeed!" so much in vogue among our London charioteers, and which is invariably punished when brought under the notice of a magistrate by a fine. Now Messieurs Palkee-bearers (like all Hindoos), being avaricious by nature, had long winced under these forfeitures of rupees, and on considering the matter, and revolving in their minds a plan for avoiding these mulcts for the future, they were not long in discovering that it was (very naturally) owing to the badge, or number, which they are compelled to wear, that the justice-seeking victims of their extortions were able to identify them, for the palanquins being hired from certain proprietors by the month, and the bearers never changing their badge during that period, the process of identification was not a difficult one. What, then, must palkee-bearer do to enable him to victimize the "sahibs" with impunity? Oh, the cunning of man! He hires his palanquin *by the day*, changing his badge and number also *diurnally*, and thus defies discovery, as is apparent to the astonished eyes of "sahib," when he drags No. 172 into court for being extortionate the day before yesterday, and finds, alas! that he is by no means the real Simon Pure. The case is dismissed; "sahib" looks foolish; while ex-No. 172, temporarily transformed into 384, is probably jogging and grunting away across the Chowringhee, and complacently contemplating "doing" the fat old "fare" who now occupies his palanquin in exactly the same manner. It is to be hoped that long ere these pages are printed, counter cunning, to meet the exigencies of the case, and tending utterly to confuse and put to shame palkee-bearer, will have been employed; but I tell the story as I heard it a short time ago, as I think the hint may perchance be of service to our "cabbies." By the way, is it not lucky that these bearers, in addition to their cunning, are not endowed with the "chaff" and impudence which form the stock-in-trade of every British cabman? When you reflect with a shudder on the altercations in which you have, doubtless, been often engaged with that rapacious class; with what a sarcastic smile "cabby" has regarded your tendered sixpence; with what minute interest he has examined it, as a curiosity with which he has hitherto been unacquainted; with what *naïveté* he has held it up to the light, as though to observe whether or not it was transparent; with what painful incredulity he has bitten it, as though to test the purity of the metal; and, last, but not least, with what cutting irony—and in such naughty words !—he has questioned your position in society—I say, when you reflect on all you have gone through on these occasions, when you had only *one* opponent, you turn pale at the bare idea of the conflict that must result every time you issued from your palanquin, were each of your four bearers possessed of equal acerbity of temper and powers of repartee!

At length we pass the "Burning Ghât," the banks of the Hooghly, one of the onions" of Calcutta. Here the last rites of fire and flame are performed on the mortal remains of many a Hindoo, and it is curious to see the crowds of huge birds of prey assembled at this spot. Great vultures, suffering from repletion, and in a state of after-dinner *coma*, doze placidly on one leg; tall and stately "adjutants" stalk about—" tritons among the minnows"—picking up the tit-bits, and actively performing their duties as the scavengers of Calcutta;* others are waiting in patient expectation, with hungry eyes, for the arrival of the next body ; and the whole scene is one calculated to afford food for reflection for the thoughtful philosopher, and to produce a sarcastic chuckle from the observant satirist. We are not Hindoos, readers, but in our own country do not vultures sometimes dispute as savagely and publicly over our remains? Are there not "birds of prey" as rapacious, who will quarrel over our "pickings" when the time comes for us "to shuffle off this mortal coil?" I have heard it said there

* These birds are so useful as scavengers, that any one in Calcutta shooting one, is, I believe, liable to a fine of £5.

are, and I have also heard it hinted that it would be more seemly if these harpies at home would follow the example of our feathered friends at the "Burning Ghât," in waiting until life is extinct before they scramble and peck at one another for the tempting morsels!

For the last half-hour our path has been through streets in all the benighted vandalism of the dark ages, among scenes painfully illustrative of the uncouth and untutored taste of the East; through squalid narrow slums, in which civilization has stagnated; past low ill-built houses, reeking with impurities, and fevers, and vile stenches; while, buying, selling, coming and going and passing to and fro, pours along the dark stream of noisy, bustling humanity, which floods to overflowing these living sewers. Here and there does some tawdry, gaudily-painted mosque dazzle the unaccustomed eye, but it is like the flash of lightning, which renders yet more palpable the darkness of the night—a bright, brief flicker, which is straightway passed. High above all this rises the jargon of tongues, many, confused, and loud; and if the reader can picture all this to himself, he will form a tolerably correct idea of the native portion of Calcutta. But see! a little further on, and as our palanquin turns a corner, the beautiful buildings in the neighbourhood of Government House, with the vast proportions and high dome of that palace itself, break upon our view; the Chowringhee, gay and glittering as ever, spreads out before us, and we are once more sunning ourselves in the bright noontide of civilization and refinement. The change has been as rapid as it is curious; it is like coming suddenly from a dark room into the light, and the sense of oppression which has weighed heavily upon us is at last replaced by one of calm enjoyment.

There are very many subjects connected with Calcutta on which I would willingly touch, were it not that I am fearful of wearying my readers with matters of so little interest to them as the luxury of the clubs, the vastness of the hotels, the public offices, and how the science of circumlocution is preached therein; the almost total absence of theatres and theatrical amusement, except when a few ambitious amateurs make occasional wild efforts to immortalize themselves; the Post Office, the prevailing feature of which, at first sight, is chaos—but which gradually, in my case, gave way to one of awe and admiration, for on first going into the Calcutta Post Office I was overwhelmed, not with civility, not with letters which had been lying *perdues*, but with wonder— wonder that people in India ever received their letters at all; and, as I found, on proceeding "up country," that I actually received about one letter out of every four, and one newspaper in every eight despatched to me—which ratio continued during my residence in the country—a feeling of respect and admiration came over me for the master-minds of those *baboos* and functionaries who had extricated these welcome little documents from confusion worse confounded, and for the clear heads and lucid intellects which, amidst official anarchy there reigning supreme, had been able to grasp the subtle and misty details of that idea, the execution of which puts me in possession of—as I said before—fully a fourth part of the letters that I ought to receive; and therefore do I respect the Calcutta Post Office, and think it a grand and noble institution, a *leetle* apathetic and mouldy it may be, and perchance a " wee bit " tardy and irregular in its proceedings, but a grand and noble institution nevertheless, and well worthy of England or of India.*

At the time I landed in Calcutta (December, 1857), though all immediate panic as to the outbreak of the mutiny in that city had subsided, and the good folk had left off sleeping in the fort and other available strongholds, there were still ample signs of its existence. The native sentries (belonging to disarmed regiments) were entrusted only with that formidable and murderous weapon a ramrod, which they made faint efforts to shoulder, after the manner of a musket, when saluting an officer, thereby presenting an appearance savouring more strongly of the ridiculous than the sublime. Occasionally little excitements were got up by some highly imaginative gentlemen fixing in their respective minds' eyes a certain day as the one on which the natives were to rise in deadly hostility, and expressing their melancholy convictions of this fact to the public at large, and the government in particular, thereby giving some

* To the English gentleman in Yorkshire or Northumberland, who at that distance from the metropolis sits down to a perusal of the *Times* the same day that it is published, it will appear almost incredible that a letter I wrote from Allahabad to Futtehghur (not more than two hundred miles) was over *sixty days* in reaching its destination, having, I believe, visited *en route* Calcutta, Madras, and Bombay.

extra occupation to the troops in the shape of night alarms, patrols, and constant admonitions to be "in readiness to turn out at a moment's notice;" in fact, the sea of English society at Calcutta was still swollen by the storm which had ruffled it so boisterously a short time back, and it heaved now and again with a heavier swell than usual. But there were sadder signs than these of the fury of the blast, which one met at every step; in the shattered, drooping shrubs which it had stripped of twig and branch—in the sturdy oak, whose every bough had been torn from it, leaving the parent stem all desolate and bare—in the tiny budding blossom, blighted and alone, so young that it knew not its loss, and cried impatiently, from time to time, for the mother whom it was never more to see on earth, and when asked its name, gave the only one it ever heard or knew, "Mamma's Pet."* These mutely told the tale of woe—told it more eloquently than cold words, or the pen of howsoever ready a writer ever could; on the pale, careworn faces, on the deep mourning, on the sad forms—look on these if you would read such lines of bereavement, and suffering, and sorrow, as would melt a heart of stone. Still down country poured this melancholy stream—day by day did fresh mourners arrive— faces more haggard still, more pale and tearful, saddened Calcutta by their presence, preparatory

* This is related as a fact of a little child who was rescued from the mutineers, whose kindred had all been swept away, and whom no one knew; while he was too young to give any other account of himself than the touching one I have recorded.

to leaving the land in which they had borne and lost so much, and returning to seek for peace and repose among the calm scenes and pleasant homesteads of old England.

During a conversation which I had with a person soon after landing, in the course of which I naturally recurred to the all-absorbing topic— the mutiny—I unwittingly touched a tender chord, for he sighed when I mentioned the subject, and said, solemnly, " Ah, sir, I have been a sad sufferer by it;"—he had lost *his wife and thirteen near relations* during the bloody scenes which had so convulsed India! Many a tale of torture and cruelty did he tell me; in some of the instances being himself personally acquainted with, or related to, the victims—tales of butcheries and the pouring out like water of innocent blood—of insults to ladies too horrible to mention—of repulsive indignities too dreadful to conceive, equalling, if not exceeding, in the atrocity of their details any of those accounts which had chilled the blood of newspaper readers at home—but I firmly believed at the time, and I firmly believe now, what this man told me; he was a person holding a most respectable and responsible office under government, and I have never seen any occasion for discrediting his statements. Why is it that by some these tales of suffering and torture are now disbelieved? Have we, since they were first published, seen anything in the Sepoy character—any unusual gentleness—any tender forbearance—any great humanity, which may justify this disbelief? If so, on what occasions? Surely not in the loathsome mutilations of the bodies of dead English soldiers which may fall into their hands—surely not in the frightful cruelties that they commit, to this day, when they have the power, on unfortunate villagers, *their own countrymen*, whose only crime has been remaining faithful to us—surely not in the taunting boast made by one of them, as he was being led to the gallows, that he died happy in the consciousness of having himself assisted and taken part in the killing of English children, and the dishonouring of—as he expressed it—" your wives, your mothers, and your daughters."* These things are not calculated to elevate the Sepoy character in our opinion, or to cause one to think that in the first flush of triumph —in the first outburst of his pent-up hate, maddened by the taste of blood, and dazzled with his temporary successes, he would think of mercy; or is this disbelief merely assumed, to goad the poor shrinking sufferers into detailing before a curious public the misery, the indignities, the humiliations to which they or their families have been exposed? I cannot think so badly of human nature as this. But why probe afresh the healing wound? why thus additionally pain the poor surviving victims, by saying, " You did not go through so very much, after all; you say you did, but unfortunately we cannot believe you, unless you give us ocular and tangible proof;" for it seems much as though

* This vile wretch was captured by a column under Sir Hope Grant at Meahgunge in Oude, a short time before the attack on Lucknow, at which place he prophesied we should be defeated and all put in chains! He uttered the words quoted in my text while being led to the death which, by his own admission, he so justly deserved.

these words were in your mouths when you give the lie to your poor suffering countrymen, when you discredit their tale, for the sake of a wild infatuation—for such it must be called—which prompts you to doubt that the hell-hounds who have filled *seventy-two pages* (of an official report) with the names of their victims, murdered deliberately and wantonly, are not capable of any atrocity which the minds of men or fiends can devise.

I do not wish by the above remarks to intimate my belief in the *whole* of the stories which appeared from time to time in the public prints, many of them being, doubtless, gross fabrications, written to satisfy a morbid craving for horrors, to which we are all somewhat prone—or for the purpose of indulging the writer's powers of romancing to the utmost; but I do most thoroughly believe, painful as is the thought, that tortures of the most revolting description were committed, and that scenes occurred the grossness of which far exceeded anything that appeared in the columns of the press, and that if all the instances were detailed, some of the stories conceived by the most lively minds would be thrown far back into the shade, and we should find another verification of the old saying, " Truth is stranger than fiction."

There are few things more striking to a person just landed in India than the extraordinary and unbounded confidence which English people appear to have in their native servants, who, to use an unclassical expression, walk, " quite promiscuous like," in and out of one's room all day—noiselessly, certainly, for there are no shoes upon their dusky feet to creak and disturb you—but the very presence of these white-clad figures flitting about one prevented me for some time from feeling that placid sensation of "at home" and retirement which every man at times must long for and seek to obtain in the privacy of his own chamber. But after a time one becomes accustomed to this; one finds a troop of domestics indispensable, and one thoroughly appreciates the removal of that restraint which is a sort of bugbear in England—the fear of talking before the servants, and of John Thomas retailing, for the benefit of Sally the housemaid, and Robert the groom, your eloquent remarks on poetry, politics, or the fine arts, minus the *h*'s; then, again, from time immemorial, it has been the custom to entrust your "bearer" (or *valet-de-chambre*) with entire control over your purse; he takes possession of the unwieldy bag of rupees containing your pay for the preceding month, he doles out to your manifold attendants their wages, he pays your bills, he settles all monetary transactions, and, in fact, acts *in toto* as your treasurer. Now, to the suspicious young son of Albion, who arrives in India with ideas redolent of Bramah locks and patent safes, this custom is a hard one to fall into. He consults some old Indian, who says, "Oh, yes! it's all right. Your 'bearer' will cheat you a little, but he will not allow any one else to do so; whereas, if you keep your own keys, opportunities will never be wanting for him to pilfer; and his reply on your frantically crying to him for 'my ducats! oh, my Christian ducats!'

will be, 'What should I know? Sahib keeps his own keys, how can I then guard his money?'"
So, acting upon this advice, griff resigns his keys with a half-sigh and a feeling of regret, which, however, soon dies away as he becomes daily more Indianized in his ways of thinking and acting.

CHAPTER VI.

"*Malbrook s'en va-t-en guerre*"—Pursuit of packing under difficulties—Howrah—East Indian Railway—Raneegunge.

"Hurrah! the order is come for us to proceed at once 'up country' by bullock-train—to join the army!" How I jumped up from my bed, threw my cheroot and the fag-end of my reflections on Indian customs and peculiarities to the winds when I heard these words! for stirring events, and deadly strifes, and glorious victories were now convulsing that portion of India familiarly known as "up country," and to join Sir Colin Campbell's splendid force, to share its laurels and its toils, was the acme of every soldier's ambition.

It is no small feat to pack for a campaign of indefinite length so that the whole of your personal baggage shall not exceed 100 lbs. in weight —such being the allowance for each officer travelling by bullock-train. No small feat, did I say? it is an impossibility! Your portmanteau alone weighs about half that, and when you fill it with shirts, socks, boots, brushes, coats, and all the manifold et cæteras, why, 200 lbs. would not turn the scale against it; not to mention a camp bedstead and some pounds' weight of saddlery. In despair you unpack it, and ponder over the contents. What is there in that heterogeneous collection that you can dispense with? Shirts?

No. Boots? Certainly not. Towels? how can you do without them? So finally in despair, you repack the portmanteau, having reduced its weight by, perhaps, one shirt, two pairs of socks, and maybe a boot. Now for shutting it: a healthy, athletic, nail-breaking, finger-pinching amusement, which occupies you for some time, and when flushed, breathless, and with dishevelled locks you accomplish it, you probably discover, carefully placed on a side-table ready for packing, your pocket handkerchiefs, tooth-brushes, and half a dozen articles equally indispensable. Gracious goodness! and must these go into a space scarcely ——Well, well, there is no help for it, and somehow or another, when the day arrives, you find yourself at the Armenian Ghât, casting a sickly smile on exactly four times the quantity of baggage that you are entitled to, and the iron of despair enters your soul as you, from time to time, bethink yourself of some important articles that you have left behind, and which you cannot possibly do without—trousers, *par exemple*. But what are your woes to those of Gunner Patrick Murphy, who comes up to you to report that he has lost his knapsack?—HIS KNAPSACK! Oh, ye gods, have pity on this Patrick Murphy, for every stitch of clothing that he possesses (except that in which his burly frame is at this moment clad), the knife and fork wherewith he eats his dinner, the brushes wherewith he cleans his boots, his pipeclay, on which rests his military reputation, nay, even the tress of hair which he sheared at parting from the head of his well-loved Biddy, all these does his well-filled knapsack contain, and one really feels as if any attempt to offer consolation, or hold out any hope to a wretched mortal who will—as far as you can foresee—have to go through a campaign of some two or three months in one shirt, and without a change of socks, would be simply ridiculous; nor are you sorry when the ferry steamer coming bustling and puffing alongside, relieves you temporarily from your embarrassment, and carries you across the muddy Hooghly to the railway terminus at Howrah, which is opposite to Calcutta, on the right bank; Mr. Pat Murphy consoling himself, the while, with reflecting on the possibility of his getting a new kit, knapsack and all complete, from the first "Saypoy" that he kills; for Private Murphy, true to the discipline which has moulded him into the machine he now is, and with a high, opaque, war-office fence of stocks, straps, and pipeclay surrounding his imagination, and somewhat limiting his ideas, has doubtless pictured to himself the Sepoy as appearing on all occasions *en grande tenue*, after the manner of British soldiers at Aldershott and the Curragh.

Howrah—the terminus of the East Indian Railway. I wonder what the frequenters of the Great Western would say, if, one fine morning on going to Paddington station, in the place of the lusty, fustian-clad porters, they were to find the platform swarming with naked Hindoos—I wonder what my friends the cabbies would say if hansom after hansom were to drive away with a nigger fare in it—I wonder what the epicures, who grumble at the refreshments provided at

Wolverton, Paddington, and Euston-square would say, if they were forced to enter a dirty little place and pay innumerable rupees for sandwiches, which, judging from their appearance, would be likely to meet with a favourable reception from no one except, perhaps, the members of an antiquarian society, as being curiosities in their line of business—I wonder, in fact, what our good friends at home would say if Howrah, with its cheerless appearance—the absence of all that bustle, hurry and scurry, which, with our English notions, we consider as inseparable from a railway station—with its semi-European character, with its snorting locomotives, typical of civilization and science on one hand, and the black, naked natives, impersonation of barbarism, on the other, were to open business in London one fine morning! Probably as I did, they would take their seats in the train slightly bewildered, and with a dreamy, nightmare-ish sort of feeling coming over them; a whistle—no mistake about that—you wake from your reverie to find yourself spinning some twenty-five or thirty miles an hour over a dead level country, which as far as the eye can reach, scarcely appears to rise or fall an inch—flat, flat, flat for miles, and miles, and miles, but rich with vegetation; on you go, getting such a jolting as few people who have not travelled out of England have experienced; dazzled with heat and glare, blinded and choked with dust, suffering in the region of your digestive organs from the effects of the superannuated sandwiches, and rousing yourself ever and anon to look out of the window, when you find the scene so unchanged as almost to tempt you to believe that you have not moved a yard for the last half-hour; flat, flat, flat as a billiard-table, wearisome to gaze upon, and you pine even for a friendly ant-hill to relieve your eye, and break this almost maddening smoothness of country—flat, flat, flat—heigho! but neither "stale" nor "unprofitable" if one may judge from the natives at work among the numerous crops of rice, and corn, and "dâl," labouring on in the scorching sun, with bare heads and shaven crowns, scarcely deigning—whether from excess of apathy or industry I cannot say—a glance of stupid wonder as we jolt and rattle past them; now a wood, or a piece of jungle—now a wide tract of sand, glaring, glistening, and white—now a half dried-up "jheel"—now a paddy-bird frightened at our approach, soaring up into the air—now a covey of small green parrots similarly employed—now a garden—now a green—now a desert—now a few bullocks in the agricultural interests—now a mud hovel, and now a solitary palm-tree—here a rice-field, and there a few isolated tufts of high grass,—these are the objects which in their turns attract one's attention during this monotonous and weary journey, and these seen only through the glassy, glaring film of sunlight, which glitters and plays about them in all the brightness of an Indian noon, and which causes one's eyes to blink and water painfully as they encounter it.

A short time is allowed for tiffin at Burdwan, when bell and whistle warn you once more to take your place, and, whisk! you are off again. Still over the flat, monotonous country you rumble and roll along—rice-fields, hovels, palm-trees, and wastes of sand—palm-trees, hovels, and rice-fields, with a one-two-three-four precision, which, combined with bottled beer consumed at Burdwan, at last has a narcotic effect, your doze being somewhat disturbed by a mosquito, who has taken a first-class ticket to Raneegunge, and by the feeble efforts of one of your comrades to manufacture a joke or riddle at the expense of the *black guard* attached to the train, but which, when he delivers himself of it, after much labour, proves singularly unsuccessful, and with an irritable " Pshaw!" you turn to the window again, hotter, dustier, more uncomfortable than ever, and wondering with savage impatience what the deuce those bullocks can mean by eating dust, for there appears to be little else upon that parched plain, where a dozen of them are placidly grazing. As we approach Raneegunge some hills become visible, and our spirits pluck up a bit accordingly; and by the time the break is put on, and its peculiar odour—which, by the way, is agreeable, as reminding you of England—becomes apparent, our temper has improved considerably, while we almost become amiable as the train draws up alongside the platform.

Raneegunge (about one hundred and twenty miles distant from Calcutta) is the farthest point to which the East Indian Railway is at present carried in Bengal Proper—the point at which one of the rays from the magic-lantern of science, now so fast dispersing the darkness of the East, ceases, and is, as it were, lost in the surrounding night; it is the point where the traveller, proceeding up country, must part with that staunch and unrivalled ally of civilization, steam, and gently lead his far-stretching imagination backward some half a century; it is the point at which the reinforcements of men, ever flowing towards the scene of action, are collected before commencing their long and tedious march, or committing their martial forms to the tender mercies of the dâk carriages provided for their conveyance; and, more important still, it is the place where we, and such as we, first stretch our limbs upon the rack of the Great East Indian Torture, yclept bullock-train!

Here, too, does one first become acquainted with the admirable working and perfect arrangements of that department, which in India soars high above surrounding incompetence and chaos, and which, arduous and prolonged as have been its duties and extensive its operations, has on no occasion, I believe, been found wanting or incapable—I mean, of course, the commissariat, to which, I am sure, no officer or person acquainted with its performances will refuse that meed of praise which it so richly deserves.

Huts built of bamboos, flattened out and plaited, are provided for the accommodation of the troops who may have to tarry here *en route*, and to these somewhat frail and airy residences, which are about two miles from the railway station, were we directed to proceed, our path thither lying through scenery more thoroughly Indian and characteristic, more innocent of bungalows and civilized houses, than any I had yet beheld. The Oriental beauty of the landscape received additional effect and was enhanced tenfold by large quantities of elephants, some of whom were tranquilly enjoying a bathe in certain shady pools, while others were lazily strolling towards the encampment, where a number of their huge companions were picketed, jingling the strong iron chains which fastened them to posts, as they consumed the ample piles of branches, and sugar-cane, and long grass placed before them by their respective *mahouts,* flapping their immense ears, or occasionally taking the bough of a tree in their trunks wherewith to drive away the flies and other buzzing insects which irritated and disturbed them, or throwing dust and sand over their enormous black bodies, or between their uncouth legs, with a similar object. What with the voluptuous repose of the charming evening; the mellowed light of the sinking sun; the tall palms casting their long, fantastic shadows over straggling but picturesque mud villages, and athwart tangled brakes, wherein lurked half dried-up muddy ponds; the sensation of relief as the heat of the day gave place to the cool, light evening air, which played softly among the tropical foliage, and swayed gently to and fro the tall yellow grass composing the wild patches of jungle, which were dotted over the country with a beautiful irregularity; the quiet pervading the whole scene; the low hum of insects, and the novel and striking pictures by which the lover of nature must have been captivated on every hand, —all these combined could scarcely have failed to gladden one's heart, and to leave a lasting and grateful impression on one's mind.

On arriving, however, upon the plateau where stand the bamboo-hut barracks, the landscape loses all this beauty, and savours once more of the sterile and the bleak. Nor does the town of Raneegunge itself impress one with any very great amount of admiration, composed as it is of a few rickety wooden huts, in which are exposed for sale, *à la* Kadikoi (of Crimean celebrity), the miscellaneous goods which merchants have been enterprising enough to bring up here, the prices of which may be briefly stated as *à la* Kadikoi also.

CHAPTER VII.

Journey by "Bullock-train"—The Fashion of it—A Night in a Cart—Grand Trunk Road—Moving Accidents.

AND now, kind reader, I think it not only charitable, but necessary, before enticing you into a bullock-waggon, to explain in a few words the nature of this mode of travelling, and the vehicle employed, in order that you may be, in some sort, prepared for the amount of suffering to which you will be subjected if you think fit to accompany me, or for the harrowing details which it will be my painful duty to lay before you.

A bullock-waggon, then, is a very strong wooden cart, on two wheels, without the faintest attempt at springs, and with a fragile roof, made of thin staves of wood, covered with painted canvas, the curtains of which may be let down or rolled up at will; the body of the cart is about seven feet by five, and with sides about one foot and a half high, the whole of this primitive conveyance being drawn by two bullocks and driven by a native, and travelling at the brisk average pace of from two to two and a half miles per hour! Into each cart six soldiers, with their goods and chattels, are deposited, two out of this six being constantly " on guard," and marching alongside the train, for the double purpose of affording protection in case of an attack, and of creating a mathematical possibility—very far removed, though, from a practical probability—of the remaining four occupants of the cart lying *comfortably* (?) down in the same. Each bullock-train consists of large numbers of these carriages, from twenty-five to forty generally, following in succession, one behind the other, travelling during the night, and halting during the heat of the day at appointed stations, which one ordinarily arrives at about eight A.M. or nine A.M., and leaving again about three o'clock in the afternoon, changing bullocks every eight or nine miles, and by this means accomplishing a distance varying from thirty to thirty-six miles per diem.

These appointed stations for rest are each under the charge of a military officer, whose duty it is to see that breakfast is provided for the troops on their arrival, to furnish them with dinner, and generally to superintend the issue of all supplies, and to supervise the accommodation of the parties of men passing through. Temporary sheds have been erected for the men at these halting-places, while there is generally a "dâk-bungalow" (post-house) for the accommodation of the officers; and I feel assured that any one who has travelled by bullock train will testify to the excellent character of the arrangements, the superior quality of the rations which are served out, the thoughtful preparations for the troops' reception, and the careful attention paid to their comfort and well-being during their temporary sojourn at these truly "green spots" in the desert.

This, then, is the manner of travelling by bullock train. Well, so much for the theory. Would you apply it to practice? Kindly picture to yourself, then, a train of some thirty of these carts, drawn up in line at Raneegunge, awaiting the arrival of the gallant body of men whom they are about to convey to "death or glory," with a funereal sluggishness of pace, which, though unsuited to so stirring an occasion, had nevertheless a somewhat ominous and prophetic character; the knapsacks and baggage are already placed in the carts; the bullocks are wriggling their necks in the thraldom of the yoke, after the manner of a young "swell" whose deportment is affected by a too tight shirt-collar: all is prepared. Turn, then, thy admiring eyes, oh! spectator, and observe us stepping proudly towards our carts, our eyes wildly flashing, our hearts beating high as pardonable emotions and thoughts of "deeds of high emprise," swelling exultingly within us, test rather severely the strength of the buttons which fasten our tight regimentals, and the nature of the sewing in the seams of our martial, short-tailed tunics; observe us with light elastic step approach the line of vehicles; observe, if you will, a slight hanging back, a temporary hesitation, when the time comes, for effecting a lodgment on the vehicles in question, but prithee attribute it not to moral, but to physical causes, such as the absence of steps—the inaccessible nature of the carts, and their other unprecedented peculiarities of construction—to which alone it is ascribable: observe us, at last, after some difficulty and shin-barking, stowed away, "bag and baggage," the party on guard (consisting, as I have before intimated, of a third of our whole number) distributed with an eye to defensive operations, if necessary, and the word being given, behold! we are off.

We proceeded without interruption for at least fifty yards, when several bullocks began to show strong symptoms of mutiny, and one pair in particular, contriving to unyoke themselves, frisked pleasantly away across country, to the immense disgust of the driver, who pursued them, muttering what I conclude was *not* a blessing—though, as it was uttered in Hindostanee, it is impossible for me to say with certainty—and equally to the astonishment of the occupants of the cart, who, in consequence of the sudden withdrawal of the two animals supporting its pole, and its emulating the example of a seesaw, on the capsize of one of the two balancing powers disporting themselves thereon, found they were very much " down by the head," or, as they graphically expressed it, " all of a slope." At last the bullocks were led back captive, and being yoked in, once more unwillingly trudged on; but, alas! the revolt had become general, and from this time forth continued to break out at intervals. Now it was a pair of hitherto loyal bullocks proclaiming their independence by galloping, cart and all, furiously down a steep hill; now it was a pair of these charming animals refusing to go up one, and with more of disaffection than fatigue in their deportment, quietly lying down, and dropping off to sleep upon the spot, regardless of an avalanche of blows and abuse; here it was a cart proceeding at an accelerated pace towards a precipice, that Quintus Curtius himself would have looked at pretty attentively before he leaped thereinto, and causing your skin to creep at the prospect of its impending and apparently inevitable fate; there it was a pair of bullocks in a perfect paroxysm of stubborn insubordination, undergoing with much philosophy and indifference the operation of having their tails twisted nearly out of their sockets by an infuriated "nigger," as an incentive to locomotion; and I never shall forget the sinking, sickening feeling which came over me when "hope deferred" *sine die* began to ripen into an awful conviction of the horrible fact, that this sort of misery, this battling with bullocks, these heart-rending delays and stoppages, must be borne to the " end of the chapter."

And then the jolting and the dust! The only way in which it may be realized at home is to go to the Arsenal at Woolwich, there borrow a wheelbarrow, and obtain the sanction of the authorities to drive therein over the surface of an incomplete pile of 24-pounder shot, while some obliging friend filling a fine sieve with sand and dust gently sprinkles it over you as you go along. It is not that the road is rough and bad that one enjoys this jolting—this is the most provoking part of it—for the Grand Trunk Road is as free from inequalities, and in as good order, if not better, than most of the highways in England; and yet, as one drives over it in a bullock-cart, one is tempted to utter an anathema upon its unoffending surface—an anathema which justice requires to be directed against the diabolical construction of the carts in which one travels.

Of course one is much too uncomfortable, for the first day's journey at least, to think about the scenery —and so you sit in a sort of dust-clad lethargy, the few remarks you make coming forth with a hop-step-and-jump motion, as some of your words are shot out spasmodically, while others, on the point of making their *début*, are knocked down your throat, like teeth, unexpectedly, whole sentences being in this manner swallowed, unpleasantly it may be, but not unfrequently; your only lucid intervals being those during which the train halts for the purpose of changing bullocks, at which times you have a respite for a quarter of an hour.

This changing bullocks at night is a peculiar business, carried on with much noise and confusion, and at no small personal risk to the mortal who descends from his cart to stretch his legs, from the horns and heels of lively young bullocks who are trotting about, on goring or kicking intent. A little extra excitement is not unfrequently created by two or three pairs of these animals availing themselves of the gloom for the purpose of setting mankind at defiance, and strolling off to a neighbouring jungle, and so delaying our departure until such time as they kindly consent to return to their allegiance, or, failing this, until another pair are procured. There is a *soupçon* of the picturesque, too, about these occasions: the great blazing wood fire, round which are gathered the bullock-drivers, and jemadars, and other niggers, and which dazzles your eyes and throws a strange, bewildering light on surrounding objects, making the bullocks, who are passing to and fro before it, look red and unearthly, and giving to the natives who are squatting round its embers a hue demoniacal; while the soldiers, as they drag therefrom blazing fagots to light their pipes withal, send a shower of fiery sparks up into the dark night towards the starless heavens, the momentary glare luridly illuminating carts, and bullocks, and groups of men, and palm and other trees, and low mud hovels, but failing to penetrate the dense ebony frame of nocturnal gloom which adds so grandly to the general effect of the picture. The bullocks, however, are yoked in at last, the stray ones captured, the refractory ones subdued, and you return to your cart, and away goes the long line of carriages once more, with a heavy rumble into the darkness—on through this wild country, on towards scenes wilder still, on past dense jungle and dark wood, on through quiet, half-deserted villages, on over vast plains, across which the wind whistles drearily, no sound save that made by the carriages and the creaking of their wheels, or occasionally the voice of a sleepy, half-frozen bullock-driver stimulating his team to greater exertions, or the shout of a soldier rousing the bullock-driver to greater wakefulness, or here and there the yells of a pack of jackals, who have evidently made up their minds not to go home till morning—the only signs of life in all this loneliness being those visible in the drowsy native police at the various stations along the road—and a yawning, eye-rubbing sort of life it is, too, less suggestive of alertness than one could wish, and hinting at sleep abruptly disturbed, and dreams unfinished, on the part of these dusky "limbs of the law." One or two solitary travellers one meets, it is true, but few and far between, or occasionally a wearied horse, who has just had a gallop of some half-dozen miles with, figuratively speaking, a tin kettle tied to his tail in the shape of a rickety dâk carriage, and who is now, with drooping head and reeking flank, wending his way back to his miserable stable, and probably speculating with fluttering and desponding heart on the very limited quantity of " gram" which will be his portion on arrival.

But I am all this time in my cart—what do you suppose I am doing? "Sleeping," did I hear somebody suggest? I think not. I should like to be, perhaps; but no, I am certainly not sleeping. What then? Being jolted to death—that is about the expression—and it is a toss-up whether my death or burial will take place first, for the latter is progressing favourably and rapidly, thanks to the dust, which even at night, and all night, continues to fall in thick, grey, suffocating clouds; there I lay, wondering how the carts, devoid of lamp or light, keep on the dark road at all, and why they do not roll down a precipice, or into a pit, or a river, and so put one out of one's misery; then I become dozy, and half drop off to sleep, but, behold! the driver, who has likewise been dozing—pretty profoundly—for some time, wakes up, and discovers that his bullocks, with an eye to grazing, have stopped by the roadside, and that the cart, in consequence, is some fifty yards in rear of the one in front of it; this involves an increase of speed, therefore does the driver hold it necessary to give a workmanlike twist to his bullocks' tails, and a savage prod with a pointed stick into their plump hind-quarters, and away we go full tilt, jolt, jolt, jolt, till there looms before me, in the distance of anticipation, a fear that the bottom of the cart will come out, or the roof come down, or a wheel come off—I am much too sleepy to make up my mind which, and I do not much care—and then once more the bullocks leave off trotting, and the driver betakes himself again to dozing, as also do I, when suddenly I hear a horn, which awakes me, and I indulge in wild fancies on the subject of being attacked by Sepoys, and, slightly excited, I sit up, lift the curtain, and look out—the horn gets nearer and nearer, there is a dull rumble, louder, closer—whish! a whirl of wheels—a quick clatter of hoofs—a cloud of dust, which falls with suffocating precision into my mouth, and strolls up my nose, or takes up its quarters in my eyes, and past us, at full gallop, goes a half-crazed horse-dâk. Thereupon do I draw in my head with nervous haste, congratulating myself that it was not carried off by the passing carriage, and wondering whether I shall ever be able to clear my eyes of the dust which oppresses them, and after a few sleepy *pros and cons*, I make up my mind in the negative; so, philosophically, I resign myself once more to my fate and Morpheus. Then away goes my cart again—jolt, jolt, jolt—if I were a package, labelled "Glass, with care!" I could hardly be worse off, or so much shaken, and the light baggage, swinging from the roof, fights a confused battle, as the articles composing it dash and jingle against one another, when down comes heavily on to my shins a well-filled carpet-bag, but which, from its weight, I am almost tempted to think must be a midshipman's chest in disguise, and I grind my teeth with rage and pain, whereby I receive additional and disagreeable proof of the quality as well as quantity of the dust in my mouth, as I crush the gritty, sandy particles—ugh!—and I lay down in despair and agony, probably, in doing so, waking up my cart-companion,* by sitting on his face, or putting my elbow or my knee into the pit of his stomach, or otherwise coming into contact with him, and he sits up moody and abusive, and wants to know where we are, and of course I cannot tell him— how can I?—not having the remotest notion myself; and all I *do* know is, that I feel as if I had been awake for a year, and shaken in a dark dusthole for a century, and I wish to goodness he would "go to sleep and not bother," confound him! and so on, throughout the livelong night, wearily, wretchedly, drowsily, with not a ray of hope to cheer one up, and one's prospects looking about as gloomy as the night and Erebus.

But it would be wearisome to the reader were I to detail the events of each day, which were monotonous in the extreme: the waking in the morning, after a wretched night— during which your sleep has resembled a curious piece of mosaic, made up of very small pieces— and with a sensation of having been drunk, or at a ball, or engaged in a wake, or an Orange row, or something of the sort, during the previous night—the arriving at the dâk-bungalow, the refreshing process of undressing and pouring cold water out of chatties (earthenware pots) over your poor dusty, worn-out body—the breakfast of ration

---

* Two officers are allowed a cart between them for selves and baggage. One generally spreads one's mattress on the floor thereof, and piles one's baggage along the sides.

tea and bread, eked out with, occasionally eggs, invariably a spatch-cock and (*cela va sans dire*) a curry—the amusement of reading the various inscriptions on the walls, being remarks on life generally, and bullock-training in particular, by officers who have gone up country before you, and who, under the influence of spleen or *ennui*, possibly both combined, have thus found vent for their feelings, in some cases rendering immortal certain of their comrades by likenesses bordering on caricatures, executed in charcoal or Cumberland lead on the whitewashed walls; while the legend of the adventures of a certain mythical major-general, illustrated by a pencil which Leech might have envied, will long be remembered by those who, like myself, had the good fortune to see it—then those dinners, following so closely upon the heels of breakfast (for one had to jumble all one's meals up into a period of four or five hours), and consisting of ration stews of the best in the matter of quality, and amplest as to quantity, of a highly-prized and priced bottle of beer, which officers are enabled—all praise be to the government, or commissariat therefore!—to purchase at one rupee, of, sometimes—*O dies faustus!*—a rice-pudding, and with bread and potatoes *ad libitum*; then, about three o'clock, having filled a bottle with tea, a flask with rum, and stowed away a large supply of hard-boiled eggs for consumption *en route*, you return to your cart, and once more undergo the jolting, and the burying alive in fine sand, as you slowly creep along; the sights, scenes, and sounds of the preceding day being exactly repeated, and with little to look forward to beyond the arrival at the next station. Wofully level is the country, except about Nymeah-Ghât, which one reaches on the second day after leaving Raneegunge, and where a high hill—one of a large range—called Parrasnaut, breaks pleasantly the monotony of the scenery; and the beautiful Raj-Mahal Hills, through which the road winds between Chouparan and Sherghotty, where the grandeur and wildness of the scenery is all the more striking from the pervading flatness of the country through which we had been passing. These hills are almost the most celebrated place in India for tigers, and Sherghotty, lying at the foot of the range, takes its name from this circumstance. While at this town, I was shown a low hovel, not fifty yards from the dâk-bungalow, into which a tiger had made his way only two or three nights previously, killing a native, seriously wounding two others, and a woman.

Oh! how interminable seems this long, long road, so hard and level, so dusty, and with so little change day after day, winding along (with the two exceptions I have mentioned) over the most boundless of plains; sometimes through shady avenues of mango-trees, or past Hindoo temples and mosques, and cool-looking tanks; sometimes through quiet villages, the inhabitants whereof are taking a sort of farewell bask in the setting sun, and naked children—oh! so shiny and highly polished!—are disporting themselves, and Hindoo mothers are talking, probably scandal, or suckling their pot-bellied offspring; sometimes past well-cultivated tracts with sugar-cane, tobacco, corn and rice growing up in rich profusion on either side; sometimes over hard, sterile moors, dreary and lone to view, and only wanting a creaking gibbet, and a few bodies swinging in rusty chains, with the wind to howl a dirge, as it seems to be doing even now, in anticipation, to render them the most awful and unbearable of solitudes; sometimes there passes you a swarthy company of merchants, with a string of camels, laden with fruit, travelling from Cabul to Calcutta (some 1700 miles), whence they will return with Manchester goods in exchange for their delicious filbert-shaped grapes, fine walnuts, and pomegranates, which they are now bearing southward; sometimes we are journeying past artistical groups of "darkies" gathered round one of the numerous roadside wells, the bright brass pots, or *lotas*, wherewith they are drawing water (and which, together with a bit of cord for the purpose, every native in India carries as surely as he carries his head), glittering in the sun, and the white dresses of the Hindoo women, fluttering against the dark green of the surrounding trees, their shapely brown arms naked to the shoulder, and covered with bright brass rings and ornaments from elbow to wrist, and their anklets ringing out a light tinkle as they walk gracefully along; sometimes past tanks wherein men are washing their dusky bodies, or alongside which, their ablutions being finished, they are seated and busily administering a polish to the dusky bodies in question, by means of oil and lubrication; a train of empty bullock-carts returning after having deposited their load, and looking rather the worse for wear, pass by you; sometimes a horse-dâk, galloping down country, bearing a couple of officers, also rather the worse for wear, if one may judge from the pale, worn faces, and the leg or arm swathed in bandages and splints; you ask them as they pass, "What news from the front?" There is none—a few skirmishes, preparations for the advance on Lucknow actively going on—but they are not *au courant* with passing events; these wounded officers for weary weeks they have laid in the hospital at Cawnpore, listless of all save the one thought which engrosses them, the thought of home—whither they are even now *en route*, and where they will be seen limping painfully about ere many months are over, and —God bless you!—how proud their mothers and sisters will be of them, and what heroes they will think them! So it is "Good-bye!" "A pleasant voyage to you!" and away dashes the horse-dâk with sounding horn, and dust and clatter, while you crawl slowly on in your jolting cart.

Now the road passes along a steep embankment, with dark-looking precipices on either side—now it passes over wide rivers, which are, however, dry and low in this winter season—now across rugged, yawning watercourses, which during the rains must be very sluices, but which at present are decidedly droughty—and now, one fine moonlight night, do we arrive at the river Soane, which in the wet season is nearly three miles broad, but is now strangely reduced in breadth, and split up into an infinity of rivulets and streams, and a vast extent of white, dry, sandy bed, which shines in the moonlight as we pass over the causeway, and the rippling waters twinkle in the same as they flow with a silent rapidity and sort of muffled splash beneath the "wattle and dab" bridges which span them, and which we cross, as we wend our way towards the old fort which guards the further bank, and in which sixty big-whiskered Sikhs keep watch and ward.

By no means destitute of incident has been our journey thus far—incidents of the nature of the upsets of carts down steep banks, and the consequent discomfort, not to say injury of the burly warriors inside—incidents of the nature of "strikes" and stubbornness on the part of bullocks, and, in one or two instances, their sudden decease (caused by excess of obstinacy, I firmly believe) in the middle of the road, and the substitution, temporarily, of human draught. I remember one bullock—but, as an Irishman would say, he was a buffalo—whose obstinacy could only be overcome by lighting a small fire of dry sticks under a fleshy part of his thigh (a plan for which I think we are indebted to "Galton's Art of Travel") as he lay recumbent and inexorable, a sort of living heraldic device of contumacy *couchant*, and when he was almost sufficiently cooked for dishing, up he rose gracefully—no hurry about it, mind you—and continued his journey, serene, composed, and happy; frolicksomeness and love of liberty, too, have been apparent on the part of these animals, which not unfrequently have prompted them to shake their muscular necks free from the yoke which held them, and, callous as to the tearing of the cartilage of their noses—through which the rope by which they are driven is passed—to tug at these hempen reins desperately, and in some instances with success; an excess of inquisitiveness, also, and love of the picturesque, greatly out of place, when, in the witching hour of night, it has put into their heads the idea of closely observing the effect of moonlight on some distant house, or temple, or tank of their acquaintance, and of going very much out of their road, and ours, and very straight across a stiff country, for the purpose of visiting it, possibly thinking that, like Melrose, it can only be " viewed aright" under these circumstances; a couple of incidents, too, of a more solemn nature as regards two natives, employed in driving the carts, falling to sleep and off their perches, and the wheels passing over their bodies, killing the wretched fellows on the spot; incidental quarrels with one's cart-companion on the subject of room, and having your proper share of the cart, which, when one wants to go to sleep is, to say the least, desirable, and skirmishes in behalf of the same; incidental grumblings on your part when, on his waking in the night, he insists upon making a thoroughfare of your prostrate body, or when desiring to strike a light, being seized with an unconquerable conviction that your foot is the matchbox, and refusing, on this plea, to let go of it; minor incidents connected with your *soi-disant* hard-boiled eggs proving soft, and consequently ill-adapted for consumption in a jolting cart, and calculated to cover you with yolk and confusion. These and various other incidents, too numerous or too trivial to mention, beguiled us by the way, and diverted our minds more or less during our tedious journey.

CHAPTER VIII.

Sasseram—Traces of the Mutineers—Benares—Fort of Allahabad
—Pen-and-ink Sketch from its Walls at Sunset.

THE day after we crossed the Soane (eight days after leaving Calcutta) we arrived at Sasseram, and here we first came within the area of visible destruction committed during the rebellion. Here we first saw signs of desolation: ruined houses, a burned village, blackened trees, and the charred remnants of carriages and other property; the very dâk-bungalow in which we rested had but lately been re-roofed and restored. Here it was that evidences, palpable and hideous, first came under my notice of the performances of the mutineers, when the house of Messrs. John Pandy and Co. failed in its allegiance to its too-confiding creditors, and became bankrupts as to good faith, charity, and pity. Although from that time to this present at which I sit inditing, I have incessantly been surrounded by such signs and scenes—sickened at the constant recurrence of the shells of burned houses and the remains of demolished churches,* yet I think this first sight of objects which seemed to paint for me a mind-picture of the reality of the mutiny more vividly than anything I had seen, or heard, or read before, impressed me more deeply than what I since beheld

* These lines were written some time previous to my departure from India.

of the more extensive dilapidations of Allahabad or Cawnpore, the desolated districts of Oude, or even than the shot-riddled Residency and buildings of Lucknow.

The second morning after leaving Sasseram, we arrived at the Ganges, and before us lay the celebrated city of Benares, looking bright and pretty in the light of breaking day, with the holy river in the foreground spanned by a rickety bridge of boats, and with a few long, snake-like river steamers and clumsy country craft lying lazily upon its muddy waters; while hosts of temples, painted and bedizened, and quaintly carved, reared here and there their many-pointed pinnacles, and a few tall, delicate minarets, carrying one back to sunny days spent at Constantinople, and to pleasant rambles on the shores of the beautiful Bosphorus—of large white stone buildings—of small brown mud ones, the latter in the majority—of waving fan-palms and dark groups of mango-trees —of fakirs, and coolies, and baboos, and merchants, and other natives who throng the crowded streets—of monkeys who climbed the trees, and chattered on the roofs of houses—of bullocks and creaking carts—of elephants, of camels, and of all sorts of other sights, some novel, some picturesque, many ridiculous, a few sublime, but all slightly dirty and bedusted, as the glories of the East are wont to be, made up the *coup d'œil* presented by Benares; and when we had crossed the rickety bridge, a feat whereby our lives were apparently placed in much jeopardy—had threaded our way through the narrow streets—had wondered at the rude grotesque paintings on the walls, and over the doors of houses, of curious objects of idolatry or mythology, possessed of the bodies of men, the heads of elephants, and some dozen arms, and half a hundred hands, sticking out like the spokes of a wheel, and distributing the *largesse* of their godlike beneficence—had passed innumerable Brahmins with faces smeared with streaks of paint, which to the initiated in such matters spoke volumes on the subject of their caste, but to our pagan minds suggested merely recollections of the "Last of the Mohicans," and war paint, and other barbarous ideas—had been half poisoned by the variety and overpowering nature of the stenches which saluted us—had been deafened by the clatter of voices—had been sickened by the sight of loathsome deformities exposed to view for the sake of obtaining charity—had been jolted into a conviction that by no means sufficient attention was paid to the paving of the streets—had been cheered by the sight of English faces and English uniforms leaning over the parapet of a fort—had admired the carved fountains, the shady tanks by the side of fine temples, and the numerous bungalows with their well-wooded compounds, which are dotted along the road after leaving the native town—and had at last drawn up in front of the Mint, a beautiful building, now appropriated to the use of the troops passing through—when we had accomplished all this, we had seen as much of Benares as, for the time being, I felt up to, though not nearly as much as there is to see in its streets, sacred to every Hindoo superstition and tradition, and as old—if one may believe the Brahmins—ay, and older than the proverbial hills, or even than Time itself. Independently of its sacred character, which has long rendered it a place of much interest, this town was the scene of stirring events at the time of the outbreak; it was here that General Neil first earned his character for firmness and contempt for danger—a character his title to which he improved and strengthened, on every subsequent occasion, up to that fatal evening when, fighting his perilous way through the bloody lanes of Lucknow, a bullet cut short his glorious career; and this at a time when England's supremacy in Benares was waning fast, and with it our feeble grasp of one of the few places remaining to us in this portion of the country, and when a moment's hesitation or indecision would have sacrificed all.

It is an exciting tale that one which tells of the disarming of the Sepoys at this place by a handful of English soldiers, who were received on their approach with a volley of rebel musketry, the first angry shots, perhaps, which had rung through these old sacred streets, and startled the dull ears of the sleek, fat, holy Brahmin bulls which dwelt therein for many a century. It is feverish work listening to how the balance in which their fate, and almost that of our empire in the East, hung, wavered, and fluctuated irresolutely from side to side. It is glorious at last to hear how Neil, rushing forward, pistolling or cutting down a traitor who was pointing his musket at his breast, set thereby an example which was so nobly followed, that the scales wavered no more, or trembled, but turned at once, and thus Benares was saved.

But I am no historian, and do not wish to trespass on his province, and shall, therefore, leave the reader, who may be interested on the subject, to find out from other sources the details and particulars of these stirring times, and to read the accounts abler pens than this have written of the deeds of the gallant Neil, and his performances at Benares and elsewhere.

At the time I passed through this city the tragedy of Retribution was being daily enacted in an open space, where, day after day, crowds collected to behold their traitor countrymen launched into eternity, and to see the arms, legs, and bodies of the murderers of women and children blown mangled and shapeless from the smoking muzzle of the avenging gun. Even the day before we arrived ten Sepoys had expiated their crimes on the gallows, and an officer of Royal Artillery quartered at this place had little occupation besides the occasional blowing away of those who had been condemned to this nature of death. A few hours' stay at Benares was all that we enjoyed, for that same afternoon saw us again on the road, while a couple of days brought us to the junction of the Ganges and Jumna, where are situated the town and fort of Allahabad, and where we halted for a few days, thus obtaining a temporary respite from the discomforts of the bullock-train.

Along a winding sallyport—through a labyrinth of ditches, and parapets, and "covered ways"— under the muzzles of guns which frown upon one at every turn—beneath a fine old echoing gateway, carved and curious, and we are in the Fort of

Allahabad, and ere long have taken up our quarters in the "Ellenborough Barracks," a handsome range of yellow buildings, "picked out" with white, and with pillared verandah and front. This fort is of very considerable size, though when I was there no more than fifty guns were mounted on its ramparts: it has two land "faces," elaborately "broken" with all the scientific appliances of bastions, demi-bastions, ravelins, and batteries "*en embrasure*" and "*en barbette*"—a detailed description of which I do not think necessary to inflict upon you; perhaps to the unprofessional eye the river fronts, over-looking the junction of the Ganges and Jumna, are the most interesting, composed as they are of the grey time-honoured walls which formed part of the old fortifications in days long before the "Feringhees" had overrun the land—in days when bows and arrows were considered formidable weapons, when the ping of a bullet or the booming of a gun was unknown—in those days, in short, when Allahabad was in its glory, and kings feasted within its gates.

True, we have touched up these old walls here and there—have added a bit of parapet, it may be, or bricked up some useless Oriental staircase—but there still are the holes through which, in their barbarous warfare, the defenders poured molten lead down on to their assailants as they advanced to scale the walls; there are the old loopholes behind which the archers bent their bows; there are the same stones, cement, and masonry, a little crumbling, and verging upon their "second childhood" perhaps, but still there, with the waters of the

ALLAHABAD. 93

Jumna washing their base, and flowing on as in those rare old days of yore.

I wonder, though, whether they were "rare old days" after all, and whether they really possessed those features of romance which antiquity lends to them. I wonder whether people in those times grumbled about the crops and grew morose when the dinner was half an hour late, or talked of the times being different when they were in their *jeunesse dorée*, and of a mythical "good time coming, boys," as we matter-of-fact, degenerate, discontented mortals do now; possibly, though I do not choose to think so, as I ramble one sunny evening about the ramparts, picking little bits of romance out of the old tumble-down walls, much as with a stick I might pick crumbling stones and mortar from out the same, and they yield it about as readily; and looking up reverentially at the aged mass of buildings which formed the *Zenaneh* (or harem) of the court. Don't tell me, sir! that the faces which looked from those old Moorish windows, that the bright eyes which had peeped—ay, and, perchance, winked!—through those sly lattices, had ever bent over a pair of stockings which required darning—that the little hands which had rested on those carved stone balconies were ever employed in knitting and crochet, with their attendant mysteries of "*drop two—purl—take up one—four rows repeat;*" in trimming, and *tulle*-ing and *ruche*-ing (if there are such things); or in that, to me, yet more unaccountable operation of making small holes in long slips of linen or calico, and then mending them again as fast as possible.

No, no, sir! real live Oriental beauties they were, whose sole occupation was the arduous one of laying their heads upon the breasts of their beloved lords and masters, or *vice versâ*, and billing when he billed, and cooing when he cooed, and fondling and caressing, and filling his pipe, and lighting it —ask your wife to light your cigar for you now-a-days!—and telling stories about barbers, and barbers' brothers, and hunchbacks, and one-eyed callendars, for one-thousand-and-one consecutive nights, and living for the most part upon sweetmeats and sentiments. Such were the fair creatures who, peering from the old windows on just such another sunny evening as this—gazing over the broad winding Jumna which seems to take its rise in that red bank of clouds with the golden fringe which is mantling in the west, whence it pours down a molten, glittering stream —gazing upon the tall-masted country boats which are floating down the river, or anchored by the banks—gazing over the town of Allahabad straggling away in the distance, its flat-roofed houses, and its tombs, and temples, and mosques (the latter with their arched frontals all staring with wistful devotion towards the Mussulman's Holy of Holies—Mecca), half hidden by the green trees—gazing upon all this fair scene, were gladdened by it, even as it gladdens us now.

But if in this present year, 1858, we go within the walls of the Zenaneh, and wander through the courts of what was once the palace of kings, what shall we find there? Princes, think you? with diamonds blazing on their foreheads, and emeralds glittering on the tips of their big toes?—retinues of bejewelled courtiers and mailed warriors in all the prismatic colouring of the "glowing East?" No! but—*O tempora! O mores!*—piles of shot, and guns, and arms, and stores of camp equipage, and ropes, and picks, and shovels, like a marine store-dealer's shop on a large scale—and calculating *baboos* sitting before great big ledgers—and mathematical-headed functionaries issuing munitions of war, summing up totals, and putting down figures, and dealing with facts, for all the world as if romance had never been—had never dwelt within these courts and walls, which are now thus barbarously converted into an arsenal. Such is the Fort of Allahabad, tempting one to indulge in pleasant dreams, and then waking you up by a "cold pig" in the middle of them—Fact kicking Fiction's shins—Romance battling with Reality, and invariably getting the worst of it; and yet it is not without a little romance of its own, this same fort—a romance, not of antiquity and the " days when earth was young," but a matter-of-fact romance of *anno Domini* 1857—the romance of mutiny rampant within its walls—of a few high-couraged Englishmen standing firm and unmoved as they stemmed the in-setting and awful torrent—of one " brave among the bravest," Brasier by name,[*] who, when the Sepoy guard of the " Loyal" 6th Native Infantry, guarding the gate, hesitated to give up their arms when ordered to—when the very Sikhs whom he commanded were rather to be feared than trusted—when the match which self-devotion had prepared to fire the magazine, and so blow the fort and all within it

[*] Now commanding the Ferozepore Regiment of Sikhs.

up into the air, sooner than that treachery should prevail, was lighted—then, like the romances of old, wherein, though all the characters are heroes, one is always found to shine pre-eminently, so did Brasier, courageous, unhesitating, and determined, brooking no delay in the obeying of the order to disarm, wrenching the musket from the grasp of the right-hand man, overawe the mutinous, reclaim the disaffected, save Allahabad, and gain for his name a high and glorious place in the annals of the mutiny.

And while this was being enacted *within* the fort, there was another drama going on without its walls, and not two miles from its gates —more tragic, alas! in its bloody and melancholy results. Who is there that has not heard the story of the 6th Native Infantry, then quartered in the cantonments of Allahabad?—how they professed the utmost loyalty, begged to be led against their mutinous brethren, swore again and again they were, and would continue, "true to their salt"—how one afternoon an order by the Governor-General, thanking them for their good faith and lauding their staunchness, was read out to them on parade—how they received it with cheers, and renewed, and yet more vehement protestations of fidelity—and how, a few short hours afterwards, they were shooting down their officers like dogs, and throwing their murdered bodies into a *nullah* to rot away, while they went forth to fill the insurgent ranks, to burn, and plunder, and destroy, and, combining with other mutineers, to subject the fort to a desultory siege and shelling, from which, after a fortnight's duration, it was relieved by General Neil. They have been known by the soubriquet of the "Loyal" Sixth ever since, and a bitter sarcasm it is.

Such is the story of their mutiny which has been told time after time in the public prints, until almost every one is familiar with it, but which I had scarcely realized till I rode past the ruined mess-house and cantonments, passed the *nullah* where those poor officers' bodies had lain—until I had seen the destruction wreaked by the traitors in the moment of their bloody triumph marked here, as everywhere, by the shells of destroyed and burned bungalows, barracks, and churches, and by a wild effort to root up all traces of the English wherever planted.*

* It is a curious fact that one of the few—very few—houses in the neighbourhood which have escaped the general destruction and demolition was the "Freemasonry Lodge," whether designedly or accidentally, of course I cannot say.

CHAPTER IX.

Allahabad—The native town—Country ride near Allahabad—
Perilous railway journey—Railway officials—Kharga.

ALLAHABAD has lately been fixed upon as the seat of government during the summer months, and a wise measure has been adopted in giving every facility to capitalists and merchants to establish an English town and English hotels at this station, laying the foundation, as it were, of an inland metropolis, sadly wanted hitherto, and more than ever desirable, and indeed necessary now that the removal of the government thither for a great portion of the year will cause the tide of civilization to set more strongly in that direction.

At present, Allahabad is a purely native town, with the exception of a few English merchants, branches of great firms in Calcutta, who have built for themselves wooden sheds on the *maidän*, whereunto there flows a tolerably steady stream of rupees, being a very large portion of the "pay and allowances" of the thirsty and baccy-loving English officers and soldiers congregated in this station, and out of which there flows another stream hardly of corresponding proportion in the matter of intrinsic value—a stream of beer, and brandy, and cheroots, and hermetically sealed canisters, bearing on the outside yellow labels, with "Fine Hams," "Real Stiltons," and "Preserved Tongues," printed in black letters thereupon.

As regards the native town of Allahabad, I have but little to say; it straggles away to—goodness knows where. A sprinkling of Hindoo temples, a tolerable supply of mosques, which, though striking and picturesque individually are apt to pall upon one when you pass fifty of exactly the same make and build in an hour's ride: oblong buildings the whole of them, with three Turkish-looking domes on the summit, and three Moorish-looking arches forming their front, and a minaret at each end by way of a finish, never parallel to the neighbouring houses, or the street, or anything, but contorting themselves ridiculously, and squinting horribly in their attempts to look towards Mecca; the everlasting clatter of the *bunneahs* and other vendors of commodities, who appear to talk, and shout, in inverse proportion to the quantity and quality of the goods they have for sale, so that the hullabaloo raised by the man, whose entire stock-in-trade consists of one earthenware pot or *chattie*, and a handful of small univalve shells, or *cowries*,* each of which represents an infinitesimal piece of money, is overwhelming in the extreme; then there is that appearance of decay about Allahabad, noticeable in all Indian towns; they are all on their last legs, utterly done for, and used up; they may be able to pull through another week, but to all appearance, that will be the limit of their existence. Nor have they any of the personal

---

* Sixty-four cowries go to a copper *pie*, or the fourth part of an anna; there are therefore, two hundred and fifty-six cowries to an anna. An anna is three-halfpence, therefore one cowrie is the two hundred and fifty-sixth part of three-halfpence!

pride or proper feeling becoming patriarchs in this their old age; occasionally, maybe, an old beau of a house pads and puffs himself out with a buttress or two, and does his best to look young and healthy, or a vain and decrepit temple takes to rouge and paint as a last resource; but, as a general rule, one misses that hoary, venerable appearance, that nobility of age, that grandeur of decay which distinguishes our English ruins, an effect attributable to the fact that, built only of brick, and stuccoed, and plastered, and daubed in their youth, as the generality of these Indian mosques and temples are—sailing through life under false colours—when the wrinkles come, and the flesh falls off, and the skeleton is laid bare, we see the littleness of the bones and joints, and the feebleness of the whole structure, instead of the stalwart sinews and sturdy frames which we are accustomed to look for among the fine old ruins at home. It is very like the glimpse you sometimes get of the *passée* beauty who has sparkled, and shone, and triumphed throughout the ball, as she steps into her carriage in the dawning morning light, looking a somewhat wee bit less beautiful than in the earlier part of the evening.

It is a curious fact, but no native ever appears to repair his house. I have never, to my knowledge, seen one so employed; they do not appear to care much whether the wall falls down or remains standing, evidently taking a very philosophical view of the case; one would hardly think they would call it "destiny" in this case, and yet I verily believe that the Mussulman, buried up to his neck in the *débris* of his fallen domicile, would complacently inform the public, that it was "Kismet," and that "Allah is great, and Mahomet his prophet," though a cartload of bricks and a hod or two of mortar would have gone far towards overturning the decrees of fate, and might, perchance, have temporarily exalted the bricklayer almost to a level with Mahomet in the eyes of our pork-abhorring friend.

Executions at this time were common in Allahabad; the energy of the gallows was severely taxed, for one, two, three, and sometimes more Sepoys were hanged almost daily. It is rather startling when enjoying a quiet country ride to come suddenly upon a body writhing in its last agonies, or hanging lifeless before you—it somewhat abruptly breaks off your train of peaceful thought, and pleasant reveries of home—and I must plead guilty to something very like a revulsion of feeling, when, sauntering along one evening, and coming upon a moderately large green, which my truant fancy immediately metamorphosed into a village green in England, I became suddenly aware that there was swinging before me, not the signboard of the "Green Dragon" or "Marquis of Granby," but the pinioned lifeless corpse of a Sepoy, which a native policeman, tulwar in hand, was guarding. The man had not been dead long, and his face, over which there was no cap or covering, was as quiet as though he had been asleep; but the silence, and the absence of any mortal beings but my companion, the policeman, and myself—the dreary, listless way in which the body kept on swinging, and swaying, and turning to and fro—

the arms—what deeds of wrong and murder may not those arms have done—now pinioned as if in mockery of the helplessness of death, made the scene a sombre one enough—sombre, and that was all; for no feeling of sorrow, pity, or remorse for the fiends who, falling into our hands after a bloody and treacherous career, meet the death which is so justly their due, can ever be roused, I should think, in an Englishman's breast. This very man now swinging before us may have dappled those pinioned hands in women's blood, or the golden tresses of a child may have been wound round those fingers, while the other hand grasped the knife which was to sacrifice it: those eyes may have looked into the trusting blue eyes of a poor little baby, and seen it smile on him and on the sharp steel, in its innocence, and yet that smile may have failed to rouse his pity. Faugh! let us be off, such sort of reflections are not pleasant, but they are apt, my friends, to occur to one on such occasions.

I should like to have told you a few other little things in connexion with Allahabad, about the state prisoners,—three captive, and once rebellious rajahs—who are, and have been for ten long years lying in "durance vile" inside the fort; of a certain gentleman who rattles his chains over the main gateway in a snug little cell, and whose prospects were anything but cheerful, if we take into consideration a pleasant murder or two which he had taken the opportunity of the outbreak to commit, and which were likely to have the effect of abridging his days very considerably and abruptly. I could have *discoorsed* you a tale or two, which were whispered in my ear about the performances of the Naval Brigade when they manned the fort of Allahabad in the absence of other "soldiers," and "did sentry" upon the ramparts, and frightened peaceably disposed people, who might be returning to the fort at night after dining with some friend, into fits, by firing at them first and challenging them afterwards, in direct opposition to the—I think preferable—custom, usually observed of allowing the challenge to *pre*cede the bullet; or of the sailor who, one night returning to his barracks, was accosted as usual by a bullet whistling past his ear, just by way of calling his attention to the main question which immediately followed of "Who goes there?" and who responding, "Oh, that's your little game, is it?" and that he "was darnged" (or something stronger) "if he'd stand being a 'umbugged in this way," and, having a musket, let fly therewith back at the sentry, and *then* proceeded to answer his challenge—a practical retort enough, and very much to the point, perhaps, but hardly in accordance with discipline. But we must be off; there is no disobeying an order of Sir Colin Campbell's, and one has come for us to proceed to Cawnpore to join the main body of the army about to advance on Lucknow.

I certainly do not look back upon the fifty-five miles of railway travelling from Allahabad to Kharga as the pleasantest or least perilous portion of my Indian career; crammed, neck and crop, into a train consisting of one second-class carriage for the officers, and about fifty open trucks, loaded with baggage, doolies, and ammunition, upon which, or underneath which, or somewhere, or anywhere about which, the men must find places as best they can—never mind tumbling off, lads, or breaking your necks or your legs, or both, so long as the railway company do not have any trouble. In with you—steam's up—look out!—wait till that man picks himself up from under the wheel—that's right—whish!—train moves away, half a dozen men, shaken nearly off by the jerk, which discomposes the pyramids of baggage on which they are seated, seem hanging by their eyelids, and such hurry and scrambling on the part of the railway officials as was anything but creditable; the expostulations of the military officers unheeded, or treated with discourteous contempt, and on we go.

Suddenly, loud shouts. We look out—train on fire—"Stop her!"—men sitting on blazing doolies, the mattresses of which, being made of cotton, burn like tinder. Fire extinguished; officials decline to take any precautions for avoiding a recurrence of the same, refuse to burn coke instead of wood, though it is clearly proved to them that the sparks from the latter, falling upon the cotton doolie-mattresses, caused the conflagration—refuse to do anything, and object to everything—huddled into the train again—a whistle—off! while you are still standing on the step of the carriage—thrown violently forward on to your nose, which is all you get for helping to put out the fire; jolt along for half an hour—fresh alarm—heads out of window—train on fire again—the men seen crawling along the burning carriages in a state of semi-combustion. Two natives, encircled by fire, adopt the principles of the scorpion under similar circumstances, and commit suicide, or do their best to, by jumping off while the train is at full speed—one killed, t'other, both legs broken. Train stopped at last; get the fire out as quickly as possible, back into your places—grumbling (perhaps not unnatural) on the part of some soldiers who have had their kits burned, or their coats and trousers, or blisters raised about their hands and legs.— Pshaw! officials laugh—" Deuced good joke"— " Soldiers—stand fire"—" ha! ha! ha!" " No real harm done—fires of this sort every day— come, in with you, men!" Off we go—no precautions, no anything—"happy go lucky"—jolt along till we catch fire again, which we do in about three-quarters of an hour, this time blazing away right merrily, three trucks and an infinity of doolies being burned, baggage, &c., destroyed, not to speak of the exertions necessary to detach a truck containing two hundred barrels of ammunition, and to prevent the same from catching fire and exploding.

I believe at last the officials began to think a little seriously of the affair, for they did not rally the men who had holes burned in their trousers and their shins, or whose heads were singed, quite so gaily; perhaps it began to strike them that the never-ceasing expostulations and protestations of the officers might possibly have some little truth in them, and that the argument which held it to be advisable not to burn more soldiers than was absolutely necessary, or more baggage than they could conveniently help, might not be so wholly devoid of logic after all;

perhaps the information that the whole business would be reported—that the gross destruction of government and other property, through carelessness—the unseemly hurry—the discourtesy—the risk to men's lives—the absence of any, the commonest precautions against fire, in a train containing a quantity of gunpowder, would be made known to the authorities, may have had an effect on them, but certainly not before it was wanted. We were this time allowed not merely to get on the steps of the carriage, but actually to take our places in the same, quite peaceably, after we had succeeded, not without some difficulty, in extinguishing the fire No. 3, and, by dint of throwing a few tarpaulins over the doolies, and some other equally simple precautions, we managed to get to our journey's end without any fresh outbreak of the flames.*

I have forgotten to mention that, during this eventful journey, we passed a tank for watering the engines at a place called Burwarree, on which seventeen persons had, at the outbreak of the revolt, defended themselves for three days against the mutineers. It is a plain oblong stone tank, some ten or eleven feet high, such as one may often see at a small station in England, barely large enough, one would think, to act as a fortress for so many, but here, destitute of food

---

* These fires on this line were of constant occurrence. Three officers of the royal artillery, who came up country shortly after me, had every stitch of baggage, clothes, saddlery and books destroyed in one of these conflagrations; a serious matter when one considers that they were about to enter upon a campaign, and the impossibility of replacing good English clothes and saddlery in this country, except at the very large towns, such as Calcutta, and then at most exorbitant prices.

or water, or with a very scanty, insufficient supply of both, exposed to the frightful heat of an Indian sun, in the heart of an Indian summer, which none but those who have felt it can realize, surrounded by a crowd who thirsted for their blood, they held out gallantly until relieved by troops from Allahabad. One of the party, a lady, died of exposure, fatigue, and want of food, but the others, I believe, all escaped.

We made but a short stay at Kharga, which was then the terminus of this little bit of railway— now continued as far as Cawnpore—arriving there about half an hour after noon, and leaving again by bullock-train about five P.M. Bullock-train again!—oh horror! the rack once more; worse bullocks, it appeared to me, than we had ever had yet; more capricious and volatile than before— greater amount of jolting—half-healed bruises on hips and elsewhere get a relapse—more dust and more intense misery. Futteypore, some seventy miles from Allahabad, and the scene of one of Havelock's fights, we passed through that night. Some skeletons here and there by the side of the road still remain to mark the gallant general's progress, for all along and up this road had he been obliged to force his way against opposing and overwhelming numbers, always doing battle against swarming rebels—ten, twenty, thirty to one—and yet never failing to snatch undying laurels, however long and desperate the odds.

The road was interesting from these reminiscences alone, but, more than this, there was the nervous, almost painful excitement of nearing Cawnpore.

CHAPTER X.

First impressions of Cawnpore—"Wheeler's entrenchment"—An every-day scene at Cawnpore—Camp followers—The remains of the "Slaughter House" and the "Well"—The Assembly Rooms, as they were and as they are—A backward glance at Cawnpore in happier days gone by.

On the second morning after leaving Kharga, I was awoke by the news that we were approaching that now celebrated place, the crowded state of the dusty road telling plainly enough of the propinquity of an army. Long strings of camels were sailing away in all directions; their heads tied to each other's tails, they stretched over the flat country as far as the eye could reach; some infantry, dusty and footsore, were trudging wearily along; elephants, with that soft cat-like tread peculiar to them, were making the best of their way towards tanks and ponds, and trumpeting shrilly every now and then in pleasant anticipation of the bath they were about to enjoy; hackeries were discordantly creaking out their complaints of the amount of baggage heaped on them, and getting jammed into a state of inextricable confusion; bullocks, as usual, were in the last extreme of one of two stages—intense moodiness verging very closely on the stubborn, or intense liveliness bordering on the reckless—either of which frames of mind, when exhibited by a fine, muscular, full-grown bullock, is calculated to drive any one having anything to do with them into a state of the wildest insanity; *sowars,* or Irregular Horsemen, with lengthy spear, huge turban, and panting steed, were spurring madly through the dust; pedestrians, carts, buffaloes, ponies, natives, soldiers, horses, officers, commissariat supplies, those inevitable light liver-coloured natives employed as scribes, accountants, &c. &c., in the public departments, and yclept *baboos*, baggage, doolies, and ammunition, all wending their way towards Cawnpore, to supply the capacious maw of that ever-greedy monster, an army, were scrambling as best they could along that dusty, roasting, crowded road, amid such a noise and confusion as I had never seen equalled.

It was when surrounded by all this bewildering mass that my attention was called to a long, low building, which loomed through the dust like a great nightmare on our left hand—a building surrounded by four or five others of inferior size—sort of outhouses—situated on an open *maidän* (or plain), and the whole battered and pounded by shot and shell and bullets, so that window and door were shattered out of all shape and outline, so that the roof had fallen in, and great breaches and fissures in the walls had reduced the whole almost to a pile of ruins. What could this wretched wobegone building be? What mortal men could have stood behind those battered walls and faced the storm of shot which must have rained upon them night and day before such destruction was wrought, or before all those gaping holes which riddle them like a sieve, were made! What men could have lived for an hour in such a place as this! Not only men, reader! but women lived here, and helped to hold these ruined walls, and faced the iron rain of shot which beat upon this house—not only women, reader! but children and babes have been behind those flimsy parapets when the fire was at its hottest and the iron rain fell heaviest, not for one hour, or for one day, or for two, but—look on these shattered buildings and be proud of your countrymen who could hold them so nobly and so long—for three long weary weeks! And even then these gallant English hearts failed not, but would have held on still, had not the falsest promise that traitor ever made, or deceived man believed—the most positive and sacred pledge that lips could utter, made only to be broken more foully and cruelly than ever pledge was yet, and, for the honour of mankind, let us add than ever pledge is likely to be again—tempted them from behind those walls, whence, battered as they were, shot would never have driven them, and delivered man, woman, and child up as victims to treachery, cruelties, and indignities which few men beside Nana Sahib could have devised, and which fewer still could have executed.

Yes! this pile of battered ruins, this shapeless mass of buildings, is the celebrated "Wheeler's Entrenchment." You may ride round it half a dozen times and not notice the tiny embankment and ditch which surrounds it; and yet that embankment and ditch, now, of course, trodden down and diminishing in size daily—but which in its best days could have been but a poor puny breastwork—this and those walls, through the great jagged holes and breaches in which the light now shines, throwing uncouth shadows on the plain beyond, was the only home* for three long weeks for that gallant garrison — for those tender women poor children, whose blood sprinkled upon the walls of this frail fort, staining the floor of the "slaughter-house," and reddening the sides of the fatal well, cried aloud to their countrymen for vengeance.

It is difficult to describe the sensations with which one first beholds such a spot as this, particularly when one visits it so short a time after the events which first dragged it into celebrity had occurred. Not more than seven months since the curtain had been raised, and the first act of the tragedy had been played; and in those seven months, upon this self-same stage—the wide, dusty scorched plain there stretching out before you—how many more scenes of the bloody drama had been acted! how many a battle and desperate strife had thereon been decided!

As we continue our journey to the quarters allotted to us—some barracks which, *mirabile dictu,* had not been destroyed—we are able to observe how carefully every building that English hands had raised was levelled to the ground; not a bungalow which a Feringhee had inhabited but had been gutted; the churches wherein he prayed, the altars before which he knelt, burnt, unroofed, and defiled; even racket-courts and riding-schools ruined and destroyed, and all in a systematic, regular manner, which spoke volumes for the virulence and *animus* of our treacherous enemies. Cawnpore was strangely busy at the time I arrived

* "Wheeler's Entrenchment" is now pulled down.

there; its pulses beat feverishly high, responsive to the rumbling of guns, the clatter and jingle of cavalry, and the tramp of regiment after regiment as they concentrated and collected here for the grand advance on Lucknow; many had already crossed into Oude; the frail bridge of boats across the Ganges creaked and trembled daily as portions of the *fifteen miles of siege train*, destined to accomplish the destruction of the great rebel stronghold, rumbled and clattered across it, and as elephants, camels, baggage, infantry, cavalry, and field-artillery pressed over it into Oude, and strained heavily the timbers, and cables, and quaint flat-bottomed boats composing it; vast canvas towns silently sprang up day after day on the hot *maidän*, announcing the advent of fresh troops, while other canvas towns as silently disappeared, announcing the departure of more regiments into Oude; one constant in-pouring and out-pouring of Highlanders with big legs, of line regiments, and riflemen, sailors, and artillerymen, of bronzed and bearded soldiers in astounding cap-covers, and with a certain tough look about them, more satisfactory, I should imagine, to the eyes of an Englishman than a Sepoy. The glittering bayonets of regiments on the move caught the eye at every turn; the inspiriting airs, such as "Cheer, boys, cheer," "Far, far upon the sea," and that well-beloved march of the Rifle Brigade, "I'm ninety-five," with a variety of other pleasant familiar tunes, which had a joyous, careless life in their every note, rang in your ears till you almost wearied of the sound, or came faintly from the far distance, so far off some-

DOOLIES.

times they sounded, that I half fancied they must have been wafted to us straight from home across the wide sea; bodies of Sikh irregular cavalry, composed of big-whiskered, swarthy, stalwart men, each one a picture down to the waist, but with something wrong about their legs—which are decidedly of the broomstick order— spurring about in every direction; sailors in the baggy-est of trousers, and with a rollicking air, not to mention certain mysterious lumps in their cheeks, possibly having some connexion with " pig-tail," were polishing up black monsters of siege guns till their lacquered surfaces glistened and shone again, or, patting the breeches of 10-inch mortars, in playful and encouraging anticipation of their services against "them there black rascals;" officers and others in the commissariat department were proving the existence of " perpetual motion" in their own persons. All was life, bustle, and excitement, and no light task must his have been who had the management of this vast machine, swelled almost beyond all bounds by the enormous staff of camp-followers, indispensable to an army in India.

It may be as well to say a word or two here on the subject of camp-followers, and to explain as briefly as possible how it happens that so large a number is necessary.

In the first place, the mode of carrying the sick in India tends to increase the train enormously. The sick are carried in "doolies," which are in many respects most excellent, affording as they do a bed, a covering, and a little temporary hospital for the invalid.* When the army has to bivouac, the sick are sheltered from the damp night air by their roof of painted canvas; when in wet weather the army pitches its camp on damp ground, the sick may be seen lying in dry beds raised some eight or ten inches above the mud by the short legs of their doolies; when a march is prolonged until the sun is hot and powerful, still are the sick to a certain extent shaded from it, as, also, they are protected from the rain by the same means. The wounded man, to whom moving from one bed to another would be agony, may for months, as many *have* done, live in his doolie; for in camp it becomes his bed, the roof and pole being unshipped, and in the morning, when the march commences, on goes the roof again, in goes the pole, and away goes the doolie on the shoulders of four lusty bearers. Moreover, when necessary, a surgeon can operate on a patient, and dress and probe his wounds, with as much ease as though he were lying in a four-poster bed; and yet with all these manifest advantages a doolie would be out of the question in European warfare, and for the following reason— each one requires six men, four to carry it and two to relieve them when necessary; thus, to every

* A *doolie*, pictures of which in the *Illustrated London News*, from time to time, must have made most people familiar with its appearance, is a bed (framework, mattress, pillow, &c., complete) with legs cut short, and from each end of this bed rise two strong pieces of wood in the shape of an inverted V, and each having at its apex a strong iron ring, through which passes the stout bamboo pole, whereby it is carried, the ends of the pole (which project beyond the *doolie*) resting on the bearers' shoulders, and over the whole of this is a movable roof made of thin laths of wood, covered with painted (red or blue) canvas, and having curtained sides of the same material.

sick man there must perforce be six bearers, a proportion which would not be procurable in any country but India, where the population is so great and wages are so small, and where we can draw to any extent on the millions of natives who are always ready to accept employment, and are well paid at from 3d. to 4d. per diem. And now I come to the point at which I wished to arrive: the proportion of doolies in war time is one to every ten men; this, in a regiment one thousand strong, amounts to one hundred doolies —six bearers to each, total, *six hundred doolie bearers* to a single regiment! Here, then, is the nucleus, and an extensive one it is, of the force of camp-followers; in addition to this is the large staff of cooks, "bhistees," "bildahs," "sweepers," &c., allotted to regiments on landing, which of course accompanies them in full force into the field.

The regimental hospitals, too, are augmented to an overwhelming size; to each tent in the huge camp is allowed a "kulassie," or tent-man, while the cavalry and artillery swell the black rabble some thousands by their innumerable "syces" and "grass-cutters," who are nearly in the proportion of one of each to every horse. Throw into the scale, also, another by no means small item in the shape of hordes of hackery-drivers, camel-drivers, and "mahouts;" add to this the bazaar establishment attached to each regiment for the purpose of supplying the soldiers and the natives of the same with any little things they may require from "gold mohurs" to "gram," and numbering, in many instances, whole legions of speculative niggers, all busily and greedily intent on one object, beyond which they have no hopes or cares, viz. the amassing of rupees; each officer employs also from eight to twelve servants, and this long list is closed with the numberless *employés* in the vast train of ordnance (which, on this occasion, extended over a distance of fifteen miles), and with the functionaries, baboos, &c., nearly as numerous, belonging to the commissariat department—*cum multis aliis*—the wives and families of the above, with interlopers, milk-sellers, do-nothings, lookers-on, tag-rag and bobtail attendant upon the whole, and then you may perhaps understand how it is that the non-combatant part of an army doubles, ay, and trebles, the militant portion.

To an Englishman, arriving for the first time in India, this gigantic army of camp-followers appears, to say the least, unnecessary; but the old Indian knows well enough that it *must* be. It is necessary for balancing the kite and enabling it to rise; for were this tail to fall off, the whole army would be helpless and impotent; and therefore he regards it much in the same light as he does the arming a soldier with a musket, or the supplying him with ammunition for the same, or the giving the cavalry soldier a horse. And "griffin," long before his first few months of hot-weather campaigning are over, finds out that the old Indian is right. And now let me proceed.

It will easily be believed that, during my short stay in Cawnpore, I visited all the chief points of interest in the place with a greedy excitement.

I rode past the spot where the "slaughter-house" (now razed to the ground) once stood, and where, when our troops first reoccupied the place, they found pieces of women's dress, and long hair, and clotted blood, and splashings of the same about the walls, and children's little frocks all dabbled in it, and other horrible signs of slaughter, too marked and real to be mistaken. I saw the well, now filled up, and with a monument to mark the spot, commemorating in simple words the dreadful deeds there done, and with an iron railing round it. It is now the only piece of brick or stone work standing amid a great sea of ruins, the buildings in the neighbourhood having been pulled down to afford a free range to our guns in the fort hard by.

There is something indescribably sad about Cawnpore, where destruction has been carried on by friend and foe with such an unsparing hand; you may yet, through the ruins of razed houses, trace the walks and beds of what once were gardens, with occasionally a few poor crushed flowers, that have slept through all these changes and tumults, and are now springing into life, wondering where the hand is that used to tend them so carefully, and vainly endeavouring to struggle up through broken bricks and stone, and mortar, and falling pillars, to look round them and find out what all this is about. You may still see the spots where our countrymen, unmindful of the dark shadow which coming events were casting over them, unsuspicious of the evil hastening towards them fast, spent many a happy day, and sat out in the cool of pleasant evenings—

you may still see the Assembly Rooms,* where erst, when Cawnpore was one of the gayest stations in India, its English inhabitants met

> To chase the glowing hours with flying feet—

a day, too, when no one was so courted, no one so hospitable to English officers and ladies, no one gave pleasanter parties or grander fêtes—no one, in short, more popular than the Nana Sahib of Bhitoor!

The Assembly Rooms are sadly altered now from what they must have been; naked and unroofed, huge skeletons, mourning over their past grandeur, pining for the pleasant strains of music which were wont to swell within them; pining for the cheerful, sparkling light which streamed forth on festive nights from their many windows, now, alas! mere square openings, like eye-sockets from which the eyes have been torn; pining for the merry faces which have smiled there, and for the joyous laughs which have rung out within those now shot-riddled and lantern-jawed old walls. Yes, the Assembly Rooms are indeed sadly altered since those times; they are roofless now, and have suffered from many a shell which has torn and crashed through them, and burst within with a loud and startling explosion, awaking harsher echoes than did the soft tones which they were accustomed to of yore, and scarcely so pleasant as the "sound of revelry" to which they had been used in nights gone by. The Nana Sahib, he has altered, too, and gone a *little* to the bad since then—an Englishman

---

* The Assembly Rooms have, since the time of which I am writing, been pulled down.

would hardly be found to accept his hospitality now-a-days, even supposing that Bhitoor, the sacked and looted, were flourishing in all its former grandeur; likewise, is he less popular than he was in those times past. And yet I should like to know if he has really changed so very much, or whether, rather, his heart was not black as now in those days of yore; whether, when his fêtes and feasts were at their height—when his smile of greeting for his English guests was pleasantest, and his welcome warmest, whether then he saw not, in the dim future, a day when he should dye his hands in the blood he was now warming with his wine; the day when his order should deliver up to torture and death, and to indignities even worse than death, those delicate English ladies with whom he was now exchanging such fair words of friendship, and who, many a time and oft, had graced Bhitoor with their kind and comely presence.*

* This is as probable as it is possible; for there is no doubt that Nana Sahib considered that he owed an old grudge to Government, by whom he fancied himself aggrieved in respect of a large pension which his *adopted* father enjoyed, but which was refused to him. This grievance rankled in his black, unforgiving, Asiatic mind, till the payment of the grudge became the dearest wish of his heart; a fact well known to many influential natives, as was proved by some of them writing on the occasion of the outbreak at Delhi to Sir Hugh Wheeler, warning him that the mutiny would extend to Cawnpore, and bidding him distrust the Nana, and make preparations for the defence of the place. Deceived, however, by the villain's promises, and by the seeming friendship which he had always borne towards Englishmen, Sir Hugh responded that he disbelieved these statements of the troops' or the Nana's contemplated treachery, and this unfortunate confidence it was that enabled the fiend to take his hellish revenge, and to commit the deed which has gained for his name such a detestable notoriety.

It is a question which is unlikely ever to be solved completely, but it occurred to me among many other reflections of a sadder nature, as I rode among those scenes which give to Cawnpore such a deep and painful interest.

CHAPTER XI.

A Ride through the Bazaar at Cawnpore—We cross into Oude—
The March—Oonao—Morose Remarks about Camels.

THE native bazaar, from its great size and the insatiable craving for everything and anything which characterizes the British army, and which must long ere this have raised the not over conscientious *buneahs* to an unprecedented state of affluence, is even noisier and more crowded than these pandemoniums usually are. The narrow, filthy streets, with that peculiar smell—I wonder what it is!—which one notices immediately on landing in India, or, indeed, in any Eastern country, and which is to be found in the highest perfection in the native towns and houses—form one huge labyrinth filled with shops of every description, in the heyday of their prosperity. English officers galloping recklessly along on their *tatts* (the Indian substitute for that hardy, hairy, half-fed animal, the Crimean baggage pony) in quest of *karkee*-coloured turbans, or coats, find themselves suddenly brought up by an elephant, whose huge carcase effectually blocks up the narrow street, while his flapping ears seem almost to brush the houses on either side, and looking, as he decidedly is under the circumstances, very much out of proportion; or, occasionally, a camel, with bells tinkling gaily, and his nose high and haughty in the air, trots rapidly down a corner, to the great alarm and confusion of the "tatt" aforesaid, who disappears backwards, in spite of the frantic kicks administered by his rider, accompanied by an irascible and not very sweet-toned " Come up (thud), you infernal brute (thud), will you?" (thud, thud, thud); about which time, the camel being close upon him, "tatt" *en route* overturns a jeweller's table, a money-changer's stock-in-trade, and steps into a basket or two of vegetables, all of which articles—jewels included—are exposed *in* the street for sale, after the manner of the baked chesnuts and veal-pies "all 'ot !" of London notoriety, and subsides into a graceful attitude among some hookahs and pipes, the property of a Cawnpore " Milo," manifestly to their detriment; the camel trots by—"tatt" narrowly escapes hysterics as it passes—after which he recovers. British officer rides forth once more, probably, with true Anglo-Saxon sense of justice, abusing the jeweller, the money-changer, the vendor of vegetables, and the pipe-man, whose shop he had ridden into backwards, for not getting out of the way!

Cawnpore is celebrated for the manufacture of harness; but, oh, what stuff it is! The saddles are not badly-shaped, being made on English trees, or correct models of the same; but the leather! I should like to see the face of a pig, if he was told that it was the skin of one of his brethren! And yet these saddlers drive a thriving trade: when a man has bought a pony—as nearly every officer in the army does—a saddle becomes indispensable; and a saddle begets a bridle, a brush, a currycomb, and various other articles of a like nature, so that the Cawnpore harness makers are generally well to do.

There are tailors, too, who have got their hands as full as they will hold, and fuller, employed as they are in making summer clothing for the troops, and turning out sun-defying but exceedingly unbecoming wicker helmets, at the shortest notice; orders from fresh regiments for eight hundred and nine hundred suits, which *must* be finished in three weeks, says the Colonel, which *shall* be finished in three weeks, promises the Tailor, and which are not finished for two months, proves Experience, pour in day after day. Gopal Doss, with orders for some thousands of helmets, coats, inexpressibles, and turbans, is literally up to his eyes in karkee, to which colour everything in Cawnpore seems, in the excitement of the moment and the flourishing state of commerce, to be rapidly turning.* Another tailor appeared to be gradually becoming a drivelling idiot, under the combined effects of pressure of business, and the prospect of incalculable wealth. As for the dyers, I believe they lived in a bluish slate atmosphere, and breathed karkee-coloured air, and, upon the whole, I think I may affirm that Cawnpore was beside itself at this particular and busy period of its existence. These shopkeepers have had a fine time of it altogether, they had probably assisted very materially in the looting of the English property at the station—a hypothesis which was encouraged by the fact that, in one's peregrinations about

* *Karkee* (a sort of bluish slate) is the colour fixed on by regulation for the summer clothing of the troops.

the bazaar, one often came across some piece of English crockery, or furniture, with a half-worn, suspicious look about it highly suggestive of looting, exposed for sale; and now they were reaping the golden harvest, and all those benefits derivable from the wants of the chastising army. Of course, to us, they would tell melancholy tales, of how they themselves had been looted by the sepoys, and how very much impoverished they were, and how they would have protected the English people if they could, and how sad it all was; and make various other speeches, which I think we may safely bracket together under the head of "humbug," and, drawing our own conclusions from what we saw, make up our minds that the effect of the mutiny on the Cawnpore merchants instanced afresh the truth of the proverb, "It is an ill wind that blows nobody any good." And now, good-bye to Cawnpore, and its thriving *buneahs*, and its forts and ruins, and, if we *can* bid adieu to them for a while, to the sad recollections which those ruins suggest, for we are about to cross into Oude.

Scene—Our temporary quarters at Cawnpore. There is a perfectly opaque atmosphere of dust, likewise gritty in its nature, and with an irresistible tendency to enter forcibly into one's eyes and up one's nose, and into every pore and crevice of one's skin; we are wildly endeavouring to effect a start; for the conveyance of our baggage the commissariat have supplied us with a few elephants (who are flourishing their trunks about, and throwing sand over themselves in a manner ridiculous to behold) and a large quantity of hackeries, which all appear to have their wheels loose, and to be in the last stage of ricketiness. The said hackeries are drawn by a very fat, comfortable, well-looking, well-looked-after lot of bullocks; but I am as convinced, as I stand eyeing those beautiful and apparently docile animals, with sleek white skin and big hump, (how good that would be salted!) and long, smooth, velvety dew-lap, which are now, pretty dears, so calmly eating their chopped straw —I am as convinced, I say, as ever I was of anything in my life, that those sleek white skins enshroud the most diabolical dispositions—that beneath those calm exteriors lurk villany and treachery; in short, that those patient creatures are fiends incarnate, and that even now they are pleasantly contemplating the possibility of precipitating our baggage into the Ganges, and anticipating and determining upon stoppages, delays, and every sort of disaster and disagreeableness which the minds of bullocks can conceive, or their muscular bodies execute. There is a man standing by me who did not come up-country by bullock-train: he doubts the truth of my assertion; he says they are "very nice and quiet to pat." Well, well, he will have the kindness to defer any very strong expression of these doubts until the evening, when I shall be only too happy to hear anything he may have to say on the subject; but at present, much as I may regret appearing to treat any opinion of his with contempt, I can only look upon him as a man devoid of experience, and I am therefore under the painful necessity of pooh-poohing him, which I do—you will observe—as good-naturedly as possible.

Baggage all loaded—everything ready—*allons!* and away we go, through an atmosphere suggestive of Scotch mist, petrified and then pulverised, and unpleasant work it is, trudging on through these grey, penetrating clouds of gritty matter. A dust storm usually blows steadily, in one particular direction, but I notice as a peculiarity of this one (and of Indian dust-storms in general), that it blows in every direction, and therefore always right into one's face; wherever one turns, however one twists, and wheels, and goes round corners —north, south, east, and west—still one is sure to have the storm in one's teeth, and the state of frenzy to which it drives one, the irritation it causes to one's eyes, and the way in which it envelopes one in a sort of light grey paletot, are worthy of observation.

My respected commanding officer, whose words, at certain periods of my career, I may have treated with less respect than the rank of the utterer demanded, and whom oft, in waywardness of spirit, "to the prejudice of good order and military discipline," I confess with shame and sorrow I have thwarted and opposed, now inspired perforce an unwonted reverence and awe. The hoary garb of wisdom had fallen upon him, in a gritty and arenaceous form it is true, but nevertheless it had whitened his beard and the ends of his hair quite patriarchally, adding some twenty years to his appearance, and giving to the sentiments which fell from his lips such additional weight and importance that words of command were metamorphosed into moral sentiments, and even the curt, gruff "Halt" seemed, as he uttered it, to embody some sage and golden maxim. So much for the dust-storm, an evil of constant occurrence in India, and making life still less endurable in this horrible country.

At length we cross the Ganges by the bridge of boats, which groans and creaks audibly, and whines out a protest against this daily infliction, this never-ceasing tramp of armed men and baggage, and artillery and stores, over its long-suffering planks; but kindly condescending to bear us in safety, we now place foot in Oude.

Miles of white glaring sand, whose component particles glitter like diamonds in the sun, stretch away along the river bank, dazzling the eye painfully with the reflected glare; and owing to this, and to having to ride over the heavy surface, our horses sinking deep at every step—owing to the hot sun, now shining with more splendour than was agreeable—owing to the dust which had insinuated itself into ears, eyes, nose and mouth, and which made life a burden—owing to a certain barrenness of country, which struck me forcibly and dismally; in short, owing to being in a very bad humour, my first impressions of Oude were not favourable. Nor was my peace of mind made greater by certain mysterious evolutions on the part of the bullocks drawing our baggage, whose deeply-rooted villany began to bud about the bridge, and to expand into full bloom as soon as they arrived on the soft white sand, where the hackeries sank up to their axles, and the bullocks gave themselves up with much zest, and in a fine acrobatic spirit, to a series of field sports and athletic performances, such as tumbling, upsetting the carts, turning so sharply that the wheels came off with a crash, tilting out the baggage, and gamboling so gaily as quite to justify (and a little more) my previous forebodings on the subject, and effectually putting to shame the sanguine, unsuspicious mortal who had not travelled up country by bullock-train, and who had found them so nice and quiet to pat, and who now begins to be sorry he spoke, and to express himself accordingly.

We get over the sands at last on to the main road, along which we rattle along merrily, passing, as we go over, the scene of one of Havelock's fights during his advance to the relief of Lucknow; a ridge of rising ground marks the Sepoys' position, and traces of a battery and small earthwork, and a semi-fortified village called Mungawarra, crowning the high ground, still exist. Up this slope towards the ridge our troops had ascended in pouring rain, and "without a check" had gallantly driven the enemy from his fine position, thus securing to Havelock a firm footing in Oude, if firm the footing can be called, which a few hundred British soldiers held, despite a trained army in rebellious opposition, despite the efforts of a hydra-headed enemy, and despite the armed and inimical population of the country in which they were. After a long and not very pleasant march we reached Oonao, celebrated as the scene of another struggle on the 29th of July, 1857, in which, after a severe "pounding match" between our own and the enemy's artillery, our troops had achieved a brilliant victory, captured nineteen guns, and won yet more laurels for General Havelock and his gallant little band. Oonao is a large village, strongly situated, and having, at a little distance, more the appearance of a large irregular fort than anything else; and the general aspect of the country, which I characterized on first crossing the river as "barren," here becomes well wooded and fertile, striking and pretty, though as level as a bowling-green.

Just beyond Oonao we found encamped a large portion of the army, consisting chiefly of the park of artillery and ordnance stores, the Naval Brigade, Hodson's Irregular Horse, some Punjab infantry, some regiments of Highlanders (as our ears soon found out to their cost), horse artillery, and a few other troops; and here we halt also, and encamp.

Ah! what "griffs" we were in those days! what poor hands at campaigning! I quite shudder when I look back on that dismal period of "griffendom" and inexperience; new to the work of picketing horses—new to the usages and customs of the country—unable to speak a word of the language—driven mad by "syces," "grass-cutters," "kulassies," "khitmutgars," "bhistees," "bearers," and others of your native establishment, who neither understand you, nor you them; burnt by the sun into blisters; fiercely hot, tired and hopeless. I look back upon that time as the most miserable I ever spent in my whole life. True, glory and distinction were before us; but what is glory when you want your breakfast, and see no chance of getting it for hours to come, if at all? What does the man, before whose mind keeps ever flitting a horrible vision of his baggage upset upon the sandy banks of the Ganges, trampled on and injured by fiendish and insulting bullocks—what does this man care at that moment for distinction and fame? Alas! but little. You feel as though you would willingly exchange glory for a mutton chop, your chance of distinction for a portmanteau, and all your "blushing honours" for one clean shirt and a little soap and water; and as you lie wearied, hungry, dusty, despairing and miserable on the floor of your badly pitched, baggageless tent, you feel sadly tempted in the bitterness of your heart, in the extremity of your wretchedness, to echo the sentiment, "All is vanity!" Mistake me not, O reader! nor look on me as a discontented, luxurious, ease-loving mortal, unfitted for and loathing the rough work and hardships of war—for it is not so. Different, indeed, is marching, when a few days' ungentle teaching has broken one in, and taught one wisdom—when the apparently insurmountable objects which so unnerved you the first day, yield one by one to the simple shifts, and happy "dodges" which experience suggests, till you fall into that regular clockwork system which is the perfection of campaigning, and which converts into a pleasure what at first was most decidedly a pain.

Even on this occasion, so elastic was our temperament, that when, thanks to the hospitality of others, we had partaken of a good breakfast, and were in a state of profuse perspiration from hot tea and military ardour, which, conjointly with "Worcestershire sauce" and curry, was burning within us, our existence, which not half an hour ago looked blank and worthless, now assumed such a delightful *couleur de rose*, that, rising superior to adverse circumstances, we looked forward with a pleasurable excitement to continuing our march, as we expected to do, on the following morning towards Lucknow. In this, however, we were disappointed. Various reasons were assigned for the delay, none of which, in all probability, were the right ones; but for several days did the force remain stationary at Oonao, the gunners and Naval Brigade rubbing up their guns and gun-drill, cavalry and horse artillery doing the like to their horses; the Highlanders disported themselves in kilts, and aired their legs, to the no small astonishment of the natives; and the force, generally, strove by a happy mixture of races and routine to while away and improve the time till the commander-in-chief thought fit to let slip his " dogs of war" upon the foe.

I should hardly have thought worthy of mention, in the midst of so many other stirring events, the apparently trivial fact of our receiving camels for the transport of our baggage *vice* bullock-hackeries, during this halt, were it not that from this event dated the overthrow (as far as we were concerned) of one of those popular fallacies which one often finds high-seated on the pinnacle of Delusion, till the rude hand of Truth, armed with a hard stone called Fact, which it throws with unerring aim, brings it toppling over. The fallacy in question is one to which from my earliest days I have subscribed without doubt or hesitation, and which two-thirds of England believe in firmly at this moment—I allude to the notion that the camel is a pleasant animal to have to do with—that he is agreeable, patient, good-tempered, gentle, docile, meek, and the like, all which facts I had hammered into me by "pictorial primers," under the head of an enormous letter C, in the first instance, and subsequently at every school I went to. Invaluable he is, I admit, likewise hardy, capable of carrying enormous loads for great distances under a frightful sun, and generally admirably suited for the purpose to which he is put—that of a baggage animal; but to say that a camel is patient, to affirm that this great, grumbling, groaning, brown brute is either docile, meek, or sweet-tempered, is stating what is simply not the case; and I have no hesitation in saying that never do I remember to have seen a camel in a good humour, or otherwise than in open or moody hostility with the world at large, at least if outward appearances are to be credited. Watch him when he is being loaded; see his keeper struggling frantically with him, only succeeding in making him kneel down for the purpose by sheer force, and when down only keeping him there by tying neck and fore leg together tightly with a piece of string; hear him grumbling in deep bubbling tones, with mouth savagely opened, and all his huge teeth grinning ferociously at you, and I think that then at least you will admit he is by no means in as amiable a frame of mind as one would wish. Observe him now that the process of loading is completed, and the string which held him in subjection loosened; up he rises—a great brown mountain—still groaning, still bubbling, and away he goes, madly dashing to and fro, and shaking off tables, portmanteaus, beds, furniture, and baggage in a scattered shower around him, and I think even his staunchest admirers will allow, that neither at this moment is he what one would call in a pleasant humour. Mr. Camel having, after some battling, been overcome, and compelled to carry the load which he so objected to, but not until he has damaged it considerably, arrives when the march is over at the encamping ground; it is necessary to make him kneel down, to have that load removed—grumbling, as much as ever, in opposition, as usual—beaten physically, but with soul unsubdued, and internally in a state of rebellion and mutiny—a sort of volcano ready at any moment to burst out.

Now, if any lady or gentleman interested in zoology generally, and camels in particular, objects to my arguments because I have taken the opportunity to sketch this animal's infirmities at a time when they were most likely to be apparent, then I answer let such sceptics come out to India, and sleep, or try to sleep, for one night in a tent outside which are squatted the camels which are to carry his or her baggage in the morning, and I think all their doubts will speedily disappear. Throughout the night do they growl and grumble solos, duets, and choruses in harsh discord; and with that peculiar and very nasty-looking water-bag, which they are able to draw up from their stomach into their mouths when thirsty, and refresh themselves withal, they make a noise exactly resembling that made in smoking a "hookah," or hubble-bubble; all which keeps you awake for hour after hour, and tempting you to curse bitterly the humpbacked gentlemen from whom these noises emanate. I may as well add that a camel's bite is more severe than that of almost any other animal; likewise that in an olfactory sense, he is far from agreeable, the aroma which he exhales being, I think, the most sickening I ever encountered; all which little trifles added together go far towards lowering "the ship of the desert" in my estimation —or rather, I should say, in my high opinion of him, for my admiration for his powers of endurance and strength has been increased tenfold since I have become practically acquainted with them.

CHAPTER XII.

The Advance upon Lucknow—Scenery and Incidents on the March.

THE delay is over at last. The idle halt has come to an end, and the army once more is on its legs. Tents struck, baggage loaded, and away to Lucknow. We do not move up *en masse*, however, but in driblets, some troops moving forward every day. The monster siege-train, with an appropriate guard of cavalry, infantry, and field artillery, travels in two divisions, the second half being one day's march in rear of the first; far along the road does the straggling line of guns, mortars, howitzers, and hackeries loaded heavily with shot and shell, and tumbrils crammed with thousands upon thousands of pounds of powder, and ammunition, and diabolical contrivances of war. Far along the dusty road, I say, does all this extend; nor are its movements by any means swift owing to innumerable break-downs, and not a litttle to certain before-mentioned eccentricities on the part of our old friends, the bullocks, who somehow contrive never to have less than about five hundred carts stuck in ditches, or inextricably jammed at one and the same time, so as always to have on hand some very fine specimens of chaos.

It is but dreary work travelling alongside this *train d'équipages militaires,* as the French would call it, but it is still more dreary work travelling behind it in the capacity of rear-guard, when you are of course delayed by and made sensible of every new break-down, or fresh bullockian caprice, more especially when your humour is none of the sweetest from the fact of your having been roused from your couch two hours before daybreak by a heartless bugler sounding the *réveillée*.

I wonder if the best-natured man in the world could be agreeable, or even civil at this unearthly hour in the morning. I have noticed that even the cheerfulest and most buoyant of mortals become grumpy and unsociable at this miserable period of their existence. One is generally in a state of vacant stupidity and owlishness from want of sleep; one is probably in a state of moroseness likewise from the barking of one's shins over an infernal tent-peg; of desperate though subdued rage from the tumbling over an accursed and tightly-stretched tent-rope, and of cold perspiration at the recollection of how, in the dark, you had walked up to a horse's heels and narrowly escaped a violent and horrible death therefrom. All this causes you to foster misanthropy to an extent which is positively terrific; your dearest friend tells you in confidence that he feels " deuced seedy this morning." Ha! ha! delightful! You become grumpily ecstatic thereupon; you chuckle over it with fiendish glee, and you make merry at your "dearest friend's" expence! Lieutenant ———'s khitmutghar failed to bring him the customary cup of tea this morning before starting, and he is consequently hungry, and even in a worse humour than yourself. He confides to you with much pathos the sad fact. Confound the man and his khitmutghar! what do you care? You are rather glad than otherwise, and you tell him so; and if he chooses to continue a conversation commenced so inauspiciously, why then—*que voulez-vous, mon cher?*—you will disagree with him on every point except that of licking his khitmutghar "within an inch of his life," because at the moment that proposition happens to suit your Timon-of-Athens-like mood.

But of all objectionable people to meet at this hour the worst I know is your *lively* man— the man who affects a sort of ghastly merriment and wide-awakishness, which resolves itself into a hideous jocularity and sleepy sort of briskness, which you know must be all a sham at this time of day, or night. Feigning jollity, he calls you "old fellow." Now I have no objection to being called "old fellow" in the middle of the day or after dinner; but when a man deliberately, and of malice aforethought, calls you "old fellow" at 4 A.M. he commits an act which ought to be made punishable by law. You rather hope that he will bring matters to a crisis by slapping you on the back, which would, of course, be an excuse for at once knocking him off his horse. "Well, old fellow! how are we this morning? Sleepy, eh?" Of course you are sleepy, and so is he, only he pretends not to be. Continued jocularity: "Cheer up old boy" &c. &c.; and so we wrap ourselves up in a cloak of grumpiness and hatred of our fellow-man, and ride gloomily along on our horse, who stumbles, the brute! at every step. By Jove! how sleepy we are. We light a cheeroot, which of course is a bad one—we watch the grey morning breaking—we watch the black shades of night peeling off, as it were, one by one, and disappearing—we watch the day dawning prettily in the east, and insensibly, gradually, we are humanizing once more. We watch the little bit of gold showing above the horizon, and growing into a great, glowing, fiery orb, which we know, ere long, will dart out such brazen heat and scorching rays that existence anywhere but in the shade will be impracticable. We watch the dark masses of troops and guns (who have hitherto been, to our eye, only as huge, shapeless masses of darkness moving mechanically onward) becoming defined and clear by slow degrees, until at last the men's faces become apparent, and you are able once again to behold private John Smith in all his glory as he trudges along, puffing away merrily at his short, black cutty, filled with the nastiest tobacco in the world, in an overpowering state of heat, perspiration, and dust. It is wonderful how dusty every one seems to have become in that hour or so before dawn, but so it is : in the wrinkles of the men's coats, on their beards and whiskers, and down the junction of their cheeks and noses—about their firelocks—in your horses' ears and your own, and on his smooth, sleek skin—upon the bullocks, yokes—upon the elephants' broad backs—thickly over the heavy guns, from muzzle to breach, in the crevices of their mouldings and carvings, over the carriages, and upon every chain and handspike, ring and bolt—as thickly, too, upon the field pieces, and taking the shine out of the harness—wherever, in fact, a grain of sand or dust can cling there will that grain be found, reducing man and beast, and wood and iron, to a sort of neutral, gritty grey.

It is wonderful, too, how with sunrise all sleepiness vanishes; often have I found in a night's march, when I have rolled and lolled about on my horse with very drowsiness the long night through, and would have given all my worldly possessions for a nap—when I have in sheer despair wound the mane round my fingers, and then resigned myself to Morpheus, and the safety of my neck to chance—when, on a short halt being called, I have thrown myself off my horse on to the soft dusty road, and dropping off to sleep before my foot was well out the stirrup have slept with all my might and main until "Attention!" was called, or in case that failed to awaken me, until a good-natured sergeant coming up roused me with "They're a moving off, sir"—I say, invariably on these occasions, when I have been thus overpowered with sleep, have I found that immediately the sun appears, long before it gets hot, does all that drowsiness vanish, and you feel almost supernaturally wide awake—the first few rays as they sparkle and gleam upon you seem to drive away every wink and blink from your eyelids, and leave you with that sort of sleepless, weary Wandering-Jew *marche-marche-toujours-marche* sensation which is scarcely more agreeable than the previous one of extreme somnolence.

CHAPTER XIII.

The March to Lucknow (continued)—Nawabgunge—Busseratgunge—Bunterah—An Alarm, "Stand to your arms"—The Dilkoosha—The First Glimpse of Lucknow.

AFTER two or three days' journeying along a road remarkable for its monotony, except when one passed through some walled village, such as Busseratgunge and Nawabgunge, where ragged shot holes denting the old gateways, and making splintered gaps in the rotten wooden gates, showed us the nature of the key which Havelock had used to open them, but which became monotonous after a time from the fact of the keys being all off the same bunch, as we had opportunities of observing at each succeeding village—we arrived at last at the appointed rendezvous for the army, Bunterah, about seven or eight miles from Lucknow.

Here such a force was collected as must have paled the cheek of Pandy's spies when they caught sight of it, and must have made the old Begum tremble in her palace at Lucknow when she heard of its approach.

Magnificent it was to see this vast assemblage of white tents stretching out for miles, and among which went hither and thither some fifteen thousand troops, English and Sikhs, full of ardour, life, and hope. Nor did this force, large as it may appear, include all the

FORCE ENGAGED.

troops who were to be employed in the capture of Lucknow; for, at the Alum Bagh, General Outram had some four thousand men, while General Franks was expected in a few days with a force of five thousand eight hundred men, after a long but victorious march through the south-eastern portion of Oude, while I suppose the six or eight thousand exceedingly useless Ghoorkas must find a place in our calculations.*

* It, perhaps, may not be out of place here to give the actual numbers of the troops employed in the capture of Lucknow, as taken from an official return; they are as follow:

Force under Sir Colin Campbell (this includes the Alum Bagh garrison under General Outram).

Artillery and Naval Brigade.	Engineers.
European officers . . . . 87 Rank and file . . . . . 1526 Horses 930	Unarmed pioneers . . . . 754 Officers . . . . {Nat.} {Eur.} 91 Rank and file 1911
Cavalry.	Infantry.
Officers . . . {Eur. 132} {Nat. 61} 193 Rank and file (N. and E.) . 3420 Horses 3587	Officers . . . . {E. 558} {N. 147} 705 Rank and file (E. and N.). 11,940

Grand total of force under Sir Colin Campbell—20,627 men, 4517 horses.

Force under General Franks.

Artillery.	Cavalry.	Infantry.
European officers . 17 Rank and file . . 327 Horses 193	Officers. {Eur. 13} {Nat. 11} 24 Rank and file . . 519 Horses. 417	Officers . {Eur. 110} {Nat. 96} 206 Rank and file . . 4800

Total force under General Franks—5893 men, 610 horses.

Grand total of force engaged in capture of Lucknow, exclusive of Ghoorkas under Jung Bahadoor (6000 or 8000):

All ranks (Native and European) . . 26,520
Horses 5,127

Well, we encamp with the rest at Bunterah; we eat our breakfast (we are no longer "griffs" in the campaigning line); we smoke a cheroot, and then lie down for a snooze in our hot tents; it is nearly mid-day, all is silent as the grave in camp, except when half a dozen well-toned *ghurrees* (a sort of native gong) clang out the hour—dozing—dozing gradually off—(a snore)—hush—" eh !"

" Hallo! get up !"

"What's the row?—what is that cry?"
" Stand to your arms, the Saypoys is a-coming !"

A hideous clatter, a rushing of men past your tent, a shouting, a neighing of horses, who possibly imagine that the noise is in some way connected with feeding—an unwonted hurry and confusion, and ringing again and again through the camp the cry of " Stand to your arms, the enemy are coming !" You are in a sort of summery *dishabille* of *pyjamas* (loose cotton trousers) and shirt sleeves, and you find it as difficult to collect your ideas, which have travelled with you from Dreamland, as it is to collect your luggage at London-bridge station after a three hours' journey from Dover; but, *qu'importe?* pyjamas, shirt-sleeves, or mental aberration, when you are going out to get shot very possibly ?

Away you rush, buckling on your sword as you go, and meeting more men in shirt-sleeves, who also cannot collect their luggage—I mean their ideas—and buckling on swords very fast, and swearing gutturally—but I fear earnestly—to themselves, or mounting their steeds in the very hottest of hot haste; and as you

A FALSE ALARM. 143

pass a tent door you catch a glimpse of a wretched mortal *à la belle nature,* or very nearly so (he having been employed in the operation of "tubbing" when the row commenced), now engaged in an attempt to perform the impossible feat of getting into a pair of trousers hind-side before, and the fastening round his waist of a revolver at one and the same moment, and vociferating madly for his "bearer," and, of course, swearing desperately. Elsewhere is another equally wretched mortal trying to get on a boot, tumbling and hopping about on one leg in a manner stupendous to behold, very red in the face, and using exceedingly strong language, and consigning all sorts of people and things, and himself among the number, to perdition and elsewhere, in a by no means Christian spirit.

I just see and hear these various domestic episodes *en passant* towards the front of the camp, whither soldiers and officers are swiftly hurrying. Everybody says the enemy are coming, some men swear they can see them, or very nearly, but they are not quite sure in which direction, nor, in fact, is any one. Conjecture is at a loss; officers are still galloping to and fro; Sir Colin, on his white Arab, starts off across country with the intention of judging for himself; bullocks and camels out grazing are coming into camp helter-skelter, urged along by their alarmed drivers, and all looks as if, in our joyous expectation of a "mill," we should not be disappointed.

It is pleasant looking at those dense masses of troops drawn up in readiness in front of their respective camps, and none the less fitted for fighting, you may be sure, because the greater part of them have got neither stock nor coats on; it is equally pleasant to look at the long array of guns with the burly detachments *en chemise* standing by them, slow-match lit, and wanting but two words of four letters each— " Load !" " Fire !"—to cause them to hurl forth flame, and death, and destruction.

A dead silence pervades the camp now, almost oppressive after the noise and confusion, and one could not help thinking, that " Jack Sepoy" would be a sad fool if he chose this moment for making his attack; and I suppose " Jack Sepoy" thought much the same, for he did not put in an appearance that day, and, indeed, I believe he had never had the slightest intention of doing so, the whole being a false alarm. We returned to our tents, cheroots, and " pyjamas," and heard nothing more of the matter till evening, when an order from Sir Colin appeared on the subject of alarms generally, concluding with a request that on similar occasions staff officers would " not gallop wildly about, vociferating to regiments to turn out, and thereby causing panic;" whereat we who were not on the staff chuckled not a little.

The following morning, March 2nd, at daybreak, a force marched for Lucknow (Sir Colin Campbell himself accompanying it), intended to drive in the enemy's outlying pickets, and open the way for the rest of the army. The 23rd Royal Welch Fusiliers, the 42nd Highlanders, 93rd Highlanders and three troops of Horse Artillery, with two or four guns of the naval brigade, and I believe some cavalry, composed the chief part of this column; and it was not very long before heavy firing told us that they were at it, and in the afternoon of the same day we had the pleasure of hearing that they had occupied the Dilkoosha, with little or no loss, after driving the enemy before them and clearing the Mahommed Bagh, a large walled garden near the Dilkoosha, in which preliminary operations the troops under General Outram had also assisted. These successes enabled more troops to push on that evening, when the 34th, 38th, 53rd, and 79th regiments, the remainder of the Naval Brigade, and six guns (heavy) of the Royal Artillery, and possibly a few other troops that I have not the names of, marched to join Sir Colin, and to occupy the ground taken in the morning. The main portion of the park of artillery had not advanced yet, it being most desirable to get a perfectly firm footing before hampering ourselves with heavy guns, and the more so as they could be of but little use yet.

Heavy firing throughout that night and the following morning, and in the evening, March 3rd, the order came for the remainder of the army, with the park of artillery, to march at half-past ten P.M. Oh, what a slow and wearying march that was! the night seemed interminable, and from having to go the whole of the way across country, the riding was none of the pleasantest. As day broke, we found ourselves under the walls of the old fort of Jellalabad, which is the right of our Alum Bagh position; it certainly was a pretty scene, for Jellalabad is charmingly situated, embedded in dark topes of mango trees, about the branches of which skip innumerable monkeys, chattering, jabbering, screeching, hanging now by their tails, now by one leg, and playing the wildest and strangest pranks. The effect of the scenery was much enhanced by the groups of men, and guns, bullocks and horses, and the thousands of camp-followers, with their wives and ponies and domestic belongings, scattered about over the face of the country for miles, or gathered in picturesque parties among the trees, a sort of ever-changing, many-hued panorama of striking character.

Under one tope of trees, where also is situated a stone well, lay twenty or thirty skeletons—a ghastly sight enough. There they lay in all sorts of unnatural and distorted positions, with their fleshless limbs angularly contorted, and the white teeth imparting a horrid grin to the ghastly skulls. Some of their old rags yet clung to them, the mouldy remains of their red coats and uniforms as decayed as themselves. Ah! many a dainty meal have the jackals and pariah dogs made over these horrible bodies, often have they in the dark nights held high feast and festival over these mutineers' bones, from which they had

> stripped the flesh,
> As ye peel the fig when the fruit is fresh,

making night hideous with their unearthly yells.

The trees under which they lay bore signs which told unmistakeably the whole tale; deep rugged dents on the trunks, boughs cut and splintered in two, and the wood so chipped and torn that it did not require much experience in such matters to enable one to see, in imagination, the case-shot as it had come crashing through the tope with that partridge-like whirr-r-r-r peculiar to a shower of this description of projectile, and laid low those wretched men.* I have since heard the tale from people who were present when these men were killed. It was during the time Sir James Outram held the Alum Bagh, and one of the almost daily attacks by the enemy on his position was going on; these men whose remains we now see lying before us had with some others occupied the tope of trees in question, where, I believe, they had brought two guns into action, which guns we subsequently captured; the enemy were driven back as usual, but these men, either surrounded by our cavalry, or fanatically determined to die, were at all events so situated that escape became impossible. The cavalry were ordered to ride in and cut them up; but directly they advanced the Pandies climbed up the trees and coolly "potted" our helpless soldiers as they rode beneath them. Thereupon General Outram ordered the cavalry to be withdrawn, and the guns to pour a few rounds of case-shot among the trees; they did so, and the Pandies' hours were numbered; toppling down they came like birds, some shot through and through, others with the branches on which they were perched cut away from under them,

* Case-shot are very commonly but erroneously, called grape, which is a totally distinct thing; the former being a cylindrical tin canister, or case, filled with iron balls; the latter being made by seven, nine, or more balls of a much larger size tied together, which, presenting a real or fancied resemblance to a bunch of grapes, have given it its name.

and some of their own accord, in the vain hope, perhaps, that there was yet time to escape. Bang! whirr-r-r-r, rattle, rattle, rattle, went volley after volley among the old mango trees, and bringing down at once a shower of green leaves, branches, and men, mowing them down wholesale, while those who attempted to flee were cut up by our cavalry. Two of the wretched devils, seeing that the game of life and death was nearly played out, and unable to bear the torture and suspense of waiting to be killed, in a mad desperation actually threw themselves down the well which I mentioned before, and where to this day, when the sun shines into it, you can catch glimpses of the white gleaming bones.

Allons! en avant, mes braves!—we leave Jellalabad some miles in our rear, and at last, about ten A.M., we receive orders to halt and encamp. We do so, and then, in spite of the fatigue consequent on our long night march, we stroll out to the front of the ridge whereon our camp is situated in order to look at the view.

What do we see? Immediately beneath us the florid and gilded "Dilkoosha" (Heart's Delight)—a strangely fantastic-looking domicile it is too—built apparently of nothing but domes, and arches, and points, and peaks, and cupolas in endless and bewildering variety, and reminding one of those crowded collections of chimney pots which one sees exposed for sale in London. Behind it are groups of Highlanders, musket in hand; and close by it is a battery of heavy guns, which is carrying on a duel with the "Martinière," that immense and very extraordinary looking establishment by the river's bank, among the trees. Martine, the liberal founder of this place, must have had some odd notions of his own on the subject of architecture, or possibly he may have been possessed of the noble idea of cutting out the Dilkoosha; in which case I must admit that he has succeeded, for even that very peculiar building must yield the palm in point of outlandishness to the Martinière.

A faint pop-pop-popping of rifles is going on between the advanced pickets, varied by the heavy boom of a mortar or 18-pounder. Every now and then a little puff of white smoke issues from the Martinière, and while we are watching the tiny cloud expand, curling up, and fading away in the blue sky overhead, we hear a rushing sound like the concentrated essence of express trains passing us at full speed; we duck—yes! I confess it— we duck involuntarily as a something lodges with a dull heavy thud in the bank behind us, and warns us that we have advanced a little too far in our eagerness to see the view. To our right lies the river Goomtee, winding about, serpent-like, in a great open green plain, fringed with dark trees. This evening our engineers will commence constructing a bridge of boats across it.

Beyond the Martinière, which lies directly to our front, we can see the golden minarets and gay domes of Lucknow, with a few snow-white buildings, and some red roofs gleaming and glittering among the bright green trees, which, by their pleasant fresh colour, set off picturesquely the much painted temples and bright looking houses, and give a sort of relief to the otherwise almost too glowing scene. We cannot see much of the fair city, but we can see enough to excite in a high degree our admiration and interest, and our longing to be inside it.

Ah! how many of us will never see the inside of that city—how many a gallant heart will lie cold—how many a noble soldier perish in the attempt! there are old battered veterans, there are young, glad, happy boys amongst us now, who will soon be lying dead upon the space there, which divides us from that town—fair young forms must lie writhing in agony as their life blood trickles slowly away—and life must have died and be dying out from what but an hour before, were sturdy healthy men in the full vigour of their manhood; and many a young Hercules will have become a cripple, helpless as a babe—and the mad gallop after the hounds, or the pleasant walk, gun in hand, over the crisp, sweet-smelling heather, will be a joy gone for ever from some among us ere that city be won. Ah! did we but know who were to be taken and who left, could we but read the dim future, and foretel events as surely as we can gaze back into the past, what a strange thing would life be— what a sad trade soldiering! Should we have so many heroes, I wonder, as we have now? It is, indeed, a kind Providence which ordains that the future should be a sealed book to us, though there may be moments when we almost wish it otherwise.

Yes, many were to fall in the capture of that doomed city, and many a mother's heart would bleed, and many a wife would mourn, when the proud tale was told at home of how the rebel stronghold fell.

CHAPTER XIV.

Commencement of the Siege of Lucknow—Night march of the Trans-Goomtee column—A pleasant morning scene—The halt for breakfast—Sir James Outram.

AND so the big guns were booming hoarsely, and rifles, matchlocks, muskets, and small-arms were popping briskly, and the bullets pinged with a soft, but unpleasant sibilation before the fair city of Lucknow, on the fourth day of March, in the year of Grace one thousand eight hundred and fifty-eight.

And now the time was come, as Sir Colin Campbell worded it in his despatch, " for developing the plan of attack which had previously been determined on," the first step of which was to bridge the Goomtee. Hereat did Engineers, Royal and Bengal, her Majesty's Sappers and Miners, and Sappers from Madras, dusky of hue, big-turbaned, and intelligent, work gaily through the night, and the following morning did the enemy appear in force upon that wide green plain, through which the little river Goomtee flows so snake-like, and they threatened the bridge, and appeared disposed to retard its completion; whereupon were field guns sent down to overawe these gentlemen by their presence, and to bark hoarsely at them, like huge watch-dogs suffering from bronchitis, and to play at "long bowls" with other and hostile guns, which they did to their heart's content the livelong day, while the big guns kept on booming and the bullets softly pinging, and the city glittered and gleamed unconsciously the while in the bright hot sun.

Swiftly did the making of the bridge (or rather of the two bridges) progress, and plank after plank was laid down with a workmanlike and pleasant celerity. With the exception of this operation, the 5th of March was an uneventful day, in the course of which much ammunition was wasted, and many a bullet fell harmless, and artillerymen and sailors grew hot with the exertion of manning the 18-pounders. And some curious specimens of hammered shot,* unsightly, and far from mathematically spherical, came spinning into the camp and crashing through the trees, beneath the shade of which the drivers and horses of Gibbon's field battery of Royal Artillery, whose guns were playing at the long bowls aforesaid, were reposing; and but little harm was done, I wot, that day to friend or foe.

But this night will a move be made, and at an hour past midnight, in the darkness and the fog which overspread the scene, and silently, without sound of trumpet or bugle, there assembled in front of the camp a dense body of men, who were about to test the efficiency of the bridges that day constructed by crossing over them. It was a

---

* The enemy's shot were chiefly hammered—*i. e.* lumps of heated iron beaten into a spherical form, and not cast as ours are —probably from want of furnaces, moulds, and other appliances.

strange scene this midnight assembly, and a sort of forced stillness pervaded the whole as the troops moved, regiment after regiment, up to the rendez-vous. I use the word "stillness" advisedly, reader, for to those unaccustomed to the noise and clamour usually attending the parading of a mass of troops it would have seemed far from still. Now the even, measured tramp of men falls upon the ear, and now the dull rumbling of the artillery guns and waggons; here, trotting briskly to the front, comes a regiment of cavalry, their steel scabbards making a light jingle as they fall against the stirrup-irons; there comes another regiment of cavalry, likewise trotting, but who jingle not as they advance, and who seem to have even muffled their horses' hoofs, so silently, almost stealthily, do they pass by. Why is this? Because these are Sikh cavalry,—who know not steel scabbards and their attendant jingle, but who wear leather sheaths, wherein the swords do not become blunt and dull, and who, though perchance they might fail to gladden the hearts of those good folks at home, who love the clatter and the clash, and the ringing of spurs, stirrup-irons, and scabbards, and look on them as part and parcel of a soldier, are able, by foregoing these same, to have tulwars, with edges like that of a razor—keen, bright, and ready, as many a deep and ghastly cut on Sepoy corpses can testify.

And so this body of troops pressed on through the darkness (with now and again the flash of a heavy gun, or a sharp rattling volley of musketry, to give a sort of zest and piquancy to the scene), finding their way—so it appeared to me—by instinct; for where we were going, how we were to get there, how penetrate the gloom, and, in fact, how anything was to result from all this, it was not easy to foresee; and, in fact, I still have my doubts on the subject, had it not been that we were suddenly favoured by the appearance of Luna looking rather pale from the severity of her struggle with the fog, but radiant with the triumph she had accomplished over the same. I have a dim consciousness of all this and all these noises—of finding myself with great, big, armed masses of shadow—for such the troops appeared to be—tramping on every side of me; of innumerable halts and delays; of being somewhere on the open plain, and not far from the river; of taking advantage of certain stoppages to curl myself up in my cloak on the ground in the warrior-taking-his-rest style, and snatch a few moments' sleep; of asking and being asked a score of times the question, which was never answered except by vague hypotheses, "Where are we going to?"—of a sort of confused notion that we were going to cover ourselves with glory; of gradually becoming insensible to the romance and picturesque strangeness of the scene which had at first attracted me, and more sensible of the cravings of Morpheus, who refused to be comforted by the light snatches of sleep above mentioned; of crossing the bridge, and of being a good deal squeezed by my fellow-man in doing so; and, moreover, of hearing a good deal of strong and emphatic language, which, as far as I could judge in the dark, sounded very much like swearing;

and, finally, of morning breaking, and of a brave and gay *coup d'œil* as one looked and saw between one and the dazzling sun the various regiments composing the force drawn up in column, and beheld how out of the nettle Chaos we had plucked the flower Order.*

Ahead are the cavalry and horse artillery, sending out skirmishers in all directions; there are the Queen's Bays, who look, in their scarlet coats, as if they had come out for the express purpose of attracting all the rays of the sun; there are the 9th Lancers, looking as they ever do, smart, neat, and business-like, with their lances slung lightly on their arms; but—hear this and weep, O ye frequenters of reviews in the Phœnix, Hyde Park, and at Aldershott ! with no little red and white flags fluttering prettily beneath the bright gleaming points; for, alas ! it must be admitted that the streamers in question, attractive though they be, have not been found to conduce overmuch to the overthrow of our enemies or the quelling of the rebellion, and considering how liable they are to attract the enemy's attention, and to draw down fire upon those bearing them, they have been wisely dispensed with on service. There are large bodies of Sikh Irregular Cavalry, big-whiskered, monster-turbaned, and, for the most

* The regiments present on this occasion were the 2nd Dragoon Guards (the " Bays"), the 9th Lancers, and one or two regiments of Irregular Cavalry ; D'Aguilar's troop Royal Horse Artillery, Rimington's and Mackinnon's troops Bengal Horse Artillery, Gibbon's and Middleton's field batteries of Royal Artillery, the 23rd Royal Welsh Fusiliers, the 79th Highlanders, 2nd and 3rd battalions Rifle Brigade, 1st Bengal European Fusiliers, and Green's regiment of Sikhs.

part, slate-coloured as to clothes, while each man presents the appearance of an armoury in miniature, what with the spear, tulwar, and pistols *à discrétion* wherewith he is equipped. There are three troops of Horse Artillery, one whereof is Royal, and the other two Bengal, all equally ready to gallop over the stiffest line of country you can point out to them, and to blaze away with perfect and deadly precision afterwards, and these complete the cavalry column, which is halted on the slope of a hill, waiting the order to advance.

Reader, a word in your ear. There is an officer among those scarlet-coated Bays, chatting away merrily enough now—a gallant soldier, full of life, courage, and hope. Look on him well, my friend, now while you can, and then seek not to look on him again, for three short hours' hence, or when you next shall see him, it will not, as now, be a glad sight which shall meet your eyes, but a ghastly and a horrible one, from which you will turn shuddering and pitying away. How bravely does the great round sun rise up!—how bravely and how bright!—gilding the gay scene and gladdening all hearts; and yet did some of us but know—did he I have just spoken of but know—that this was the last sunrise he would ever see! and that when to-morrow the round sun rises up as brightly and gilds the green plain and the waving tree-tops as now, its rays will light up and fall upon a dank and mutilated corpse lying away there towards the city upon the dewy grass—where, then, would our gladness be?

Plumes of Highlanders waving gaily, dark coats

of Riflemen, the red uniforms of the Royal Welsh
Fusiliers, the blue of the Bengal Fusiliers and of
the Artillery, and the serviceable karkee-coloured
vestments of the Sikh regiment of infantry, are
clustered pleasantly *en masse* below the ridge on
which the cavalry are halted. There is an everlasting glint and glitter from the bright locks of
the rifles, from steel ramrods, and polished belt-
plates and burnished buckles, as the sun's slanting
rays fall upon them, and the whole makes up a
scene in which the pomp and circumstance of
war are so blended with its stern reality that it
will not readily be effaced from the beholder's
memory.

I like to look back upon all the picturesque
details of the same, to see in recollection the
horses, with their heads deep buried in their nose-
bags, feeding greedily—the men carving away
with their pocket knives at the hunch of bread,
or sucking down the " go of grog " which com-
poses their frugal breakfast—the officers gathered
in knots round doolies, wherein are pieces of cold
beef and mutton, pleasant to the eyes of hungry
men, but which are rapidly becoming " small by
degrees and beautifully less:" while the meat
receives a peculiarly racy and *prononcé* flavour
from somebody insisting on carving it with the
same knife that he uses for tobacco. The tops
of innumerable flasks, both wicker and leather,
are being unscrewed, and the " dew off Ben
Nevis " is fast evaporating, while it is astonishing
how many people find it necessary to " correct
acidity " by " nips " of " Exshaw's No. 1." There
is a large display of cigar-cases, and short, black

pipes, accompanied by a strong smell of tobacco, very sweet and fragrant in the early morning air, and——But why dwell on trifles such as these, and leave unnoticed a very pleasing and prominent feature in the scene? A little to the left are gathered a group of officers "of high degree," and among them is one who, at this moment, is attentively observing through his glasses some of the enemy's videttes and cavalry, who are visible at a distance on some rising ground——a short, strongly built man, black haired, with a keen, twinkling eye, and a cheerful bright smile, and a kind word for all——dressed in a blue frock coat, and everlastingly puffing away at a cheroot—— quiet in manner, cool, unwavering, and determined; ——one whom neither the hottest and most deadly fire, the gravest responsibility, or the most perilous and critical juncture can excite or flurry——a knight *sans peur et sans reproche*——the "Bayard of India." ——General Sir James Outram——of all the host here assembled the kindest hearted and the gallantest.

General Outram's character and services are too well known to need any praise from my pen; but there were many among us who, as they looked on him and thought of his brilliant career of forty years——thought of his exploits in days gone by against the rebels of Khandeish, the wild and savage Bheels——of his many deeds of personal valour and the bright romance which attaches itself to them——of his performances in the Affghan campaign, and in Lower Scinde, among the Mahrattas, and in Persia——of his political, as well as of his military, services——and more recently of the noble part he has borne during this rebellion, in the annals of which no act will stand out more gloriously, than that which, prompted by a chivalrous generosity, this noble soldier performed, when he served where he might have commanded, that he might so avoid robbing a gallant comrade, now, alas! no more,—the illustrious Havelock—of the glory of leading the troops he had commanded so well to the relief of Lucknow—I say, there were many among us who, as they looked on the hero of all these deeds, felt that it was in truth an honour to serve under such a general.

All the world know the public services of General Outram; but all the world do not know by how many little acts of kindness and generosity he has endeared himself alike to officers and men;—they do not know that, thanks to him, many of the regiments who entered Lucknow with Havelock and himself, and who were subsequently under his command at the Alum Bagh, enjoy at this moment books, papers, periodicals, cricketing things, and other amusements, wherewith to beguile the weary hours in camp, and which Sir James has provided them with at his own expense. These and many other like acts, I say, are not generally known, they have not been trumpeted loudly forth, but they are none the less appreciated by those who are acquainted with them: they are jewels which neither lose their lustre nor their value because enclosed in a case, or hidden in the mine; and to the warmth of devotion which they, and his many other qualities have called forth among all ranks, those who have served under him will readily testify.

There is one other characteristic of General Outram's which I must mention, for it is one which, alas! is far from universal—I refer to that courtesy of demeanour which he invariably exhibits in his conversation with the lowest, as with the highest, of those with whom he may have to do; never for a moment forgetting in his position of commanding officer that he is a gentleman, or that he with whom he may be conversing, or to whom he may be giving an order, be it general or private soldier, has feelings and sensibilities like himself, which no rank, however exalted, gives the right to insult.

CHAPTER XV.

Pandy's Tactics—Outline of the Plan of Attack on Lucknow—
Cavalry Skirmish on the Race-course—Charge of the Queen's
Bays—Death of Major Percy Smith—A Touch of Roughing it—The Night of March 6th.

By this time the nose-bags are empty, and the maws of the hungry ones are filled—the black pipes have been smoked down to mere ash, and the cheroots are beginning to burn the lips that hold them—and, in short, our hasty meal is over. " Attention !" and in a moment the mass of men are reformed in their even ranks, the cavalry are upon their horses, and all is ready for a start. It would be difficult to describe the route we took that day without a plan on which to mark it out, and my best course will therefore be, to endeavour to explain the movements we were intended to execute, and the results which were expected to be derived therefrom.

I must first, however, observe that Pandy's knowledge, or at least his practice of strategy and tactics is exceedingly limited; and that, luckily for us, he judges of his opponents by himself, never anticipating any originality of conception on their part, or giving them credit for more than one idea on any one given subject. Acting upon this, therefore, he obtusely imagines that the same operation must on all occasions be performed in exactly the same manner, and that if we wish to fight a battle or

M

capture a city, we shall invariably go through the same steps, over the same ground, and, in fact, set about it in identically the same way as we did last time we attempted it. Thus, after Havelock had thrown reliefs into Lucknow, the enemy set to work energetically to erect defences along the road by which he had entered the city, so as to foil any troops who might again attempt to enter the place by the same path. Very naturally Sir Colin, when he rescued the beleaguered garrison, sagaciously declined to advance his troops by the way which they had so carefully prepared for his reception, and by making a slight *détour* to the right, he steered tolerably clear of these defences on which the enemy had expended so much time and trouble. It was scarcely courteous, perhaps, but decidedly wily, and I doubt not Pandy lamented much over the gross incivility which prompted us to decline so fair an invitation, and must have thought the "Feringhees" sadly uncomplaisant and *brusque* when he saw them come bustling in past "Dilkoosha," "Martinière," "Secunderabagh," "Mess House," and "Shah Nujeef," which fell one by one into their hands till the Residency was reached, the garrison relieved, and the feat of arms accomplished, without ever once troubling his well-prepared fortifications.

No sooner had Sir Colin gone, than the enemy again commenced their old plan of locking the stable-door after the steed was stolen, and vigorously did they work at repairing the unfortunate gap which they had before left open; thus when we advanced for the capture of the city, we found the defences along the line of Sir Colin's former route greatly enlarged and strengthened, and fortifications grown up where previously none had existed. This was all well and good—Pandy was perfectly happy; in blissful ignorance of the art of taking defences in reverse, or of the many cunning devices and resources of engineers. In the fond hope that this time he was ready for us, he reposed behind his huge mud parapets, or popped away from numberless loopholes and embrasures in charming confidence; or threw up trenches, ditches, and batteries in all sorts of sly streets and roadways; and set a thousand traps in a thousand unexpected corners wherein to catch the unsuspicious infidel.

Alas for Pandy, he had quite overlooked one thing; the side of the city along which the little river Goomtee runs (a side against which no hostile demonstrations had been made on former occasions—a fact which, according to Pandy's reasoning, inferred that none ever would be made,) was left bare, naked, and comparatively unguarded. True, there was the river, and was not that a defence in itself? *Nous verrons*. And, in the meantime, my black friends with the black hearts, child-killers and murderers of women, lie calm and happy within your fortified palaces; set your sly traps, and blaze away with matchlock and booming gun, and heap fresh insults upon those two English ladies whom you hold captive within your walls; and be merry, my friends, over the coming fall of the " Feringhees," for have not your *fakirs* and *gooroos* told you that the sun of the infidels is set, and that they shall be confounded and put to shame? And is not Allah great, and Brahma good and powerful?

It was a pity, to be sure, for your sakes, that Sir Colin should have had a head upon his shoulders at all, or that any of our generals should have been capable of logically putting *this* and *that* together, and that it should have occurred to us to make a demonstration on that particular side of the city where the Goomtee is the sole defence. It was likewise somewhat unfortunate that there should have been a general of Sir James Outram's experience and ability to conduct these trans-Goomtee operations. But so it was; and now, reader, perhaps you begin to comprehend why bridges were built, and why the troops crossed over the river as I have above described. It was not, however, with the intention of actually effecting the capture of the city in this direction, but in order to assist it very materially by diverting the enemy's attention; and then by establishing batteries, which should enfilade and take in reverse their line of defences (chiefly erected at right angles to the river), and thereby render them untenable.

This movement had also another important effect—viz., that of keeping the enemy in a state of chronic alarm lest all outlets to the rear should be closed, and all means of escape cut off. Doubtless the bloody scene which had been enacted in the "Secunderabagh," at Sir Colin's relief of Lucknow, where two thousand Sepoys were caught like rats in a cage, and whence, I believe, *not one escaped*, thanks to the keen bayonets of the Highlanders and Sikhs—doubtless this bloody scene, and the recollection of the two thousand corpses, as they were taken

PLAN OF ATTACK. 165

out on the following morning, was ever dancing and flitting a horrible vision before their eyes, and fostered an unconquerable dread that, did they stand their ground on this occasion, a similar fate might befal them; and that as Sir Colin advanced against them on the one side, Sir James Outram, forcing the passage of one of the two regular bridges across the Goomtee, would take them in flank and rear, and that thus the tragedy of the 16th November* would be re-enacted; and to this dread, very probably, do we owe, in a great measure, their rapid desertion of their elaborate defences, and our comparatively easy capture of the city.

It will thus be evident that the army was now divided into two great divisions, the one under General Outram on the left bank, the other under Sir Colin Campbell on the right, both moving in the same direction, and parallel to one another, but the former always so far in advance of the latter as was requisite for the establishing of the batteries which were to drive away Pandy from his fortifications, by a deadly enfilade fire of shot and a dense shower of shell which night and day they poured incessantly into them. After they had accomplished this, Sir Colin would push forward his troops, capturing position after position in regular succession, General Outram the while moving forward, repeating the operation. bombarding and enfilading further defences, until they in their turns became untenable, and were captured.

And now, having as best I can, without plans

* The day on which the Secunderabagh fell.

or drawings, explained the principles of attack adopted, let me return to the force which I have kept waiting all this time in a very hot sun, impatient to advance.

We are in the middle of a plain. On our left lies Lucknow. We do not, however, continue parallel to the river, but make a wide sweep to the right, which occupies us for some time, and then again turning to the left, advance in our former direction at a rapid pace. It was now about eleven o'clock; the cavalry and horse artillery were far ahead, having trotted on, and we were, therefore, unable to see what they were doing; but reports began to be circulated that they were engaged, nor did these reports long want confirmation, for the sound of brisk firing became audible, and we shortly came upon some of their handiwork, and a sickening sight it was. Some women were sitting weeping bitterly over a half-dozen gashed and mangled corpses, the bodies of a small picket of the enemy whom our cavalry had surprised. The poor women first looked up at us imploringly, with tearful eyes and clasped hands, as we passed, and then sadly down at the wretched, mutilated remains of perhaps all that was dear to them in this world. Some of them had covered the still warm bodies over with a cloth, as well they might, for many of the cuts were the most trenchant and ghastly I had ever seen; while others gazed, mute and horrified, on the disfigured features and severed skulls, and on the great red-gaping wounds, as idiots look upon a sight which fascinates while it terrifies them, and as though they

DEATH OF MAJOR SMITH. 167

sought in vain to realize the terrible and awful truth.

In the mean time where are the cavalry? They have swept onward, away past weeping women and dead men; away in hot pursuit of a flying rabble! A portion of the "Bays" and 9th Lancers are called upon to charge, and headlong they ride, dealing death around them with their long flashing swords, and cutting up a large number of the enemy. But, unfortunately, the "Bays," who were the leading regiment, advancing with that wild and reckless courage which the sight of blood stirs up, galloped on their work of destruction farther than necessity demanded or prudence prompted, till, in scattered groups of twos and threes, their ranks broken by the rugged nature of the ground, they reached the "race course," where the gallant Major Percy Smith with one or two privates (I believe) fell victims to their temerity. Sir Hope Grant, seeing the disorderly nature of the charge, and fearing the results might be disastrous, had halted the 9th Lancers, and at last the "Bays" were checked in their mad career. But, in spite of the courageous self-devotion and strenuous efforts of Ensign Sneyd and Corporal Goad,* they were unable to bring away Major Smith's body, which had to be left on the field to the mercy of a ruthless enemy, a circumstance which added greatly to the grief we all felt for this officer's loss; and sad were the faces of

---

* This man has, I believe, received the Victoria Cross for the gallantry he displayed on this occasion. Captain (now Colonel) Seymour brought away Major Smith's helmet, medals, and watch.

his regiment as they rode back exhausted and with breathless horses to join the rest of the column.

It is a sad moment that, when the excitement which hurried you on, and bore you unshrinking through the heat of battle, has died away, and you have nothing left but to count over the friends who are gone, and to familiarize yourself with the cruel thought that never again will that hand grasp yours, and that the dear eyes are closed for ever. A wretched waking it is on the morn which succeeds an action—a blank and joyless day that follows. It is hard to seek in the glory you have won for the companions you have lost, and poorly does the success of yesterday fill up the gaps which shot and steel have made—the "old familiar faces" that you miss—the well-known footsteps that you hear no more—the kind voice, with its cheering accents of friendship and brotherhood—where are they now? Oh! who among us soldiers has not in the course of his career had to ask this pitiful question? How few among us are there who, in the course of this wretched rebellion and its attendant war, have not felt that dreary blank and vacuum in their hearts as they mourned over some dear and well-loved comrade? It is not when the blow first strikes upon the heart that it is felt most keenly, but it is the bruise which it leaves behind, and which refuses to be healed, that is the hardest to be borne. How cruelly in those days of sorrowing do we apply nature's probes—truth and affection—to the gaping wound, and search into it, and feel its depth, and measure its extent, and realize for ourselves the greatness and the fulness of our grief! Then it is, as day follows day, and the void remains still unfilled, and the slow cure seems still to stand aloof, that we suffer most; then, while the world rolls on as it did before, and folks around us pass to and fro upon their several paths, careless and gay as ever, and heedless of our loss, that the anguish gnaws fiercest at our souls. War is but poor work after all—a little glory, a little glitter, to season much sorrow, grief, and woe!

In the above skirmish the main body of the force had taken no part, but as we arrived on some rising ground we saw the horse artillery densely enveloped in self-created smoke, and firing away very fast in the direction of a large yellow bungalow (the "Chucker-wallah Khotee," which I shall have occasion to mention again more than once in the course of this narrative), situated on the "racecourse," and from which some guns were replying, and making the most unsatisfactory practice. I use the word "unsatisfactory" here in a selfish sense, for the shot which were, or ought to have been, intended for the Horse Artillery, would occasionally insist on plumping in among our poor selves, in by no means an agreeable manner. We were halted, and had the supreme satisfaction of standing, or sitting quite still to be shot at for some few minutes—a period not wholly devoid of excitement, as thus: there was a cloud of smoke, then a distant report, then a few moments of comparative silence, then half a dozen cries of "Here comes another!" a small dark speck visible against the blue sky, a rapid hurtling through the air of the approaching missile, a whish-sh-sh-sh which became every moment louder—louder—louder, till it passes you with a sort of scream, and lodges in the ground behind. Hardly has it passed when another puff of smoke, and another distant report, announces the arrival of a fresh iron messenger. It was curious to hear the various speculations while the ball was still in flight, as to where it would fall. "Here it comes, straight at us." "No, it'll go over us." "By G—d, it's into the Highlanders." Whish-sh-sh-sh-sh-sh. "Just cleared them, by Jove!" And a deep breath of relief is drawn as it falls harmless, tearing up turf, and stones, and dust, and ricochetting away in the distance, carrying dismay and causing confusion among the stragglers and spare horses. However, our chief object, viz. that of making a reconnaissance of this portion of the enemy's position, and of establishing ourselves upon this side of the river, was effected; and General Outram ordered the troops to retire about two miles, and there to await the arrival of the baggage, which had been directed not to cross the Goomtee until we had sufficiently cleared the neighbourhood of the enemy to ensure its safety. The position to which we retired was on the Chinhut road, and not far from the village of Chinhut itself—consequently on the site, or very nearly so, of the fight of the 30th June, 1857, the disastrous consequences of which (attributable mainly to the treachery of a portion of the hitherto seeming loyal native troops,) had probably hastened in a great measure the complete investment of the Residency of Lucknow.

Here, after watering our wearied nags, we sought shelter from the fierce rays of the sun in some friendly topes; and about one P.M., protected from Sepoy intrusion by the pickets which had been thrown out, thoroughly tired and exhausted, we lay down to take a "nap," after being some eleven hours in the saddle, six or seven of which, it must be remembered, were passed in the full glare and heat of an Indian sun. Hungry though one may be, and hungry as we were, eating becomes but a secondary consideration on these occasions —every other feeling yields to the all-absorbing one of intense fatigue—alas! to return tenfold when one awakens, as I did in about two or three hours' time, only to find—like Dame Hubbard—that "the cupboard was bare," or comparatively so, for our united contributions amounted to a few potatoes, with a modicum of grease! which we fried, and contented ourselves withal. Such is campaigning.

When the heat of the day had in some degree subsided we issued from our tope, and amused ourselves by "laying out" our camp, and grooming the poor horses (who were thoroughly "done," all of them having been in harness for two whole days, and some of them for three,) for the baggage had not yet arrived, nor, indeed, did it all come up that night; so we e'en bivouacked, and made what beds we could in the soft, sandy soil, at the imminent risk of being stepped upon by a camel or an elephant, which animals bearing baggage, together with some horses who were wandering about all night in a state of semi-somnambulism, kept strolling through the camp from "dewy eve" till morn. How any one ever found their own baggage, or the baggage its owners, it is hard to say, but the noise and confusion which continued all night was something past belief; long strings of camels with great piles of tables, portmanteaus, tents, and chairs, which looked in the gloom like houses, on their backs; and elephants bearing, apparently, whole cities, kept on passing continually, and treading alarmingly near one's face. Camp-followers and others shouted without intermission, and it seemed without ever drawing breath, for their "bhaies" (friends or brothers) the long night through; and there was an individual called "Mattadeen," who seemed to be in the bonds of friendship and brotherhood with all the world, and to be "bhaie" in ordinary to humanity at large, judging from the constant cries of "Ho, Mattadeen! Mattadeen, h-o-o-o-o-o-o!" which echoed through the darkness; these, and various other little noises, tended to sour one's temper and disturb one's rest. But at last, spite of baggage-animals, camp-followers, and Mattadeens, and of an undercurrent of snoring which was going on, I fell into a sound and delightful sleep.

CHAPTER XVI.

Attack on our Camp—Repulse of the Enemy—Outlying Picket
—Advance of March 9th—Jungle Fighting—*Horrida Bella!*
—Another glimpse of Lucknow.

ON the following morning, March 7th, while preparing to go on outlying picket, and fortifying the inner man by laying in as good a breakfast as time would permit, we were astonished by a sharp fire, which commenced in our front. At first we imagined that it was only the pickets disporting themselves, and getting up a small fight on their own accounts, as pickets are ofttimes wont to do; but the sharp rattle of musketry becoming louder and nearer every moment, and then some shot coming whistling among our tents, warned us that something was really going on, and before many minutes were over an orderly came galloping down to tell us to "turn out immediately," and move up to the front, as the enemy were attacking the camp in force. We got ready as soon as possible, and moved smartly up, but too late to take any part in this affair, in which our casualties were very few, but those of the enemy considerable.* It appeared

* Among our casualties must be included a few occasioned by the shot which the enemy sent into our camp; one, a man of the 1st Bengal Fusiliers, who lost his leg while in the act of "falling in."

that the enemy had made a systematic, and, as it seemed at one period, a formidable attack, advancing with cavalry, infantry, and artillery, in very good style until checked by our pickets. Doubtless they expected that, on seeing them approach, the little handful of men who composed these pickets would have immediately bolted, and that so our camp would have fallen a surprised and easy prey. What, then, must have been their astonishment (possibly tinged with horror) when they beheld the pickets, instead of fleeing, extend themselves in skirmishing order, and boldly advance to meet them! This gave time for reinforcements to come up, and for the artillery to open a brisk cannonade on them, the result of which was that the Sepoys were almost immediately driven back, and pursued by our troops for some distance, while we extended our position by advancing our outposts a distance of half a mile or so.

It was during this pursuit that Major Percy Smith's body was recovered. But even respect for the dead is unknown to our barbarous enemies, and the body was found, as we feared it would be, with the head and legs severed from it and the trunk otherwise horribly mutilated.* During that day there was not much done; a good deal of desultory firing was kept up by the pickets, but beyond this little or nothing. We occupied ourselves by taking long shots at Pandy whenever he gave us a chance; and as we soon

---

* The Sepoys gave out, by way of advancing their interests, that it was the Commander-in-chief who had been killed, and that this was his body: such were the shifts to which they were obliged to have recourse.

found out that we received *our own shot back again*, instead of the lumps of hammered iron, to which he ordinarily treated us, we changed our tactics, and favoured himself thenceforth with shell instead of solid shot.

Of course that night on picket we had innumerable alarms, for as long as there are soldiers in the world, so long will they insist, while on sentry, on dark nights, in the presence of an enemy, in mistaking cows, stumps of trees, dark bits of shadow, and the rustling of the wind through the long grass, for advancing foes. And so surely as they do will there be heard either the sharp crack of the alarmed sentry's rifle, or a hurried whisper of "Stand to your arms!" to rouse one from one's slumbers, when one jumps up, peers into the darkness for about ten minutes, momentarily expecting to hear the whistling of bullets, and eventually discovering that the approaching enemy existed only in the sentry's fevered imagination, upon which one lies down again, mentally consigning said sentry to a place unmentionable.

On one occasion that night, however, we were much surprised by hearing some sharp firing going on *in our rear*, and by bullets pinging past us, or falling at our feet. What could it mean? Could the enemy have got round us? Oh, moment of horrible suspense! it was pitch dark, nothing could be distinguished; we stood to our arms, and brought one of our guns into action to the rear, in order that we might be ready for them, and then set to work to discover the interpretation of this mystery. It transpired that our supporting picket, some seven or eight hundred yards behind us, were suffering from nightmare, bad dreams, indigestion, or something which had deluded them into the idea that it was their bounden duty to fire a volley or two into us, which they did accordingly. Matters were, however, soon set to rights, nobody was hurt, and with a polite request that, if it was all the same to them, they would abstain from repeating the performance, we once more lay down, and were not further disturbed that night.

On returning to camp on the morning of March 8, we found that some siege guns had arrived from the other side of the river, and that preparations were being made for getting some of them into position that evening. In the afternoon, an order arrived for the greater part of the cavalry and horse artillery, and one field battery (Middleton's), to recross the river, to assist in the operations which were to take place on the morrow. In speaking of these operations, I can of course attempt only to describe those in which I personally took part, viz., those on the left bank of the river, so that my readers will have to look elsewhere for a detailed description of the performances of the troops under Sir Colin, whose movements I shall only refer to from time to time, in a general way, and wherever I may find such reference necessary to make the successive steps leading to the fall of the city clearly understood.

At daybreak, on March 9, the force under General Outram assembled on the ground occupied by our advanced pickets, and when all was ready, the word was given, and away we go. The Rifle Brigade throw out a cloud of skirmishers, the sharp crack of whose rifles ere long told us that our work had commenced; we were now advancing towards a thick wood, over some open, but broken ground, and a very pretty sight it was—the green-coated Riflemen running quickly forward, and springing actively over the rugged nullahs and streams which crossed our path, loading and firing as they go, and ever and anon completing with the bayonet the work which the bullet had left half-finished. After advancing thus for some three-quarters of a mile, we find ourselves at the entrance of a dense jungle occupied by the enemy; the skirmishers are checked for a moment; we bring our guns into action, and bang! go half a dozen shells, whistling and crashing through the trees and long high grass, bursting inside with a loud report, and scouring the wood effectually; this precautionary measure enables us again to push on. "Hark forward!" and away we go, the little Riflemen dashing into the high vegetation, followed by the rest of the column, and pop! bang! crack! crack! with now and again the ping of an inimical bullet, soon tell us that the enemy are about.

It is strange work this jungle fighting, where you know nothing of what is going on around you; where, for aught you know, sly gentlemen behind bushes may have their fingers upon the trigger which, once touched, would send you tumbling from your horse, a corpse; where foes and friends, Highlanders, Riflemen, and Sikhs, alike are lost to view among the trees, and of whose whereabouts you can only form an idea from the sharp and constant firing which is going on. Hush! there is a breaking and rustling of the leaves; and, look! a Sepoy in full flight dashes wildly across your path; but, even as he goes, the barrel of an Enfield is covering him—bang! a sharp, quick report—a whistling of a bullet—and now he is down, rolling a confused and bloody mass in the dust and dirt—a few convulsive struggles—a little clutching at the grass which is beneath him, and which his blood, as it wells forth, is fast dying a dark red—a low moan or two, perchance, and all is over. Then, breaking through the bushes, follows a hot and excited Rifleman, his rifle still smoking, his lips black with powder, biting another cartridge as he comes, and scarcely glancing, as he passes, on the man whom he has done to death. Ping! ping! close to your ears! Where are the enemy? —who can see them? There!—there, away to the right, see, lurking behind the mud walls of that village. Ping! bang! "Halt! action right!" In a moment the trail of a howitzer falls heavily upon the ground—ping! ping! ping! again close to your ear, and crack! bang! bang! from the responding rifles. "Shrapnel-shell, my men—look sharp!" Boom! almost splitting the drum of your ear, and there burst from the muzzle a gritty volume of smoke, and as it clears away, and the startling noise rings echoing through the wood, see the faint puff, and hear the report of the bursting shell, the fragments of which fly whistling into hidden nooks and corners—and "Hurrah!—now, riflemen, over with them!"

JUNGLE-FIGHTING.

—crack!—bang! in quick succession, as a shower of bullets rattle in among the disorganized rabble whom the shells have driven from the village, and who are fleeing for their lives, few of them turning to exchange shots with their assailants.

Hark! to that cheer—a wild tally-ho. What! is this, then, fox-hunting? No—but not unlike it, only more madly and terribly exciting even than that—it is man-hunting, my friend! and that cheer proclaims that we have "found." Hark! to that quick volley which follows it, with death in its every note! See here and there a flying Sepoy, and here and there a dust-stained, still warm corpse—see, through the trees, the bright-glancing barrels of the deadly rifles as they are raised to deal the fatal blow; see the dark plumes of the Highlanders, and the grey turbans of the Sikhs, and the red coats of our men flitting to and fro—see that soldier fiercely plunging down his bayonet into some object at his feet—see, is it not red as he uplifts it for another blow? Raise yourself in your stirrups and look down and behold that living thing, above which the steel is flashing so mercilessly: is it a dog, or some venomous and loathsome reptile? No—but a human being: it is a man who lies at that soldier's feet—a man disguised with wounds and dust and mortal agony, with blood gurgling from his lips, and with half-uttered curses upon his tongue, who is dying there; and the reeking bayonet is wiped hurriedly upon the grass, and the killer passes on, to drain, in the wild excitement of his triumph, every drop of that cup of blood which this day the God of War holds out to him, and which he sees foaming and brimming over before him. Ugh! it is horrid work at the best; but that thought comes afterwards, and not now, when mad with excitement, your pulse beating quickly, and I fear me glad at the work of death, as the veriest butcher among them, you press forward, amid smoke, and noise, and cracking rifles, and burning houses and burning jungle, through an atmosphere thick with sulphurous smells, and choking dust, and heavy heat, while the scenes which I have just attempted to describe are going on, in all their licensed fury, on every side.

Strange that I could then gaze, without shuddering, on a sight which it sickens me, now as I write of it, to recal—strange that excitement should so deaden one's sensibilities, and draw such a film of callousness and indifference over one's eyes. But so it is, and many a soldier, as he "fights his battles o'er again," must shudder as he thinks of the scenes which he then beheld unmoved, and almost doubt as he recals the bloody tragedies in which he actively—nay, willingly—took part.

But, by this time, we have emerged from the wood into the open, and before us, at some eight hundred yards' distance, stands the yellow bungalow (Chucker-wallah Khotee), which I have before mentioned. Already a large body of the enemy were flying from it, but their retreat, though decidedly rapid, was a tolerably orderly one, and they seemed determined that, if they must run away, they would do it in as dignified a manner as possible; so, with heads erect, and even ranks, these Sepoys (six or seven hundred, I should think) passed away out of our sight. I must, however, do the leading files—*i.e.*, those who were furthest from danger—the justice to state that their bearing was much more philosophical and calm than that of the hindermost, among whom, I regret to say, there appeared to be a *leetle* more pushing and indecent haste than there should have been.

The Bengal Fusiliers have been pushed forward, and advance at a "double" across the hot sand; but, arriving at the house breathless and exhausted, they are unable to take a steady aim, or do as much execution as might have been wished, and Pandy escapes comparatively scathless, though some few of them fall beneath the deadly Enfields to rise no more, and lie writhing in deadly agony among the mud cottages away there to the right. The 23rd Royal Welsh Fusiliers, some Highlanders, Sikhs, and three guns have pushed on in the mean time yet farther to the right. From our position over the river we get a sight of the enemy (the body above mentioned) hurrying away below us, and we are enabled to bowl a few shot very pleasantly among them—a performance which accelerated their movements considerably; while the riflemen are keeping up a steady fire on the buildings on the opposite bank, among which stands conspicuous the celebrated Secunderabagh.

There is a splendid view of the city from this point, its domes and hundred temples, the vast courts of its palaces, the fine structures of the Shah Nujeef, Tara Khotee, Mess-house, Kaiserbagh, and Chutter Munzil, or old palace, by the water's edge, and many another begilt and gaudy building. There they all are, stretching, a glittering mass, beyond the little stream, and looking even more bright and beautiful than I had hitherto imagined them to be. Yes! there lies the prize for which we are fighting, and for the possession of which so many lives will be laid down, and so much blood will flow— there it lies in all its glory before us, seeming proud of the high value which is set on it, and the price at which it is being won; little recks it whether Feringhee or——" Look out, sir!" ping past your ear, and "Bedad! but that fellow's a dangerous kyaracter," in rich Hibernian brogue, make you suddenly alive to the fact that there are moments when it is as well not to indulge in one's love of the picturesque too freely, and that even the contemplation of the beautiful is not always unattended with risk; and, moreover, that your services are required for the purpose of throwing some shell into those mud suburbs to expel several "dangerous kyaracters" therein assembled, who are keeping up a tolerably smart fire on our position, and whom it would be as well to silence. This is done accordingly, and for about an hour is a quick cannonade of round shot, shell, and rifle bullets directed upon the opposite bank. We could see but little of the enemy from the way in which they crept behind walls and houses, but we were cognisant of their presence from the continual dropping of bullets all around us, varied by an occasional round shot, the number of casualties on our side, however, being extremely small, owing to the excellent cover afforded to the men by some banks and mud walls.

CHAPTER XVII.

Fight at the "Yellow Bungalow"—Captain St. George—Sharp Work—A Frightful Scene of Cruelty—Capture of the "Badshah Bagh"—The Ghoorkas—Engagement of March 11th—More Jungle-fighting.

AT last we found that we could be of but little more use here, and our guns were withdrawn to make room for heavier metal, the siege guns having been brought down for the purpose of pouring a reverse fire on the enemy's entrenchments. We therefore retired, and stationed ourselves as spectators near the "Yellow Bungalow," where a fierce combat on a small scale was still going on. In the lower story of this house were some ten or twelve of the enemy, who had either not been aware of their comrades' departure at the time the bungalow was evacuated, or had purposely remained behind with the fanatical determination of dying in the defence of the place; but be the real reason what it might, there of a surety they were—a dozen or so of desperate men, for whom there was now no escape, and before whose eyes the bright-eyed houris of paradise were already waving their green scarfs and beckoning to eternal bliss. They occupied, as I have before said, the lower story of the house whereof we held the remainder, and many an attempt had been made to drive them out. There, however, spite of every effort, they held their own, having already succeeded in killing some six or seven men, who had advanced with more courage than caution into the dark rooms in which they were located, and where (from the fact of their entering from the out-door light and glare) they were comparatively blind, while the Sepoys' eyes being accustomed to the partial darkness, our soldiers had fallen an easy prey. Shells with long fuses were thrown through holes cut in the floor of the upper story into the rooms they occupied, but with little or no result, as, by moving from room to room, they were easily able to avoid them. An attempt was made to burn them out, which partially succeeded, one man being burned to death, while some others, driven out by the fire, were shot as they fled; two or three more also had been killed, but still there were some remaining.

Captain St. George, 1st Bengal Fusiliers, accompanied, I believe, by another officer of the same regiment, then entered the house and shot two of the rebels with his revolver. Passing on, he found, as he imagined, the house empty, and concluded that the Sepoys were now all killed, but at last he came to a small and very dark room, which he entered, when two men—one on each side the doorway—fired, and a ball struck him in the lower part of the chest. He walked out, looking giddy and sick, with eyes glazed and heavy, and faintly assisted in unbuttoning his own coat, when it was found that the ball had passed completely through his body, from his chest to his back, whence it was afterwards cut out, being found buried very little below the surface. It was of course imagined that he was mortally wounded, no hopes whatever being entertained by the doctors of his recovery, and keen was the sorrow we all felt for the loss of an officer universally beloved in his regiment and by all who knew him. But I am happy to say that he has since gone home, with every prospect of ultimate recovery, and I sincerely trust, ere these sheets are published, that he will have obtained in Old England a return of health and strength, and have got over the effects of his frightful wound; a result which, under Providence, may be attributed in a great measure to the " pluck" and cheerful spirit which he exhibited throughout the whole of the weary period when he lay hovering between life and death. A young officer of the Sikhs (Anderson, I think, by name,) was killed in this house while endeavouring to expel the desperate occupants, but his life, like that of several other brave men who were killed here, was laid down in vain, for still did the few who remained inside hold out.

At last, General Outram, seeing that it was death to any one to attempt to enter, and thinking that enough lives had been sacrificed in the attempt, ordered some guns to be brought to bear on to the house; five accordingly came into action, and fired about twenty shells, in quick succession, at the windows and doorways of the building, and as the smoke of the last round cleared away, the Sikhs, who had been held in readiness for the purpose, received the signal, and dashing forward entered the house *en masse.* It was most exciting to see them racing up to the place, where, when they reached it, there was for a moment a confused scrambling at the doorways, then a sharp report or two, then a sort of shout and scuffling, then again bang! bang! sharp and distinct, and finally there burst from the building, with loud yells, a crowd of Sikhs, bearing among them the sole survivor of this garrison, who had made such a gallant defence—for gallant it was, be the source whence the courage sprang, fanaticism, despair, or whatever you may choose to call it. How many the Sikhs had killed inside I do not know—not more, I heard, than two or three—but this one, alas for him! they had dragged out alive. And now commenced one of the most frightful scenes I had ever witnessed.

Infuriated beyond measure by the death of their officer, the Sikhs (assisted, I regret to say, by some Englishmen) proceeded to take their revenge on this one wretched man. Seizing him by the two legs, *they attempted to tear him in two!* Failing in this, they dragged him along by the legs, stabbing him in the face with their bayonets as they went. I could see the poor wretch writhing as the blows fell upon him, and could hear his moans as his captors dug the sharp bayonets into his lacerated and trampled body, while his blood, trickling down, dyed the white sand over which he was being dragged. But the worst was yet to come: while still alive, though faint and feeble from his many wounds, he was deliberately placed upon a small fire of dry sticks, which had been improvised for the purpose, and there held down, in spite of his dying struggles, which, becoming weaker and more feeble every moment, were, from their very faintness and futile desperation, cruel to behold. Once during this frightful operation, the wretched victim, maddened by pain, managed to break away from his tormentors, and, already horribly burnt, fled a short distance, but he was immediately brought back and placed upon the fire, and there held till life was extinct. It was his last despairing effort, and very sad to see; but I thought it sadder still that those hoarse, choking cries for mercy should have been disregarded as they were; his shrieks, his agonized convulsions, his bitter anguish alike unheeded; that those upturned eyes, searching for pity in the swarthy faces which gazed with savage pleasure on the frightful scene, should have searched in vain, and that so—with the horrible smell of his burning flesh as it cracked and blackened in the flames, rising up and poisoning the air—so in this nineteenth century, with its boasted civilization and humanity, a human being should lie roasting and consuming to death, while Englishmen and Sikhs, gathered in little knots around, looked calmly on. No one will deny, I think, that this man at least adequately expiated, by his frightful and cruel death, any crimes of which he may have been guilty.

Such was the state of excitement and rage that the Sikhs were in from the loss of their officer, that I firmly believe it would have been quite impossible to prevent this act of torture; and that many did make the attempt I have no doubt, but the whole business was done so quickly, and with such noise and confusion, that, to me who beheld it from a short distance (occupied as

I then was on another duty), it seemed almost like a dream, till I rode up afterwards and saw the black trunk burned down to a stumpy, almost unrecognisable cinder.

The Yellow House was now ours—our heavy guns, from their position on the river's bank, were spinning shot into the enemy's entrenchments, and there was little more to be done, as far as we were concerned, beyond every now and then throwing some shells among and dispersing the enemy's sharpshooters, who, owing to the excellent cover they obtained in buildings and woods on the other side of the river, were still able to annoy us. But all this time we have lost sight of the portion of our force which had earlier in the day parted from us, and pushed on to the right. Continuing their course parallel to the river for about a mile, through brushwood and jungle, burning villages and houses, and here and there getting flying shots at the Pandies as they flitted past them, they had at last found themselves at the Badshah Bagh (king's garden)—a large walled enclosure containing a handsome palace for the use of its regal owners. All the elements of Oriental romance were here: dark passages and latticed windows to the Zenanah, suggestive of sparkling, love-glancing eyes, and "moonlight nights," and stolen interviews, erring Oriental Venuses, and amorous Hindoos. Cool marble halls, too, there were, gilded and carved in a manner miraculous to behold, filled with mirrors, chandeliers, damasks, and furniture of the most startling and *outré* description; there too were pleasant wide-spreading trees,

THE BADSHAH BAGH. 189

—With seats beneath their shade
For talking age and whispering lovers made;

there were stone tanks and fountains, and marble baths (the sight alone of which refreshes one); and dark, secret hiding-places, where naughty "beebees" carried on their little witcheries, and set mamma, or the proverbial "big brother," at defiance; while a million summer insects were for ever buzzing noisily around; long shady walks, too, where the scent of citron and orange-blossoms hung heavy on the air, till the whole place was redolent (as some one graphically expressed it at the time) "of a strong odour of Arabian Nights."

Such was the place in which, after a sharp fight, our troops found themselves—not, however, to lounge indolently beneath the shady trees, or to indulge in a pleasant *dolce far niente* and dreamy reverie in the cool rooms of the palace, as the luxurious couches and chairs, with the generally indolent character of the place, would naturally prompt one to do, but to continue the work of death in which, since daybreak, they had been engaged, and to screen themselves by rough barricades, or as best they might, from the heavy fire to which they were exposed. In fact, during the whole day, fighting, more or less, was kept up in and near the Badshah Bagh, from which place, however—once in our possession— the enemy found it impossible by even the most strenuous efforts to drive us. And so the day came to a close, and evening fell, and found us in possession of the whole of the villages, buildings, suburbs, detached houses, and walled gardens on the left of the Goomtee, from the point at which we had crossed up to the Badshah Bagh, while our heavy guns, placed in advantageous positions by these operations, were already at work demolishing, and rendering untenable, the defences on the right bank of the river.* Now mark the immediate effect of this: Sir Colin quietly waited until the Martinière and the defences in front of it had been subjected to an efficient pounding, when he advanced, and, instead of having a severe fight, and losing several men, as would probably have been the case had said pounding not been administered, he captured these works *without opposition*, or, at least, with very little; for such of the enemy as had braved the destructive reverse and enfilade fire of our heavy guns, and made a show of holding out, became nervous at the first glimpse of the red coats and dark plumes of the Highlanders, and fairly ran when the glitter of the bayonets caught their eyes, firing only a few desultory shots as they went.

Thus, on the 9th March we had taken the first really decisive step in advance, and were now fairly settled down to our work; the Martinière and the somewhat formidable works in rear of it were ours; Outram's column occupied a strong position on the left bank of the river, and we were able to place our heavy guns so that from front and flank they could pour a destructive fire into the Begum Khotee, Shah

---

* It is curious to observe how, in the construction of these defences, the enemy had ignored or overlooked the possibility of their being subjected to an enfilade fire, a fact evident from the complete absence of traverses, or any protective works of that description.

Nujeef, Kaiserbagh, and other of the enemy's strongholds, and so pave the way for their capture. These great results had been attained with an almost miraculously small loss of life on our side, while it is probable that sustained by our opponents was considerable.

I may here mention that, a few days previous to this, Frank's column and Jung Bahadoor's Ghoorkas had joined the army, and taken up their position on the extreme left; and it will perhaps be as well to take this opportunity of informing my readers what part the Ghoorkas took in the capture of Lucknow. From my own knowledge, I do not speak, but I will merely relate the substance of a conversation I have repeatedly held with officers who *have* had the opportunity of judging, thus: "You were near the Ghoorkas at Lucknow, tell me what they did." "What they did—that is easily answered—nothing!" Nor have I ever been able, though I have taken some trouble on the subject, to get any other reply; so that I fear these *soi-disant* desperadoes, these much-talked-of, bloodthirsty little men, of whom I had often heard it said, " By George! just wait till the Ghoorkas get among the Sepoys with their kukeries" (long curved knives), must have somewhat disappointed their admirers. It seems probable, indeed, that if we had waited until they "got among them with their kukeries," we should have had to postpone offensive operations *sine die*, for, if the truth must be told, these diminutive gentlemen proved failures, distinguishing themselves more by their dirtiness than their devotion, their boasted gallantry being of a mythical and fanciful nature. I fully believe, however, that had these men been led by English officers, they would have done their work as well and pluckily as did their countrymen at Delhi; and that to the misconduct of the native officers, which I have often heard spoken of in no measured terms, together with their prevailing want of discipline, may be mainly attributed the short-comings of this *auxiliary* force.

The night of March 9th was chiefly spent in getting guns into position on the ground we had captured, and with these on the following morning we opened fire.

There was some fighting here and there on both sides of the river, but nothing of any importance took place until the next day, March 11th, when we of General Outram's division again advanced. This time our force was divided into two columns, one of which, the left, moved from the Badshah Bagh in the direction of the Iron Bridge, the other through the woods and villages on its right, driving the enemy from any strongholds they might have there, while some cavalry and horse artillery were still further to the right, to cut off stragglers, cover our flank, and otherwise assist operations. It was my lot to accompany the second-named column, of whose doings I will therefore speak first. We had not advanced very far before we found ourselves in a narrow road leading into a thick wood; here operations commenced, for, hidden in the jungle, or in the small cottages, which, snugly embosomed among the trees, formed excellent temporary fortresses, were parties of the enemy, who opened a smart fire on us as we advanced. Skirmishers were pushed forward, and two guns brought into action abreast, on the road, to riddle the woods with case-shot, and so drive out our hidden foes. Again were the scenes of the day but one preceding enacted—that sort of confused banging and popping on all sides which I have before endeavoured to describe, with the difference that this time the Pandies *did* stand for a while, secure in their invisibility, and popped at us in return.

What noise and wild confusion and excitement then prevailed, what a smell of gunpowder, and what hurrying about of skirmishers, and bursting of shells, and the like; and yet from this mass of chaos how clear and distinct do certain little incidents stand out in my memory: the flitting Pandies as they dodged about among the trees, their white garments making them visible for a brief moment, and then they were gone; the loud ear-splitting boom of the guns, as round after round of case-shot went tearing from the muzzles, crashing through the brushwood; the hot and dusty skirmishers leaning against trees in order to steady their aim; the constant cracking of their rifles, a sort of running accompaniment to the noisy guns; the whistling of bullets, which came thick and fast among us; the contorted form of the dead Sepoy lying out there on the road in front, ghastly enough; next a burly gunner, while in the act of sponging out a gun, with a sudden start, would turn white and giddy, and stagger, wounded, to the rear; then the short fragment of conversation which ensued: "Man hit, sir." "Badly?" "No, sir; shot through leg." "Put another man in his place, and blaze away." Ping! ping! bang! right royally on all sides, while now and then a sharp cry would proclaim that a bullet had found its billet in some unfortunate, who would come bleeding past; a minute ago that man was the best runner, or the best jumper, or cricketer, it may be, in his regiment, and now he is a cripple for life. Quick work, is it not?

Some of the enemy had crept into a dry drain which ran underneath and across the road, and there, crouched in abject terror, mingled probably with the hope that we might pass them unseen, huddled up, one getting behind the other for shelter, they were discovered by our men, and a volley of bullets sent in among them. It was horrible to see, through the semi-darkness, these poor wretches trying to screen themselves behind the corpses of their comrades, but trying in vain, for pitilessly did bullet after bullet whistle in among them, striking to death those in this doomed and dying mass of humanity who still lived; while their groans and shrieks seemed, reverberated as they were by the echoing, sonorous, arched roofs of their underground retreat, to acquire a strangely deep and awful tone. There was no escape, no pity; there, in their self-chosen grave, they all died, and there, for many a day after, they lay, a horrid heap of rottenness, and worm-eaten abomination.

I remember, as we went along, seeing a woman, who had been wounded, sitting by the roadside, endeavouring to stanch a wound in her head, whence the blood was trickling and clotting her long black hair. Poor creature! she had been hit, I imagine, by some stray shot, while endeavouring to escape from us; and this to my mind is one of the most melancholy features of the war, that so many comparatively innocent beings should have suffered, as many have done, and that so little distinction should have been made between the cowardly mutineer, red-handed with the slaughter of women and children, and the Oude villager, or "budmash," who, whatever other acts of injustice and rapine he may have committed, and whatever his private character, cannot be said to have been guilty of rebellion, nor had done any of these deeds, but simply taken advantage of a great revolt to strike a blow for his country, which we had taken from him, and who was fighting—whether wisely or not is another question—with at least a show of right upon his side, and in a cause which was not wholly vile. I do not mean to say that we did wrong in shooting down, *in open fight*, any man, Sepoy, budmash, villager, be he whom he might, that used arms against us; but I do mean to say that it would have been more satisfactory, if for the people of Oude—Sepoys excepted—there had been some mercy and quarter, that they at least should be treated as fair enemies, and that, unless proved to have participated in, or connived at, the murder of Englishmen, captives of this class should not necessarily be put to death, but treated as prisoners of war usually are. At the time of the capture of Lucknow—a season of indiscriminate massacre—such distinction was not made, and the unfortunate who fell into the hands of our troops was made short work of—Sepoy or

Oude villager, it mattered not—no questions were asked; his skin was black, and did not that suffice? a piece of a rope and the branch of a tree, or a rifle bullet through his brain, soon terminated the poor devil's existence. Short shrift was his, and but little time was given him to make his peace and pray, and close his soul's accounts, ere he was hurried off to die the death of a dog. Very strange, unreal and sad, does all this seem, but on reflection it is hardly to be wondered at, for the war had, at its commencement, most naturally assumed all the horrible features of a war of extermination, a war in which pity was unknown. Where such is the case, where blood-shedding and slaughter have once become universal, it is no light task to check it, and an impossible one to stop it entirely; so that from this and a hundred other causes, which must at once suggest themselves to the reader, the impracticability, or at least the difficulty, of drawing the line between the wholly and partly guilty, will be apparent.

CHAPTER XVIII.

The Musjid—*En avant!*—A Large "Bag"—Capture of the Stone Bridge—Loot—Capture of the Iron Bridge—Should Officers be Executioners?

AFTER going some distance through the wood, we came to a large and handsome Musjid, with an extensive walled garden attached, and altogether presenting a formidable appearance. Here, surely, we thought, the enemy must make a stand; but no, ere the gate was blown open, the bird had flown, and, without a struggle, it fell into our hands. It was a place which might certainly have been held for some time, and which, if they *had* defended it with any amount of resolution, we might have had some trouble in taking; but Pandy, ever true to the maxim that "he who fights and runs away, may live to fight another day," had, as I have before said, made his exit directly we approached.

The 1st Bengal Fusiliers were left to guard this important post—situated at the meeting of four cross roads—and to complete the clearance and capture of the surrounding houses; while the rest of the force continued its route, still moving through jungle and wood, and in many places through burning sand; still firing at flying foes, and occasionally being fired at in return; still carrying all before them, though momentarily expecting to meet with opposition, and still finding none. We marched on, somewhat after the fashion of a party of sportsmen, who, having come out equipped with completest sporting paraphernalia, in all the pride of Joe Mantons and Westley Richardses, and with powder and shot sufficient to blow all the game in the universe to perdition; burning with ardour, and pregnant with a laudable desire to wipe (in sporting parlance) each the other's eye; find, to their disgust, the birds unapproachably wild and wary, and by no means inclined to give them an opportunity of testing the force and penetration of an Eley's cartridge. So it was with us, until suddenly a wild cheer rings through the wood—much the sort of cheer you may hear any hunting morning by woodsides and pleasant copses in merry England, but, alas! mingled now with cries, and shrieks, and fast-falling shots—the hounds have found, true enough, the chase is up, and the work of death has commenced!

We had, in fact, taken by surprise a large mass of the enemy, who were engaged in cooking their dinners under the trees, and who, panic-stricken at our unexpected appearance, fled precipitately. But few of them escaped; the toils of the net were round them ere they were aware, and many a body lay there long afterwards, stark and ghastly, under the pleasant trees (which cast a fitful trellis-work of light and shade upon it), to mark the spot of battle, and to tell how truly the Enfield and the bayonet had done their work.

An order to push on quickly was given, while companies were detached from the main body to assist the skirmishers, who were *unable to kill fast, enough,* so numerous were the foe!

How vividly do I remember this moment, perhaps the most exciting in my life!—how clearly do I see the regiments running forward to join in the work of slaughter—how clearly hear the deafening din, the shouts now of terror, now of triumph—how clearly see the Sepoys, as they fled in wild affright, throwing away arms, clothing, cooking-pots, and all or aught soever that might tend to hamper their movements; while, ever high above the tumult rose the cheers of our men, as they drove the enemy before them like so many hares, and shot them down by dozens as they went. Following them up, we at last emerged from the wood into an apparently boundless plain, over which a multitude of men were flying for their lives, at a frantic pace.

We had now captured two guns, several colours, and a quantity of arms, while the slaughter of the enemy must have been really immense, to judge from the way in which their bodies strewed our path, so thickly that the gun wheels at times passed over them; but this "bag," successful as it was, was not yet complete; our bloody offering at Bellona's shrine did not yet suffice. "Kill! kill! kill!" was still the burden of the cry; "bring forward the guns!" and away we roll in hot pursuit after the scattered fugitives—away, jolting and bumping, at a mad gallop, leaving infantry and supports far behind—away, over a country which, though level to look at, bore upon its smooth-seeming face more lumps and pimply inequalities than there are plums in a Christmas pudding, as we found out by bitter experience—away, over some two miles of ground, strewn with clothes, brass pots, matchlocks, tulwars, rags, powder-horns, and other emblems of a flight—away, over drains, and mounds, and dried-up water-courses, rugged bits, half-broken walls, and the like, till the wretched gunners, seated on the limbers, must have cursed the day they were born, and yet more bitterly the day on which they enlisted. At last, to the great relief of "pumped" horses and bumped gunners, we were ordered to "Halt—action front!" We then let fly shell among the fugitives, apparently with some success, judging by the way in which our foes disappeared, and by the hurried manner in which certain little knots of these gentlemen dispersed, radiating off like the spokes of a wheel, on our making them the objects of our particular attention, and favouring them with a notice to move on, couched in the form of a shrapnel shell.

We had now gone to the extreme end of the city, and the stone bridge was in our possession (as also the iron bridge, which had been captured by the left column), with a great extent of country; but General Outram decided, very wisely, that the smallness of his force did not justify him in attempting to hold so extended a position, and that it would therefore be good policy to retire from the stone bridge, and rest satisfied with the iron bridge and the approaches leading thereto, with the ground on the bank of the Goomtee, up to, and on a line with this point.

We were therefore ordered to retrace our steps, upon which the enemy, with much boldness and spirit, seasoned with bluster, bringing out a gun or two, treated us to some long shots immediately they found our backs were turned! But they did no damage, and we marched on, taking a slightly different route from the one by which we came, and going *direct* towards the Musjid, instead of making a *détour* as before. On our way, we passed through a large village (where we destroyed immense stores of powder and half-finished gun-carriages, and other munitions of war), which, in its then deserted state, "afforded an eligible opportunity for parties" fond of looting to indulge this propensity. I am bound to admit that the British soldier proved himself equal to the occasion, and fully appreciated his position, to judge from the way in which he burdened himself with articles of every conceivable nature, and of no conceivable value. If I recollect right, fowls were great favourites, likewise pigeons and green parrots; some men positively smothering themselves with these feathered captives, presenting, I fancied, somewhat of the appearance of Æsacus, the son of Priam, Cygnus, Dædalion, and other mythological heroes, (who, according to Ovid, underwent an ornithological transformation,) when in the intermediate stage, and while the metamorphosis was as yet incomplete. Others, again, bore along in triumph a chaotic mass of tobacco, glass, lamp-shades, books, bits of silk, scent bottles, plates, brass pots, and utensils of all descriptions; of which, if the quality was inferior, the quantity amply compensated, there being, on a rough calculation, a sufficiency of miscellaneous articles to set up about fifty marine-store dealers in a good business.

It is by no means safe work, this looting. The soldier who strolls so unsuspiciously into these little cottages, or tempting shops, runs a very good chance of never strolling out again. Behind many a door lurks an enemy, tulwar in hand, and in corners where least expected; while from under bales of cloths and heaps of rags, matchlocks have been known to explode, in a suspicious and decidedly unpleasant manner, in the face of the looter; and a desperate man, the lootee in person, who has hidden there, to rise suddenly and strike a deadly blow before the intruder has time to recover from his surprise.

Among the captives on this occasion was a large leopard, who was discovered in a cage by the roadside, and immediately shot for the sake of his skin, which was claimed by the whole force. I have also forgotten to mention that, with the two guns which we had captured, the draught bullocks belonging thereto likewise fell into our hands. Oh! those bullocks—never were their likes seen for stubbornness and headlong obstinacy —never in this world did prisoners of war prove so refractory as these horned gentlemen, so deaf to reason or cajolery. Unanimously and strenuously they refused to have anything to do with drawing the guns after they had once fallen into our hands, vigorously opposing us in every possible way, and baffling the efforts of some score of men who tried to yoke them in and bring them into subjection. We, however, succeeded in leading the brutes back with us for some distance, but only to lose two of them again ; these, *vi et armis,* made good their escape, and I caught a farewell glimpse of one of them, as head down, tail erect, he disappeared down a road and charged the 79th Highlanders, much to their consternation. There is an amount of lively facetiousness, which is anything but pleasant, about bullocks even when they recognise you as their liege lord and master, but all the saints defend me from them when serving against their will ! Their humour is then too grim and determined to contemplate without a shudder. When we got back to the Musjid, which we had taken possession of in the morning, the bulk of the force was sent back into camp, a sufficient number remaining behind to furnish pickets and guard the ground we had taken.

And now let us turn to the left column, and see what they had been doing all this time. This force, which consisted of the 2nd battalion Rifle Brigade, 23rd Royal Welsh Fusiliers, and Green's Sikhs, with three guns of Gibbon's battery, had advanced, after leaving the Badshah Bagh, towards the Iron Bridge, through a series of intricate streets and narrow winding lanes, under a galling cross-fire from the enemy, who, hidden in the surrounding houses, were able, with comparative impunity, to annoy us rather seriously. However, they did not make any determined stand, except in isolated cases. Here and there the small garrison of a house would be seized with a sudden access of courage or fanaticism, and defy for some time our efforts, generally succeeding in killing several of our men before we could drive them out;

enabling us to form a tolerably correct idea of how bloody and desperate would have been the contest, how prolonged and formidable the siege, if our opponents had been brave and determined men— Russians for example, instead of Sepoys. The iron bridge and neighbouring suburbs were at last captured, and a strong force remained behind to hold them, the enemy keeping up a furious cannonade from the other side of the river, as (in every-day life, as well as in war) weak and cowardly-minded people, when they are beaten, not unfrequently use much noise and bluster to compensate for their short-comings.

Sir Colin, on his side, had also advanced, capturing, I believe, the Shah Nujeef, mess-house, and the buildings in that neighbourhood, and (either on this day or early the following morning) the Begum Khotee; but of the movements of this portion of the army I cannot speak with any great accuracy, not having been an eye-witness of them.

No time was lost in taking advantage of our freshly-captured ground, for that evening two batteries of heavy guns and mortars were established close to the iron bridge; one to the right, and the other to the left of it; the duty of these guns being, as on former occasions, to keep up a severe fire upon the works on the other bank, preparatory to Sir Colin's force attacking them. Thus, on the 11th of March, another important step in advance had been taken, and we were in possession of the whole of the left bank as far as the iron bridge, and of the right bank up to the mess-house, with the defences and fortifications included in this space. True, the citadel of the place, on the elaborate defences of which so much labour had been expended—the Kaiserbagh—was still uncaptured; but we already had our guns busily at work, rendering it untenable. A constant and deadly fire of shell was fast destroying the large and beautiful buildings composing it, and making cruel havoc among the fair mosques, and gilded domes, and ornaments with which it was replete.

I spent that night on picket at the Musjid above mentioned, much of our time being passed in shooting or hanging prisoners taken during the day; or men whom our soldiers, while wandering about in search of loot and adventure, discovered lurking near, and hiding in the old houses and gardens in the neighbourhood. Many a poor wretch breathed his last at this spot, dying, for the most part, with a calmness and courage worthy of a better cause. I am sorry to say that, in one instance, an officer took upon himself the office of executioner, and shot with his revolver two prisoners whom we had brought up to him in a cold-blooded, deliberate way, which was most repulsive. I do not mean to infer that the men were unjustly put to death, for, independently of this being a time when no quarter was given, there was the additional argument that we were then occupying a very exposed and important post, surrounded by the enemy, and it was but justice to ourselves to exert the utmost vigilance, and adopt the extremest precautions, treating as spies any whom we might find prowling about near our position. That these two men were spies I have not the slightest doubt, so that it was not their fate which surprised or distressed me, but that an *officer* should choose to take upon himself the unpleasant duty of an executioner, and so far lower himself as to stain his hands with these miserable beings' blood. It was not as though an example of severity was needed—the men were ready enough, God knows, to shut their eyes to prayers for mercy, to kill and destroy whoever they might catch—perhaps too ready; and it was scarcely necessary for an officer to come forward as fugleman, and foster this thirst for blood among his men; and I think, when I used the word "repulsive," I expressed not only my own feelings on the subject, but those of the rest of us who were standing by when these men were shot. We passed a quiet enough night on picket, being but little disturbed by the enemy, who were lurking about in the woods around, though we half expected them to attack us, and had placed guns sweeping down the different roads in case they should feel so disposed.

CHAPTER XIX.

On Piquet at the Iron Bridge—"Loot"—"Kaiserbagh" Captured—The Fight in the "Engine House"—Horrors of War—The Little Drummer Boy.

On the morning of the 12th March we were ordered down to the Iron Bridge, there to remain, a sort of permanent piquet, for several days. The enemy were still keeping up a smart fire of every description of missile, from round shot to matchlock balls, upon our side of the bridge, doing however but little damage, for we, as well as the other troops stationed down here, were not called upon to do more than guard the position. For this purpose it was scarcely necessary to expose ourselves, except occasionally, when the enemy by an increase of bumptiousness and much firing, made it advisable for us to favour them with a volley; or, by bursting a shell adroitly among the buildings where their sharpshooters found shelter, check the outburst of impetuous valour in question. Their principal fire, however, was directed upon the batteries of heavy guns to the right and left of the bridge, and it required no slight exertion on the part of a detachment of our infantry, picked shots, and told off for the purpose, to keep down Pandy's fire sufficiently to allow of our artillerymen serving their guns without great loss.

From the iron bridge runs a wide street, up which there came constantly a pelting fire of case-shot and bullets, rendering the crossing in no slight degree unsafe; while in the small sheds, shops, and houses on either side our men found cover. Curious enough holes many of these buildings were, and very miscellaneous the goods which they contained; *par exemple*, the house which we occupied, and behind the jutting corners of which we sheltered ourselves from the bullets, had been an old curiosity shop, or theatrical property warehouse, or some such establishment, to judge from the heterogeneous articles discovered therein. It must not be imagined that the goods were laid out in shelves, or that its riches presented themselves ready to the hand of the looter; no!—a spade and pickaxe were necessary to bring to light the hoards, buried as they were in copper and earthenware vessels, some feet deep in the ground; when, behold! silks, old books, bits of lace, nautch girls' trousers—be-spangled and pegtoppy—cloths, turbans, pieces of carpet, bottles of attar of roses, drinking vessels, and a good deal of half-made gunpowder, with great quantities of sulphur and other ingredients for the manufacture of the same, were exposed to view, greatly to the delight of the finders, and stimulating them to further exertions. How the men did dig, and delve, and burrow, to be sure! And with what ecstasy—after some two hours' vigorous excavating in an atmosphere like a vapour bath—would they hail the discovery of any little bit of glittering tinsel, value twopence, which might present itself. All day long and for many days did the sound of axe and shovel continue, while hot and extremely dirty British soldiers laboured excitedly at and under the floors of those stifling, musty rooms, turning up now an old brass pot, and wondering if it was gold, and now some bit of the crystal pendant of a chandelier, and never doubting but that it was a diamond. In spite of an extensive system of mining, very little of any value was found, the principal discoveries consisting of crockery and glass, and among other things several plates bearing the mark and number of H.M.'s 32nd regiment, which had evidently been plundered at the time of the first outbreak at Lucknow. In one house was found a large store of clay-toys, purporting to be models, but practically being caricatures, of guns, swords, and other warlike weapons, intended I suppose for the purpose of implanting in the infant mind of young Oude the rudiments of the science of shooting, and of fostering in the breasts of the noble youth of that province an early love for war and its appliances. It is not to be supposed that the Sikhs were content with such trash as I have just named for loot—that these masters of the art of plunder were to be satisfied with clay guns and nautch girls' silk pyjamas; no! in the *dhotees* (or waist cloths) of the corpses which lay thickly strewed about here, did they carry on their researches, bringing to light occasional rupees, gold *mohurs*, and sums of money of frequently no despicable amount. This, together with the pickings of one or two respectable bungalows in the neighbourhood, constituted the plunder in this quarter, which was by no means a rich one, and appeared very bare and profitless when compared with other places which I shall have to mention presently.

Upon the whole, I can hardly look back on the time of my sojourn at the Iron Bridge as a pleasant one. In fact, I think if we take into consideration the heat which was everyday increasing, the clouds of dust which there was no withstanding, which established sandy particles in the works of one's watch, greatly to its detriment—which penetrated one's system, equally to its detriment, and to the banishment of all the softer feelings of one's nature, and which, in fact, kept one perpetually in a state of fluctuation between raving madness and drivelling idiotcy; then the hot winds which were just beginning to blow; the impossibility of performing any very extensive personal ablutions, or changing one's clothes during the whole of the six days that we were down there; and last, but not least, the horrible stench arising from the numberless corpses which lay festering in every house, and about the street, and on all sides of us: when we, I say, take these facts into consideration, I do not think I shall overshoot the mark when I say that this period was an exceedingly *un*pleasant one. Still, there was an amount of excitement in it which kept one up, and which we eked out with a certain amusement that we derived from the fright of *khitmudgars* and other native domestics. These poor devils when bringing down their masters' dinners, or employed in similar duties, were unable to keep entirely under cover, but were forced to cross the street, and so run the gauntlet of the enemy's fire, exhibiting during this trying period an amount of terror very entertaining to behold. Their fright we increased sometimes (to our shame be it written) by throwing handfuls of stones close to their feet, which, such was their dismay and confusion from the variety of noises and perils wherewith they were surrounded, they readily mistook for showers of grape, and were driven by this appalling conclusion almost into hysterics. If, at any time, some one of a bolder nature, or less suited for rapid movements by reason of obesity, a corpulent Khansamah or Baboo, for instance, thought fit to put on a stately and unruffled demeanour, as he stalked across, we immediately took stronger measures, and rolled swiftly towards his legs, a round, black, wooden pipe-bowl (used by the natives), which, while in motion, and especially to a mind in a high state of nervous excitement, bears a strong and terrifying resemblance to a cannon-ball, and which never failed to have the desired effect. Dignity was not proof against the pipe-bowl—Bob Acres stood revealed—away went courage and corpulent khansamah at a rush, in a state of inconceivable dismay. It may be remarked that the amusement was considerably heightened if the missile was made actually to strike the shins of the victim, when he of course concluded that he was mortally wounded, and seemed much surprised, on arriving at the opposite side of the street, to discover that life was not quite extinct.

On the afternoon of the 14th, we received information that Sir Colin had taken the Kaiserbagh, and that in consequence we were to cross the Iron Bridge, and so complete the discomfiture of the enemy. All was got ready for a move, the horses hooked on to the guns, and, in obedience to orders, the infantry opened a heavy fire upon the right bank of the river, the enemy responding briskly, and making great gaps, and fissures, and rugged breaches in the houses we occupied, by a quick, but happily not very sanguinary cannonade of round shot, shell and case, till the whole scene became smoky, gunpowdery, and exciting. Lieut. Wynne (Royal Engineers) with a few men now dashed forward, and removed the breastwork which we had erected across the bridge, a duty which they performed splendidly, and although under an exceedingly hot fire, without losing a man.* All was ready for the advance, when General Outram and staff arrived, and ascending to the top of one of the houses proceeded to take a bird's-eye view of the state of affairs, and hold a council of war; the result being that Sir James came to the determination not to cross the bridge to-day, but to wait till the following morning. He then came down and said, "I'm afraid, gentlemen, you'll be disappointed when I tell you that I am not going to attack to-day"—explaining to us, at the same time, that Sir Colin Campbell had ordered him not to cross, if he saw a chance of *losing a single man!* a contingency which we could hardly expect to avoid, as the enemy had a nine-pounder gun sweeping the bridge,

* This officer, who, I regret to say, died in Lucknow a few months afterwards, was recommended for the "Victoria Cross" for the admirable manner in which he performed the above-named duty.

ATTACK DEFERRED. 213

a discharge or two of grape from which *must* have made some havoc among our advancing troops.

I shall always think that it was a pity not to have crossed on this occasion, when we might, with a very small loss on our parts, have struck a heavy and decisive blow, and effected immense destruction among the enemy: coming upon them, as we should have done, while they were in a state of confusion and depression from the loss of their grand stronghold, the Kaiserbagh. I imagine few among us regretted more than General Outram himself that the orders he had received were so positive and precise, as to prevent him from leading us over to the attack. Our hearts, which at the thoughts of action had jumped up into our mouths, now quietly subsided into their proper places; the various applications we had made in our excitement to the brandy-flask, might have been spared for all the profit they were likely to be to us now; while further applications had to be made to prevent the excitement from subsiding too quickly, and in order to let us down, as it were, easily. Pulses slackened their racing speed into a respectable jog-trot—the heavy fire died away into the usual occasional and uncertain popping, bursting out, however, now and again, into great loud angry volleys, which became less frequent towards evening, as if the guns had been suffering from intermittent fever, from which they were slowly recovering; till at last we fell back into our primitive state of listlessness, and were obliged once more to have recourse to our old amusement of accelerating the movements of timid natives, and damaging the nerves and shins of fat Baboos by pipe-bowls, as aforesaid.

It will perhaps be thought that I have passed over the capture of the Kaiserbagh too lightly, and not treated of this operation as its importance required; but the fact is, so many accounts of it have appeared, and I am moreover so little acquainted with what actually did occur there, that I have purposely abstained from dwelling upon it. But there was another operation carried on, this day, of which I will speak more fully, for the reason that though it involved a great amount of desperate fighting, and was perhaps the severest struggle which took place during the whole siege, it has nevertheless been hitherto entirely "unhonoured and unsung." I refer to the capture of the "Engine House" by H.M.'s 20th Regiment.

There was a large building surrounded by several smaller ones and out-houses, situated between the Kaiserbagh and the river, and occupied by the enemy, which it was necessary to clear, and two companies of the above-named regiment, under Major Ratcliffe, were detached for this duty, the remainder of the regiment, with some of the 38th, being posted outside. In some way or another the detachment became divided, and the greater number entered by a narrow passage at one side of the house; the smaller party with Major Ratcliffe entering at the other side; the former pressing along this passage, in which they had two men killed, arrived at a small room filled with a motley collection of Pandies. Detachments of every native regiment in the service seemed to have assembled here: the blue and white uniforms of the Bengal cavalry soldier were mixed up with the red coats of the Sepoys of the Line and with the dark blue of the "Goolundaz" (or Artilleryman), while others were dressed in the plain, white cotton clothes usually worn by natives. Equally various were the weapons wherewith they were armed—matchlocks, muskets, old cavalry sabres, tulwars, and pistols, flashed before the eyes of our men as they entered, and drove the surprised rebels, cowed and trembling, before them into another small inner room. A fierce interchange of volleys was now carried on through the open doorway, the men on each side watching their opportunity to deliver a hasty shot round the corner of the door, without exposing themselves. This, however, could not last for ever, and after some time, Captain Francis, the officer in charge of the party, ordered all his men to load; they then made a rush through the doorway upon the foe, and in spite of two of our men being shot, and two more cut down, they succeeded in effecting an entrance. A desperate fight now took place; the small room was so crowded by the enemy, who were as thick as standing corn, that there was hardly space to move, our men having literally to mow their way through this living mass,

"And like reapers descend to the harvest of death;"

plying their bayonets busily and unceasingly: blow succeeding blow—flash following flash, in quick and deadly succession, till they had hewn for themselves standing room out of this mass of struggling, bleeding, panic-stricken mutineers.

It must have been an awful scene—a mob of friends and foes crowded into a few square yards, hacking and hewing at one another, reeking bayonets and reddened tulwar blades flashing high in air — occasional pistol-shots breaking in sharp and clear upon the hideous chorus of groans, and curses, and shrieks, which resounded through the air. Throughout the whole the work of death slowly, but surely progressed, till the floor became red and slippery with warm blood, beneath the quick trampling feet of the combatants. The wretched Sepoys at last made a desperate attempt to escape, by flying from the small room into a large central apartment, filled with engines, cranks, pipes, furnaces, boilers, and other appliances of machinery; just as they entered it, however, they were met by another body of rebels, who were trying to escape from the party under Major Ratcliffe, which I have before said had entered at the opposite side of the house, and which had fought its way through just such another scene as that above described, to the central room. And now, hemmed in on all sides, with all hopes of escape cut off, with nothing left for them but to die, the miserable Sepoys seemed to have become perfectly paralysed and helpless with terror, and to have made no further efforts, or very feeble ones, to defend themselves from our men. From the doorway at the opposite end of the room, a leaden shower rained in upon them, our men actually piling up in the doorway the corpses of those they had killed, as a barricade against the shots, few and far between, wherewith the miserable wretches who still lived,

THE ENGINE HOUSE CAPTURED. 217

feebly replied to those murderous volleys which were striking them down by dozens.

The scene of horror at last began to draw to a close; the shots becoming less frequent, told that the work of death was nearly over, while our men, exhausted and sated with carnage, were firing a few last shots down the pipes, and among the machinery, to put an end to the small number of Sepoys remaining, who were attempting to hide therein. Just then, as though to magnify this overwhelming accumulation of horrors, a fire broke out in the building, the beams and door-posts of the room having become ignited from the constant discharge of fire-arms, and the flames communicating with the clothes of the dead and dying Sepoys who lay piled on one another on the floor, and spreading rapidly, owing to these clothes being in great part cotton, soon reduced the whole, as it has been described to me, to a sickening, smouldering mass of disfigured corpses.

When I add, moreover, that mixed up with, and among these corpses were several *living* Sepoys, who had hidden themselves underneath the dead bodies of their comrades, in the hopes of so escaping the general slaughter, and that these wretched creatures were thus roasted alive, my readers will agree with me that it would be scarcely possible to imagine a more terrible and ghastly scene.

The number of the enemy killed in these rooms amounted to *three hundred;* while fifty or sixty more fell outside the buildings in endeavouring to escape, having fallen into the clutches of the remainder of the 20th Regiment, and the two companies of the 38th, who were stationed round the house. This large slaughter of the enemy was effected—incredible though it may appear— with a loss to us of only about eight or nine killed, and some fifteen or sixteen wounded !

In connexion with this tragedy, I have heard related a melancholy anecdote, which, as far as I can recollect, was as follows: either in the "Engine House" itself, or in a building immediately adjacent, a body of Sepoys were holding out desperately, and one or two of our men had already been shot at the place, when General Franks ordered that no further assaults should be made on it; but that other measures, such as shelling, or setting fire to the building, should be resorted to, to drive out the occupants, in order to avoid, if possible, further loss of life on our side. This order was attended to, and any one seen approaching the house was warned off. A little drummer boy, of the 38th Regiment, who had greatly distinguished himself in the morning at the capture of the Kaiserbagh, where he had unfortunately been given grog by some officers —witnesses of his conduct—who were delighted with the courage he had displayed, returned to camp, and after there obtaining more drink, now made his appearance on the scene. Elated with his achievements of the morning, with the promises of promotion and distinction which had been made to him, madly excited by drink, and probably with a bright vision of a certain bronze cross, with the words "For Valour" embossed on it, dazzling his young eyes, the poor boy lost all command over himself, and was seized with an uncontrollable desire still further to distinguish himself. Drawing his small toy sword, for it was little else, he threw himself with a sort of shout into the building the enemy occupied; his horrified comrades tried in vain to stop him; the rash act had been done too quickly and unexpectedly for any intervention to avail, and once committed, no human power could have saved him; hardly had he set foot within the house when he fell, and the poor child's body was ruthlessly hacked to pieces where it lay.

So much for this day, the 14th of March, the evening of which saw us in possession of what may be looked upon as the Citadel of Lucknow; and though there was much remaining to be done, several more strongholds to be captured, the great mass of streets and buildings composing the vast native city to be cleared out, still the Kaiserbagh once in our hands, it was not likely that the remaining operations would be either prolonged or difficult; as indeed the result proved.

CHAPTER XX.

Our Sojourn at the Iron Bridge—Extracts from Journal—A hasty Trial, and a rough Execution—Reflections—Further Successes—Capture of the "Muchee Bhowun," and Stone Bridge—the 16th March.

OF the movements of Sir Colin's force on the 15th I am ignorant; but any operation that might have taken place on that day, or any advance which may have been made, was trifling in its nature; while on our side affairs equally remained *in statu quo*. The crossing of the river, which my reader will recollect had been postponed from the preceding day, was again for some reason or another put off. And I will here quote a short extract from my journal which refers to this, and speaks further to the extreme discomfort which we had to endure during this period.

"Monday, March 15th, 8 A.M.—We are still in our old quarters near the Iron Bridge, and at present anxiously waiting for the column to arrive, with which we are to cross the bridge and commence the attack; in an hour we shall probably be 'at it,' 'hammer and tongs;' one's sensations are much like those experienced before running a race, or going up for an examination—a certain intense but pleasurable excitement, which any assumption of coolness rather exposes than conceals, but withal a desperate longing to begin. The Bridge during the night has by us been to a great extent protected from the effects of a cross fire, by means of an embankment of planks and earth hastily thrown up on either side; and I cannot help viewing this proceeding much in the light that a tight-rope dancer may be supposed to behold the sprinkling with fresh sawdust of the arena in which his agility is about to be displayed—an operation which though soothing when regarded from one point of view, is apt to suggest, with unpleasant distinctness, the horrors which such precaution is intended to mitigate, but which one feels, alas! it is unavailing wholly to avert."

Later in the same day I find the entry.— "The attack is again put off; a report that the Pandies are bolting is current; orders issued for the 23rd Royal Welsh Fusiliers, 79th, and 1st Bengal Fusiliers, who will be joined by some cavalry and artillery, to be in readiness to march to-morrow morning in the direction of *Seetapoor*, there to cut off, or cut up, or cut down, or attack the fugitive rebels, or do something of the sort. * * * * The heat is really becoming tremendous, number of flies terrific, amount of mosquitoes at night unbearable, and the whole affair generally unpleasant. The stench from the dead bodies is also terrible, there are some hundreds of them buried about the village every day; but under ground or above ground is all the same; the stench of a dead Sepoy would baffle the most strenuous sanitary measures, and the atmosphere is rapidly becoming pestilential; so much so, that ere long this spot will be untenable from that cause."

It was curious at night, while on picket here, where we were only separated from the enemy by the narrow little Goomtee, to listen to Pandy's bands playing on the other side "reveillé's" "retreats," and marches, as if in defiance—to hear him posting his guards, relieving his sentries, going his rounds, and even the voices of the sentries as they challenged "hookum dar?" (for so they pronounce our "Who comes there?") All which duties they performed with as much noise and ostentation as possible; probably with the view of showing us not only that they were on the alert, but that though they might have forgotten many of the military habits which we had taught them,—how to fight, for instance—they still retained and went through some of the old forms and ceremonies as in bygone days, when they served "John Company."

I have before adverted to the hardness of heart which in some cases was shown by our men, and to the carelessness and callous indifference with which they took away human life; and I will here relate one of several instances which came under my notice, as being illustrative of this fact. After we had occupied the Iron Bridge for some days, and when we supposed that the houses immediately in the neighbourhood were quite clear of the enemy, we were astonished one evening by hearing a shot in one of the very buildings which we occupied, and directly after, some of the soldiers rushing in, dragged out a decrepit old man, severely wounded

in the thigh. It seems that the sentry having
heard somebody moving about the house, had
challenged, and receiving no answer, fired, and
shot the poor old wretch in question in the leg.
He was brought out, and soon surrounded by a
noisy, gaping crowd of soldiers, who clamoured
loudly for his immediate execution; expressing
themselves in language more remarkable by its
vigour than either its elegance or its humanity.
" Ave his 'nut' off," cried one; " Hang the brute,"
cried another; " Put him out of mess," said a
third; "Give him a ' Cawnpore dinner,' "* shouted
a fourth; but the burthen of all these cries was
the same, and they meant "death." The only
person of the group who appeared unmoved, and
indifferent to what was going on, was he who certainly had every right to be the most interested: I
mean the old man himself, whose stoicism one could
not but admire. He must have read his fate,
a hundred times over, in the angry gestures and
looks of his captors, but never once did he open
his lips to supplicate for mercy, or betray either
agitation or emotion; giving one the idea of a
man rather bored by the noise and the proceedings
generally, but not otherwise affected. His was a
case which hardly demanded a long or elaborate
trial. He was a native—he could give no account
of himself—he had been found prowling about
our position at night; stealthily moving among
houses every one of which contained a quantity
of gunpowder, and where, for aught we knew,
and as was more than probable, mines may have
existed, which a spark dropped from his hand

* The soldiers call six inches of steel a "Cawnpore dinner.'
The expression needs no further explanation.

would have ignited—or he was a spy, or—but
what need of more? In this time of stern and
summary justice, such evidence was more than
ample; he was given over to two men, who
received orders to " destroy him," (the expression
usually employed on these occasions, and im-
plying in itself how dreadfully common such
executions had become,) and they led him away.
This point being settled, the soldiers returned to
their games of cards and their pipes, and seemed
to feel no further interest in the matter, except
when the two executioners returned, and one of
their comrades carelessly asked, " Well, Bill, what
did yer do to him?" " Oh," said the man, as
he wiped the blood off an old tulwar, with an air
of cool and horrible indifference which no words
can convey, " Oh! sliced his 'ed off," resuming
his rubber, and dropping the subject, much as a
man might who had drowned a litter of puppies;
but it was disgusting to see any man—an Englishman especially—so callous after just launching a
soul into eternity. I may perhaps be wrong in
relating this anecdote; but I have endeavoured,
throughout my narrative, to describe as faithfully
as possible what I have seen, and the impressions
such sights may have made on me; and my object
in selecting this instance has been, not to vilify
the British soldier, or to show that *ordinarily* he
is cruel, bloodthirsty, or callous to human suffering, for I am sure he is not so; but merely to
point out the bad effects which war generally,
and this war in particular, tends to produce on
even the most civilized of those employed in it, in
banishing those nobler feelings of compassion—

in stifling those generous throbbings of the heart, nay, even in overcoming that love of fair play which is usually so characteristic of Englishmen, and which is a point on which as a nation we have always prided ourselves. That this war has had, in a great measure, such an effect is undoubtedly the case, and perhaps one hardly to be wondered at, if the earlier scenes and horrors of it be considered; the Sepoys have none but themselves to blame that they have found no quarter; and their misdeeds entailed a large amount of misery on comparatively innocent people. The Oude people have, as I observed in a former chapter, been invariably confounded with the mutinous and blood-stained Sepoy; and a spirit of ferocity arose among our men whenever they recalled the tragedies of Cawnpore, Delhi, Bareilly, and fifty other places, which little disposed them to discriminate between one black face and another. It would scarcely be reasonable to expect a man whose wife had been put to death with every atrocity and indignity conceivable—whose children perhaps had been crucified,* and whose home made bare and desolate, to retain in his breast any merciful feelings towards those who had thus wronged him, or to forget and forgive, when his day of triumph came, the cruel deeds of his enemy while *he* had had the upper hand. But however easily deducible the cause of the above-described bad

* I have before expressed my opinion as to the torture alleged to have been perpetrated, entertaining no doubt that it had in many cases been inflicted, and I have heard nothing since that time to make me alter that opinion.

effects may be,—however much they may be the natural consequences of this rebellion, they are none the less deplorable, none the less offensive where they come under one's notice; and I should hardly have been describing these operations as faithfully as I have wished to do, had I left unnoticed this feature of them, which however hideous, was so prominent that it must have been remarked by nearly every officer in the army. Indeed, the incident I have selected as illustrative of my argument, far from being an isolated or uncommon case, is, alas! not nearly so conclusive as some others which, if I had chosen to treat my readers to unpleasant and sickening details, I might have related.

On the morning of March 16th, we received orders to take a gun on to the Iron Bridge, and endeavour to keep down the enemy's fire; we did so, but found ourselves exposed to so heavy a fire of musketry, and moreover we could do so little execution, that it was not advisable to remain there, and after firing half-a-dozen rounds we retired. In the mean time affairs began to assume that appearance of forced stillness, which generally precedes important operations; as water becomes swollen and turbid before a storm, loud angry volleys burst out now and then, like peals of thunder; or solitary shots boomed from heavy guns, like the first large drops of rain of a shower, and everybody seemed to be waiting for, or expecting something, which it was evident was near at hand.

About 10.30 A.M. our attention was attracted by large bodies of the enemy moving out of the town across the Stone Bridge. We imme-

ADVANCE OF MARCH 16TH. 227

diately got our guns into action again, and blazed away at the foe vigorously, the riflemen on picket abetting us by keeping up a hot fire from the roofs of houses, but the range (about one thousand yards) was too great for us to do much more than frighten them; this, however, we did most successfully. It was highly ridiculous to see, now a body of infantry, now a horse artillery gun, and now a detachment of cavalry, scampering across the bridge as fast as their own or their horses' legs would carry them, while the Enfields rattled out their sharp and never-ceasing volleys, and our field guns joined their harsh voices to the growing din and clamour. Some said that the enemy were flying, others that this movement on their part meant that they were about to endeavour to get on our right flank and attack us, and a dozen similar reports were current.

About noon, the 23rd, 79th, and 1st Bengal Fusiliers (whose march to Seetapore had been countermanded, and who during the morning had crossed to the right of the Goomtee, by a rough bridge of boats which had been hastily thrown across the river, some distance below the Iron Bridge for that purpose) appeared on the opposite bank, advancing rapidly and driving the enemy before them, killing large numbers as they came, and capturing, among other positions, the old yellow, shot-riddled ruins of the far-famed Residency. The streets up which they were advancing brought them at last to one extremity of the Iron Bridge, where a brass nine-pounder gun of the enemy's fell into their hands, our victorious troops continuing their course unchecked towards the "Muchee Bhowun," which all who are well acquainted with the story of the siege, and defence of the Residency, will recollect had been partially blown up and evacuated by Sir Henry Lawrence after our disaster at Chinhut, as being untenable, from its necessitating the occupation of too extended a position.

CHAPTER XXI.

Scenes in the Streets and about the City—Tragedy and Comedy—A Sketch at Eventide from the Iron Bridge—The Residency—Lucknow is Ours at last—A Legend of the Iron Bridge—Remarks on the Siege of Lucknow, with some criticisms which it is hoped may not be considered presumptuous.

WE had now two field guns and one eighteen pounder on the Iron Bridge, and were keeping up as heavy a fire as we could upon the Stone Bridge, across which the enemy continued to pass and repass, and also upon the buildings which they still occupied, while the whole scene became intensely animated and exciting. A desperate fusilade was kept up on all sides, bodies of troops might be seen constantly pressing forward to the attack along the narrow streets—now hid from sight by the houses, now rushing with a cheer of triumph up to some building larger than usual, and driving the Sepoys panic-stricken before them. Smoke and flames were rising up from several quarters of the town which had caught fire, heightening terribly the general effect. The Stone Bridge presented a scene of confusion glorious to behold, owing to the crowds of the enemy, who in every garb and variety of uniform were passing over it, the greater number in headlong flight, but some few—nerved by desperation, or drunk with *bhang*, returning towards the town, to strike another and a last blow in its defence. Shot tearing with a crash through domes of temples and walls of houses, and showering bricks and stones into the street below;—shell bursting high and harmless in the air, or dangerous fragments of the same spinning whistling past;—the blazing sun overhead shedding a fierce glare and heat, which added to the smoke, and gunpowder, and noise, the wild confusion and excitement was enough to drive one mad.

A running fight was going on in the streets all this time; little knots of desperate rebels, here and there, shut themselves up in houses where they fought fiercely, necessitating an infinity of small sieges on our part to drive them out. At one house in particular, I remember, close to the Iron Bridge, six Sepoys made a determined stand; our men at last got in, killed three, and dragging the others into the street, placed them in a row against the outside of the building, and fired at them. One man, hit in the chest, sank down in a half sitting posture against the wall, and when I saw him life was not quite extinct; his dull eyes were wide open, and stared horribly into vacancy, and his head turned in a slow and ghastly manner from side to side, (much like those waxwork figures with moveable heads, which my reader may have seen,) as though he were mourning over his comrades, whose bodies, pierced with several bullets, lay at his feet; the whole making one of the most terrible pictures I ever saw. We got a soldier who was passing by to send a bullet through the poor wretch's head, and so put him out of his misery. There were many sights this day of an almost equally awful description; but none which has remained so indelibly impressed on my memory as this one.

Sepoys who had been dragged from their hiding-places, lay stretched in the open street, with their throats cut from ear to ear, and with every gaping wound exposed, by the nakedness of their bodies, in all its depth, breadth, and hideousness. Nearly every house had been the scene of some short but desperate tragedy; up every lane and turning lay two or three bodies; and frequently on entering a house did one stumble over, and start back from, the mangled remains of one of its miserable defenders.

It was quite a relief to turn from these scenes to the English soldiers, who, extremely dirty, dusty, and hot, with their mouths black with powder, their faces radiant with triumph and wild excitement, were toiling along under heavy loads of loot, buried in silks and gilded cloths; a dozen chickens strung on their firelocks—their havresacks full of pigeons, or green parrots—and probably leading a rebellious goat or two behind them, quite indifferent to the fact that said goats were on the verge of strangulation, owing to the tightness of the running noose round their necks, by which they were held, and which their struggles for freedom in no wise tended to relax. Sometimes a man, out of whose head *all* ideas of discipline had not been driven, would pass by and make a desperate effort to salute you from beneath his plunder, struggling to free a hand for the purpose, or in happy forgetfulness, bringing a cackling hen up to his cap with military precision. Never, I should think, were tragedy and comedy so interwoven and mixed up one with the other as on this occasion; never was there a scene in which a moralist might have found better matter for a discourse, than this: the dead bodies as I have just described, lying about the streets among the glittering plunder; soldiers telling their gains alongside the corpse of him with whom, five minutes before, they had been engaged in deadly combat; rich mirrors, carpets, silks, bright turbans and valuable arms piled up, so to speak, on one side—" carrion men, groaning for burial," heaped together on another;—knots of noisy looters, flushed with triumph and mad with plunder, opening out to let a doolie, with its pale and groaning occupant pass through. Here, careless Life, with no thought for the morrow, laughing, triumphing, and making merry—there, Death, cold, horrible, and ghastly, a silent Mentor—a dreadful satirist, like the skull, which we read of, at those banquets of old times. Such were the leading pictures of the panorama: incongruous and inharmonious enough, like a sombre picture, which the artist has clad in bright colours, or like a funeral where the mourners appear in wedding garments.

As I stood, towards the evening of this eventful day, on the Iron Bridge, and looked on the surrounding scene, I could not but be impressed by the striking appearance of the city generally, which, with its magnificent buildings, stately mosques, palaces, minarets, and gilded turrets; with the little river Goomtee running alongside it, among shady trees, and pleasant villages, and rich cultivation, must have satisfied the most fastidious spectator, and realized whatever of ideal and beautiful his "mind's eye" may have suggested to him in connexion with the "glowing East." Turn towards the Stone Bridge, and behold on your right the small villages, imbedded in jungle and fine trees, which line one bank of the little stream; then to your left, and see the stately city with its hundreds of domes, and masses of buildings, clustered confusedly together, and almost bewildering one by their extreme grandeur; turn here, turn there, and on each side behold, in the rich, mellow light of sunset, scenes ravishing in their beauty, and in which, sketched, as they for the most part are, by the pencil of that cunning limner Nature, no touch or tint of loveliness is wanting.

Did you ever, my friend, look on a charming view through a telescope, on the glasses of which there were a few black spots of dirt, or perhaps some slight flaw? if so, you will know how, whichever way one turns it, the flaw remains there still; however fair the view which one is examining, the little spot will constantly appear in the midst of it, to mar its beauty. So it was as I looked on Lucknow, each picture had its spot. War with his dreadful finger had daubed the canvas, and left his mark upon it everywhere. There was the old Residency, battered and deserted, recalling long months of stubborn courage, patient endurance, and anxious suspense; its ruined walls marked with many an honourable scar, and speaking with mute eloquence of the scenes of death and suffering which they had witnessed, as the head, prematurely grey, and the furrowed brow, tell of care, and grief, and of a bleeding heart. There, by the bank of the river, stood a small sad knot of English soldiers, hastily committing the body of some "dear brother" to the dust; there, down the quiet stream, lazily floated black, distorted corpses, sometimes collecting together in ghastly companionship in bends of the river, or holding horrible *réunions* beneath the arches, and against the buttresses of the bridge, while huge, obscene birds seating themselves upon them, tore away the flesh, and then soaring away with it towards the blue sky, enjoyed uninterrupted their beastly meal. These, with the flames uprising from burning buildings, with now and again an exploded mine, rolling its dense volume of smoke, with loud and long-continued reverberations into the air; these, with the rugged shot holes through the parapets of the bridges, through the walls of houses, through the gilt domes of temples; these, with the battered minarets and palaces half destroyed, and such other evidences of War's handiwork as presented themselves on every side, were the dark spots which marred and tarnished the beauty of this otherwise brightly coloured scene.

Lucknow might now be said to be ours,[*] though its capture was not properly complete until the 19th; but there was little more to be done, the town as far as the "Constantinople Gate" ("*Rom i*

---

[*] It is said that Sir Colin—on the capture of the place—telegraphed thus: "I am in *luck now*." Hardly as good a despatch as that of Sir Charles Napier's when he conquered Scinde, "*Peccavi*."

Durwaza") was in our hands; our troops were revelling in the rich loot of the "Choké Bazaar," or turning it into money, by selling it back to its original owners, the Jewish merchants, who, with outstretched trembling hands, and quivering lips, were bidding for and buying back again *their own goods*. The following morning, the last building of any importance—Hoseinabad, with its beautiful ornamented gardens, gaudy pagodas, tombs and statues, fell into our hands; the immense native city, composed chiefly of squalid lanes and closely packed houses, stifling and stinking, and into which light and air hardly appeared to penetrate, was nearly deserted, except by fowls, old women, pariah dogs, and a villanous budmâsh or two, who remained behind, in the hopes of getting a sly shot from the top of a house, or from behind a corner, at an unsuspecting "Feringhee." A few of our troops who were ordered to march through the streets, in order to make a military demonstration and go through the form of taking possession, described it as being like a "city of the dead." But of these operations I am not qualified to speak; the capture of Hoseinabad, of the Dowlut Khana, and the "Moosa Bagh,"—the bursting into a room in the last-named palace of some of our troops, and there finding the Prime Minister of Lucknow, with his throat cut, and just breathing his last, having been murdered by the Moulvie—the flight of the enemy—the fruitless, and, I fear, mismanaged pursuit of them by our cavalry—the failure of all attempts to capture either the Begum or the Moulvie, of these things I was not an eye-witness and only know of by hearsay, so that I fear, by endeavouring to describe them, I should not only run the risk of giving an inaccurate account, but be moreover swelling my narrative to a great length, and making it more a history of the capture of Lucknow, than of my own personal adventures.*

Before I leave the vicinity of the Iron Bridge, I will relate an anecdote immediately connected with it, one of the most extraordinary I ever heard. After this bridge had been captured on the 16th March, two companies of the 20th Regiment were left there, partly as a guard and partly to stop all looting. They occupied some houses about a dozen yards from the extremity of the bridge which touches on the right bank of the river; the neighbourhood had been entirely cleared of the enemy, and, with the exception of the corpses—there was nothing bearing a resemblance to a Sepoy in the vicinity, the only persons besides our troops, and the passers-by, being a very, very old woman, "a wrinkled hag with age grown double," a miserable, decrepit wretch, so feeble that she could with difficulty drag herself along. This old lady remained down at the Iron Bridge, near the picket there posted, who at first hardly noticed her presence, until the morning of the 17th, when the suspicions of the men,

---

* The story of the capture of Lucknow should never be told without allusion being made, and a tribute paid, to the gallantry of Captain McNeil and Lieutenant Bogle, who rescued Mrs. Orr and Miss Jackson from a long and cruel captivity. The story of this feat, which is too long for me to insert, reads more like a romance of the bygone days of chivalry than of this present time. It was a right noble deed, worthy of the palmiest days of knight-errantry.

roused in the first instance by seeing her mysteriously picking up little bits of rag and rubbish, and making small heaps of them with no apparent object, were subsequently strengthened by her continually hovering round their fires, as though watching her opportunity to carry some away unawares. This led them to wonder and inquire among themselves as to who and what she could be, and so strong was this feeling—fostered possibly by her witch-like appearance—that one of the sergeants went to the officer in charge of the picket, and reported the case. The officer knowing how prone men are to make mountains out of mole-hills, and, for want of other occupation, to imagine all sorts of ridiculous and undefined dangers, laughed at the sergeant's fears, and told him just to keep his eye on the woman, and see that she got possession of no fire, but not further to interfere with her; that perhaps she was half crazy, and it was improbable that she could do any harm, with more to the same effect. The sergeant then returned to his comrades, and nothing more was thought of the matter until about ten o'clock the following morning, when the old woman was nowhere to be seen; a search was instantly ordered to be made for her, and at last she was discovered in a house hard by, in a little back room or closet, which was full of shot and shell, and a quantity of rubbish and dirt.

The old hag, when found, was in a stooping posture, bent nearly double, with her head almost touching her feet, as though she were picking up something, and *she was quite dead*. Close to her hand lay a piece of cotton, like a candle-wick, and partially burnt, while, nearly hidden by the rubbish, appeared through the floor, close to where the dead woman's hand rested, a bamboo containing a slow match, and on being examined it was discovered that this bamboo led down to an enormous mine of barrels of gunpowder piled on one another, and communicating with the extremity of the bamboo by means of a train of powder, carefully laid and prepared; and as though to make the affair still more miraculous, the slow match in the bamboo had been lighted, and had actually burned about half way down, and then gone out! Here then was the explanation of this old she-devil's mysterious conduct; hence her attempts to get hold of some fire; and that, spite of all our precautions, she had succeeded in doing so unobserved, was evident, for it would seem that having, somehow or another, lighted the piece of cotton wick, which lay half burned on the floor, she had with it communicated the spark to the slow match in the bamboo, and then, either from excitement, fear, and horror at what she had done, or some other such cause, she had fallen down dead, when, by the merciful intervention of Providence, her diabolical project had been frustrated by the going out of the match. If this had burned down to the train of powder, it would, by exploding the mine, have caused the death, not only of the old hag herself, (who was probably some crazy fanatic, with a certain terrible "method in her madness,") but of the whole of the Iron Bridge and the neighbouring houses, with perhaps two or three hundred British soldiers. The truth of this anecdote is undoubted, and the details, which I took some trouble to get correctly, I heard from an officer of the very regiment which was on picket at the time when it occurred.

I have now said all I have to say about the capture of Lucknow, which my reader will have seen was effected in eighteen days, viz., between the 2nd and 19th March, (both days inclusive,) and with much less difficulty and loss of life on our side than the most sanguine of us could have expected.* It is easy to trace the causes which produced these satisfactory results, and chief among them—whatever may be said to the contrary—must be placed the masterly plan of attack which Sir Colin Campbell and his generals had devised, and the perfect maturity to which these plans, in the minutest details, had been brought. The *trans*-Goomtee movement was in every way an important and successful one: as I have before stated, it enabled us to take the enemy's defences in reverse, and enfilade; it distracted and divided their attention, and gave us an opportunity of effectually shelling their strongholds before assaulting them; it exposed them to a severe cross fire—their left flank was constantly threatened by it—and by keeping them continually under the apprehension of having that flank turned, and their retreat cut off, it had much to do with their relinquishing so easily position after position, until the whole were in our hands. To these primary causes must be added the careful way in which each separate

* I believe the loss on our side was not more than 1500 *hors-de-combat*.

operation had been planned, and the determination and skill with which they were carried out, like a beautiful piece of carpet-work, each square of which, complete and defined in itself, will bear a minute and close examination, and exhibits the same attention to details which characterizes the whole. Whether with Sir Colin Campbell this attention to minutiæ—this examination of every operation microscopically, is not carried to excess; and whether the rapidity, and hence much of the success of his movements, is not affected by it, is an open and much disputed question, the decision of which I will leave to abler judges than myself; but certainly at Lucknow we did not suffer by it, nor, that I am aware of, in any other of Sir Colin's operations considered *separately;* though it is possible that, taken in the *aggregate,* his movements have lacked that promptness and continual progressive motion which has always characterized Indian warfare. Since the glorious day of Plassey, this has been the policy invariably adopted by our most successful commanders. If our operations in this last campaign be, as I before suggested, like a piece of carpet work, made up of squares laboriously and patiently finished, the comparison may be employed still further to illustrate my meaning by saying that, owing to this extreme attention to details, so much time is expended over each, that the colours of one square have faded before the next is completed and ready to stitch on; so that the beauty and effect of the whole is to a great extent lost, or, in other words, that the combinations do not sufficiently repay the amount of time and labour bestowed upon each of the various operations composing them. Indeed I do not think we can do better than to describe this failing of Sir Colin's by one word—pre-Raphaelitism, towards which he seems to have a strong and unconquerable leaning; and as in painting this school has by no means produced our most successful artists, so in war, its disciples have never risen to the greatest eminence, and in neither science has it produced such triumphant results as a bolder and a freer style has effected. My space will not permit me to discuss this subject more at length, and I am, moreover, fearful of being considered presumptuous in thus venturing to criticise the performances of a General of Sir Colin Campbell's known ability and experience.

CHAPTER XXII.

Rides about the Captured City—The "Kaiserbagh"—A Scene of Destruction—The Residency—Alterations and Improvements in the City—The "Great Emanbarra"—A View from its Minarets—Lucknow after the Siege—A Stroll up the Choke—Return of its Inhabitants.

It will be easily understood that, whenever I got an opportunity, I availed myself of it to ride about Lucknow, and visit the most celebrated buildings in it, and of these the chief is the Kaiserbagh. This is properly speaking a succession of vast courts, palaces, and mosques, decorated in the *outré*, florid style, and with the same absence of taste which characterizes, more or less, all Eastern structures. It is lamentable to observe how the beautiful buildings which have so attracted one's attention and admiration at a distance, dwindle down into comparative insignificance on close inspection. Marble halls shrink into indifferently plastered, and rather commonplace edifices; gorgeous palaces when looked into exhibit an undignified amount of stucco; the beautiful mosques and minarets which seem at a distance as if none but angels or fairies could have built them, exhibit as one nears them unmistakeable signs of mortal handiwork, and that none of the best, and prove, alas! in many instances, to have an amount of brick in their composition which is neither fairy-like nor angelic. The beauty of the magnificent gardens departs when one enters them, and they present the appearance of a bad Cremorne seen by daylight, and without even a grotto with its beery hermit to cheer one's lonely way; while the statues placed here and there by way of ornament turn out to be execrable and very indecent productions of some Hindoo Phidias. In fact, the whole affair is a delusion and a snare, and never was the expression, "'Tis distance lends enchantment to the view," more applicable than in this case.

But though we may not admire the Kaiserbagh, on better acquaintance—though its glories fade one by one when we examine them—though we may stand aghast at the Vandalism which meets one at every turn, at the vile taste which daubs absurd, flaring pictures on the outer walls of the king's own apartments, like a Greenwich show, and which knows no higher standard of beauty than the crowding together as many little finnikin pagodas, gew-gawy bridges over contemptible little tanks, and miserable tinselly decorations as space will admit—though one laughs hysterically at the grotesque carvings and the monster fish, meeting like a pair of eyebrows, which in their capacity of the Oude crest, are painted, and sculptured, and plastered on every gateway—still, spite of all this, a visit to the Kaiserbagh, shortly after the capture of the place, well repaid the trouble, if it were only to see the ruin and destruction which here reigns paramount. No words can describe the scenes of havoc and desolation which successively startled one's sight; never was a place more thoroughly " turned out o' windows" than this one. Smashed chandeliers; huge gilded picture-frames, with the pictures which they contained hanging in tatters from them; magnificent mirrors against which our men had been having rifle practice; silk hangings torn to rags; rich sofas stripped of their coverings, and their very bowels ransacked in search of hidden loot; the gilded legs of chairs wandering about quite separate from and independent of the seats; statues *minus* their heads; heads *minus* their noses; marble tables dashed to pieces; beds in the last stage of dismemberment; carriages without wheels; buggies with their panels smashed in; oil paintings through which half-a-dozen bayonets had been thrust, in sheer wantonness; books with their backs ruthlessly removed; magnificent ' *howdahs*' with everything bearing the semblance of silver or precious metal torn roughly off them; broken glass; pieces of crystal goblets; old shields; fractured spear staves; doors which had been broken through, or torn from their hinges; with, here and there, to make the scene complete, a half-putrid corpse. Such were the sights which greeted one on every hand—such the utter ruin which one met with in every building of this immense palace.

Everywhere, on every side, appeared symptoms also of that monomania for scribbling names and drawing faces, so peculiar to us English—no place was spared the infliction, the humble outhouse and the lofty council chamber, the king's stable and the innermost and most mysterious recesses of the love-breathing Zenanah, alike bore on their walls the British soldier '*hys marke*' done in the blackest charcoal and biggest characters, or scratched with the point of his bayonet, with a startling prodigality of capitals.

When a few days after this, we, with a number of other troops, were ordered to take up our quarters in the Kaiserbagh, the old walls presented a most extraordinary appearance: accoutrements hanging in festoons upon the painted walls, and muskets resting in the niches where statues were wont to dwell; artillery horses picketed across the gardens; the English linesman lounging indolently in his shirt sleeves about the long corridors, and discussing his "tot" of rum and his rations in the chamber where kings had banqueted; or taking his siesta on the couches whereon the dusky beauties of the Oude court reposed in days gone by their dainty limbs, while the smoke from his black 'cutty' scented the air once redolent only of musk, and sandal wood, and well-flavoured spices, or rendered dim the light of chambers sacred erewhile to love, and, may be, scandal! Oh, Lucknow, how is thy glory departed!

The number of dead bodies lying about the place was very great; and though the Quartermaster-General (on whose department this unpleasant duty devolves) had taken some six hundred Sepoy corpses out of the Kaiserbagh alone, still, when we took up our residence in the place, our men were continually making complaints about the stench in their rooms, which we generally found to result from a human body, in a state of putrefaction, lying hidden in some out-of-the-way corner, and poisoning every breath of air within a hundred yards of it.

One thing which must have struck very forcibly any one who was possessed of the least observation, was the careful way in which the Kaiserbagh had been fortified, with the evident intention of making it the citadel of Lucknow; and the constructors of the immense parapets which surrounded it must have had some vague ideas of defending it inch by inch, dying in the breach, selling their lives dearly, and all that sort of thing, if one might judge from the way in which each street leading to it was prepared for defence, with guns placed so as to sweep narrow road-ways, with loopholes on every side for flanking fires of musketry, and various other devices for giving the assailants a disagreeably warm reception. How much, or how little use, Pandy made of these elaborate defences, readers of the despatches relating to the capture of the place will know; how his parapets, huge as they were, sufficed not to keep up his courage, and his multitude of guns seemed rather to inspire him with terror than confidence; how his loopholes never smelt powder; and how, in short, that chivalrous valour, whose creed is to shoot down women and children in cold blood, or, backed by some twenty kindred spirits, to attack and murder, where opportunity offers, solitary Englishmen; how this, the valour of the bully and the coward, paled before the steady courage of British troops, receded ever from the red-coats and glittering bayonets, and relinquished with scarce a struggle that almost impregnable citadel, with its much-laboured and extensive fortifications, are facts to which any one who was present at this siege will readily speak. So may rebellion and mutiny ever meet with their deserts!

In a ride about Lucknow, however, there are many other places as interesting, if not more so than the palace, some attractive by reason of the associations connected with them, others from their extreme beauty, which, unlike that of the Kaiserbagh, was such as would bear inspection; specially among the former was the Residency.

I will not attempt a sketch of this celebrated spot, for it has been so often and so ably described by members of its illustrious garrison, that most of my readers must be conversant with its appearance, and at the time of which I am writing the greater part of it was in ruins. But it was, and ever must be, an interesting place to an Englishman, and I was fond of riding amidst its yellow, shattered walls, with a friend who had had the honour of being one of its defenders, and who pointed out to me all the most noted buildings in it. That long, windowless, shot-riddled ruin, for it is little else, was the hospital; this old, haggard skeleton of a gateway, pitted with bullet marks, and with the ragged plaster dropping bit by bit from its sides, as though it were dying by inches of the thousand wounds which it had received in our service, is the well-known "Bailey Guard Gate;" the Racket Court—the house which the ladies occupied; Mr. Gubbins' house; you may see them all, all more or less injured, and you feel that you are standing among the ruins of buildings each of which has some tale of thrilling interest connected with it; each of which is replete with associations, half-mournful, perhaps, or only half-joyous, but always glorious.

But very soon after we obtained possession of Lucknow, the all-powerful hand of the engineer was at work, pulling down walls and houses, levelling whole streets, and raising at intervals earthen forts which might defy all future attempts to wrest Lucknow from us. Among other places, the time-worn and time-honoured Residency felt the pressure of this ruthless hand, completing the work which shot and shell had commenced, and over many a tottering wall, or battered house, pregnant with interest, might be seen waving the engineer's little red bannerol, ominous of coming evil, and marking the building upon which it was placed as one that was to fall. So, fast crumbling into dust was the poor old Residency, when last I saw it—the friend that had stood by us so truly and so well in the day of our adversity—elephants and coolies, (I place the most intelligent animal of the two first) busily reducing it to a mass of *débris*, while new parapets, sleek, well-made, and strong, rose, phœnix-like, from its ashes. That these new defences, if called upon, may do their work as well as the veterans they replace, is my fond and earnest hope.

How often is this so, in the world—old, honoured friends elbowed on one side, and put easily away to make room for allies, younger perhaps, and more vigorous, but untried;

VIEW FROM THE EMANBARRA. 249

how are past services forgotten, or disregarded, when the storm has ceased, and the stout old ship which rode out the gale so nobly, looked on almost with contempt, when we lie snug in port, and our eye is caught by some new launched vessel with freshly painted sides, and clean trim look—and how beautifully has our Great Poet expressed this, when he puts into the mouth of Ulysses those noble lines:—

> "Time is like a fashionable host,
> That slightly shakes his parting guest by the hand;
> And with his arms outstretch'd, as he would fly,
> Grasps in the comer; welcome ever smiles,
> And farewell goes out sighing."

I have said that some of the places in Lucknow were attractive from their beauty, and the "Great Emanbarra" may be cited as an example. This magnificent place of worship is something between a mosque, a cathedral, and a palace, to arrive at which one has to ascend a succession of fine broad flights of stone steps, and terraces, when one finds oneself in a labyrinth of lofty halls, like the naves and chancels of some enormous church. In my opinion it as far surpasses in beauty any other buildings of Lucknow, as its tall and beautiful minarets exceed all others in height. The view from the top of these minarets was one of the most charming I ever beheld, and fully repaid one for the exertion which one had to undergo to obtain it, than which I hardly know how to give it *higher* praise. It was very interesting thus to obtain a bird's-eye view of the whole of this fine city, fourteen miles, or thereabouts, in extent; and to see at a glance the Kaiserbagh, the Tara Khotee, Furhut

Bux, the Begum Khotee, and the Residency; to be able to cast the eye, at once, from the battered Alum Bagh, to the shady walks of the Badsha Bagh, on the left bank of the Goomtee, from the dark trees which waved over the Moosa Bagh, to the fantastic but beautiful gardens of the Martinière, and away over the flat, but fertile country, stretched out beyond, and all round, with pleasant topes of mango trees, or graceful palms, and small mud villages and browsing camels dotted here and there over its smiling face.

Seen in this way, the Kaiserbagh looked itself again, truly regal and beautiful, a worthy palace for so fair a city; seen in this way, the plastered buildings became marble halls once more, and gaudy tinsel shone in the dim distance like gold; while a hundred gilded domes beneath glanced and glittered in the sun, and the tapering minarets and massive mosques again established their claim to be considered as the work of spirit hands; and the beauty of the whole was so dazzling, that one felt at a loss how to give expression to those feelings of admiration and delight which were kindled at the sight.

So should Lucknow be viewed by those who would form an idea of its extreme beauty; so, indeed, should all Indian cities be viewed—not dissected, nor criticised bit by bit, for they will not bear it, any more than the drops of water which compose a clear, silvery lake, will bear the prying scrutiny of a microscope; but seen *en masse*—and viewed, not as a miniature, but as a large picture, or rather as a piece of exquisite tapestry, there is then a gayness of colouring about them, and they have such ever-changing prismatic tints, like shot silk, as they lie beneath the blue, unclouded eastern sky, basking in the sunlight; ever flashing and sparkling, like champagne, in the brightness of their beauty, or continually dyeing the warm sunny rays, as they receive them, many lustrous hues, and then, like a polished mirror, reflecting them back more resplendent than before, that they throw all the European cities I have ever seen far into the background.

I have now little more to say about this interesting city, save that ere long it resumed its busy aspect. At first a few miserable deformed beggars, then an old woman or two, with a few equally old men, were the only people who ventured to return; but, by degrees, the inhabitants flocked back to their homes, where they, very possibly, found their furniture rather out of repair, and their household gods and goods in some confusion. In some cases it is not improbable that there was a little difficulty in finding—say, the teapot (if Hindoos ever use such things, which they don't;) nor should I have been surprised to hear that a few little articles were missing, the spoons for instance, when we take into consideration how many British soldiers with easy consciences, and nimble fingers, prone to loot, had had the run of the town, for so many days, with free admission into every house.

Fuller and fuller every day did the city become, till the deserted streets were thronged once more; and when last I rode through the "Choke" Bazaar, filled as it was with shops, and merchants; with strings of commissariat camels and elephants; with gangs of coolies returning from, or going to their labour; with noisy beggars, and chattering children; with the buggies and ponies of the English officers, with the syces running before them shouting in Hindostanee "make way, make way;" with Sikhs and nautch-girls, pariah dogs and palanquins, fakirs and baboos; and with all those other miscellaneous sights and sounds which make up the noontide life of an Indian bazaar— I say, as I rode through all this din, this mixture of Babel and Bedlam, this high tide, so to speak, of confusion and noise, I found it difficult to realize what different scenes had been enacted here—what scenes of blood and death—of man tearing man to pieces—of festering corpses which birds and dogs unmolested fed upon,*—of regiments hurrying to the attack, and booming guns and whistling bullets, and all the wild and terrible excitement of war; and how short a time since all this had been, in these very streets which now throbbed only with bustling commerce and busy life, and showed no further signs of all these so lately passed evils, than here and there a rugged shot-hole through the top of a house, or—which was not uncommon—a dark splash of blood upon a white wall.

* It is a fact that at Lucknow the dogs fed upon the human corpses; never before had I seen this horrible and almost unnatural sight. It seemed a sort of cannibalism. At any rate, no one can dispute my right (with the assistance of a little *dog*-latin) to designate the taste as *cani*-balic.

CHAPTER XXIII.

Reaction—Great Heat—Job's Comforters—Cool Contrivance—Languor—Up and Doing again—The Summer Campaign in Oude—The March.

HARDLY had Lucknow fallen, when a fresh disposition of the army was made, one large column moving off towards Bareilly for the purpose of clearing Rohilcund; another returning towards Cawnpore, and the south-east corner of Oude; while a third was appointed to remain in Oude, under the denomination of the "Oude Field Force;" and a fourth, consisting of two troops of horse artillery, two field batteries, two companies of garrison artillery, the "Bays," a quantity of irregular cavalry, the 20th, 23rd, 38th, 53rd, and 97th regiments, two regiments of Sikh Infantry, and a proportion of engineers, were posted in Lucknow, as a garrison, or to be available for operations in the neighbourhood, if necessary.

With this last-named body of troops it was my fortune to remain.

Now came the terrible reaction consequent on all the excitement of the last few weeks: it was the calm which succeeds the storm; and the hard work which the men had been engaged in now began to tell on them painfully. The heat too was becoming almost unbearable: the thermometer stood at 100°, the hot winds were beginning to sweep like the blast of a furnace over the face of the country, bearing with them searching clouds of dust and sand, while the sick lists and the doctors' faces lengthened daily, and by the 1st of April it was evident that the much dreaded Indian summer had commenced.

Still the old Indian officers—as a rule, the most systematic "Job's comforters" in the world —endeavoured to cheer us "griffs" up by telling us as we lay panting and bemoaning our fate, that it was nothing to what it would be, and begging us to "just wait for another month or so," and then we *might* call it warm perhaps!

I cannot say these remarks had any very inspiriting effect, nor did the prospect of being burnt alive in June, at all reconcile me to the fact of being scorched in April, but it is, I have noticed, a "way they have" in India of consoling one for present torments, by pleasantly anticipating, and setting forth, the yet greater horrors to come. The Anglo-Indian Prometheus, chained down, is cheered by a friend who stands by him, and constantly calls his attention to a succession of fresh vultures with larger appetites, a greater liking for "*foie gras*," and sharper bills than their predecessors, looming big and dark on the horizon, and is urged to keep up his spirits in consequence!

We did what we could to make ourselves comfortable: established *punkahs*, with a large staff of black gentlemen, with no clothes on, to pull them; we placed "*tatties*"* in every window and

* Screens or mats made of *kuskas* (a peculiar description of sweet-smelling grass), which, by being kept constantly wet, cool the hot wind as it passes through them, thereby reducing the temperature of one's room some eight or ten degrees.

doorway, and had *bhistees* (water-carriers) continually running to and fro with pig-skins (yclept *mussocks*) full of water, wherewith to drench them; we invested in bottled beer at the ruinous price of twenty-four rupees (2*l*. 8*s*.) the dozen, and made strenuous, but in most instances futile efforts to reduce its temperature to something below 90°; we adopted the lightest attire consistent with decency, and so arrayed, "or," to use the words of old Spenser, "rather disarrayed," lay on our backs from 8 A.M. to 4 P.M. daily, panting like dogs, and longing for the moment when the blazing sun should disappear beneath the horizon, and leave us, comparatively speaking, cool. But all these preparations were in vain; higher and higher rose the thermometer, fiercer and fiercer blew the hot winds, till visions of congested livers, with a course of blue-pill and blisters, floated with unpleasant distinctness before our eyes; the punkah coolies too were another constant source of annoyance, from their very lax notions of duty, and the fanatical devotion with which they worshipped the god Morpheus; in fact they were like a series of Pickwickian Fat Boys, whose shortcomings in the way of pulling the punkah, and long tarryings in the arms of the above-named drowsy deity, kept one in a perpetual fever of impatience and bad humour, which, combined with the hurling of boots and other missiles at the delinquents in question, throughout the night, did more to heat one than the punkah did to cool. The bhistees likewise seemed completely to ignore the fact that they were engaged for the purpose of wetting our tatties, and were for ever absenting themselves at times when the hot winds blew strongest; "*Khana ko gya,*" (gone to dinner,) we were informed on each occasion was the cause of their non-appearance, in which case I can only observe that at a moderate calculation, each bhistee must have eaten from nine to fifteen dinners *per diem*. The state of indolence attained by oneself was almost incredible: all amusements were necessarily thrown on one side, while even reading became a labour, turning over the leaves being found to be much too heating an occupation to be indulged in with safety, and a wild attempt I made at this season to write some of the earlier chapters of my narrative, at once stamped me as a lunatic, with a tendency to commit suicide.

Such was the state of utter prostration, mental and physical, which we found ourselves in when, at the close of April, an order came for us to join a moveable column, under Major-General Sir Hope Grant, then employed in scouring Oude. We had since the fall of Lucknow more than once marched out, and encamped in the neighbourhood, to act as sort of scarecrows to any rebels who might be prowling about; and each time, on our return, were sanguine enough to imagine that we should be left in peace for the future. The prospect therefore of spending the summer under canvas was, to say the least, startling; it was however not to be disputed, and the idea of a little excitement had rather a favourable effect than otherwise, in stirring up within us a small, but *very* small amount of activity, just enough to enable us to pack up our things, and load our revolvers, and but barely sufficient to support us as far as Bunnee Bridge, (about twelve miles from Lucknow), at which place we joined the column in question.

Our force consisted of McKinnon's troop Bengal Horse Artillery, Gibbon's Field Battery, Royal Artillery, Talbot's company of Royal Artillery, with heavy guns and mortars; the 7th Hussars, some Irregular cavalry, a few Engineers under Major Nicholson, the 2nd Battalion Rifle Brigade, the 38th and 90th regiments, and one regiment of Punjaubee Infantry: amounting in all, I suppose, to about three thousand men. Our route lay towards Roy Bareilly* (Oude), which place I have no doubt it was intended we should capture, had not circumstances, which I shall mention hereafter, occurred to prevent us.

About the end of April, we marched from Bunnee Bridge; the heat was terrific, the thermometer at this time ranging at midday in our tents from 110° to 114°, and even at daybreak standing as high as 100°.

Had it not been for this we might have enjoyed the march; even as it was, I think it was pleasanter than remaining passive in Lucknow, for our way lay through an extremely pretty country; in some places long shady avenues of mango trees, through which, as one peeped into the leafy distance beyond, one half expected to see fair creatures in spotless muslins, and undeniable hats, tripping lightly along to welcome us to a jolly old English Hall, the Elizabethan turrets of which should have been visible between the dark branches, while deer should have been browsing on the lawn,

* This must not be confounded with the Bareilly in Rohilcund.

or pricking up their antlered heads, and diving into the thick brushwood, scared and terrified at our approach. " Should have been," indeed ; alas ! lawn, Elizabethan turrets, deer, young ladies, and muslins, alike are myths, the inventions of a fond and heated imagination ; this is no park in merry England, this is no pleasant English summer's morn ; through these glades wherein the chequered sunlight, fantastic and ever changing, is dancing so gladly, moves a panorama very different to those home scenes which we loved to picture to ourselves, and which we longed to be among: a panorama stern and uncompromising, the pageantry of war, painted in the bright colours of the East; in the foreground, guns, cavalry, and infantry, dusty and travelworn, backed up by a confused mass of hackeries, doolies, camels, elephants, bullocks, spare horses, and camp followers, such were everlastingly the component parts of the pictures. Features which must be familiar to every one who has marched a day in India, and which now that they had lost the charm of novelty, hardly sufficed to reconcile us to getting up at 4 A.M. daily, and marching in a temperature of 100° and upwards, after an enemy who could travel as far in one day as we did in three, whose " grace was only in their heels," and who were " most lofty runaways."

There used to be some little excitement in arriving at a village ; the bare possibility that it might hold out against us acted as a sort of tonic for the time being, but this soon died away ; the mud forts (of which each village generally had one) proving invariably untenanted, and the streets being generally deserted, except by the peaceable part of the population, who squatting toad fashion before their doors, as is their wont, gazed at us as we passed with a sort of stupid wonder, which might have been the offspring of imbecility, or sulkiness, or both combined, but they did not seem to trouble their heads further about the matter. It is not impossible that many of these peaceable-looking natives were Sepoys or budmashes upon occasion, but they were too wise to think of disputing our passage, or showing fight now; and so we went roaming on through jungle and woodland, villages and rice fields, day after day, in this stifling Indian summer weather, hot, weary, and disgusted, nor ever came upon such a thing as a Sepoy or his shadow; though, to make matters worse, we were always supposed to be quite close to large bodies of them, and in daily expectation of meeting some ten or twenty thousand in mortal combat, being told at nearly every village we came to, that our foes had quitted it only the day before, or thereabouts, till our hearts sickened with "hope deferred."

It would have been all very well if only our hearts had been affected, and we felt inclined to say with Touchstone "I care not for my spirits, if my legs were not weary;" but, unfortunately, our livers began to follow the heart's example, and our constitutions generally exhibited various weakly symptoms. The heat, fatigue, and exposure told with terrible effect upon our little force, and this dance which the

Sepoys were leading us through Oude, proved a "dance of death" to many; one or more fatal cases of sun-stroke occurred every day, principally among the cavalry, who, from the nature of their duties, rear-guard and such like, were necessarily more exposed than the rest of the troops; and the sickness throughout the column increased to an alarming extent.

261

CHAPTER XXIV.

A Day in Camp during the Hot Weather Campaign—The Heat
—Morning—Noon—Night—A Weary Time—Our Meals—
A few Words about Beer—Dress and Appearance of the
Troops—I give Vent to my Feelings in a Growl.

LET me sketch a day in camp; it will serve to give an idea of what our life was. I will take one neither better nor worse than many others, let us say May 4th; we are encamped near a village called Morawon, rather a large place, with disgustingly narrow streets, and a bad smell. Well, it is 9 A.M. our day's march is concluded, the camp is just pitched, and we are lying down exhausted in our respective tents; the thermometer by this time is about 106°. Rendered irritable by heat and fatigue, we are making the lives of a large number of black servants burdens to them; we have—that is I have—twelve of these gentlemen who all appear to be hard at work, and yet are unable to give me satisfaction, or to do things quickly enough.

I regret to have to record that, within five minutes of the time to which I refer, I have thrown a boot with diabolical precision at my bearer (or *valet-de-chambre*) who is smarting in consequence, and seems inclined to be sulky; I have hurt the feelings of my "*Kulassie*" (or tent man) by calling him in his own vernacular " a pig," an epithet, be it observed, which receives additional force in India from the fact of said animal being the very essence of uncleanliness; two coolies who have marched the whole weary distance from our last camping ground, and are now employed in fanning me, have called down my wrath by daring to exhibit premonitory symptoms of fatigue, and are in the expectation of momentarily being led to execution; I have destroyed the peace of mind of my "*syces*" (grooms) by accusing them of defrauding my horses of their proper amount of "gram," and appropriating the difference, disregarding at the same time, their protestations of innocence, and being proof against the flattering allusions they have made to my being "Lord of the Universe," such being the title wherewith they love to honour me; my *bhistee* (water-carrier) in reply to some incoherent remarks I have been making to him in a mixture of Oordoo, English, French, and gibberish, on the subject of his shortcomings, complacently informs me that I am the "Protector of the poor," a soft answer which however is powerless to avert my wrath; while my "*mehtur*" (the lowest class of household servant) attempts to escape chastisement, by letting fall hints that he regards me as the "apple of his eye;" with my "*Khitmudgar*" (table servant) I am morose—with my "grass cutters" violent—towards my "*dhoby*" (washerman) abusive, and, in short, I am decidedly splenetic, and my domestics one and all stand and crouch, under my testy humours. By this time breakfast is announced by our *khansamah* (butler,) physically a tall, goodly gentleman, in snowy linen, but morally a deformity and —metaphorically speaking—arrayed in an impenetrably black cloak of extortion and villainy; and

I have an unpleasant consciousness that he looks upon us as a sort of large sponge, to be squeezed, and pour forth rupees, at his pleasure, while I feel bound to confess, as I recall these times, that his view of the case was by no means an incorrect one.

We stroll into the mess-tent, feeling in this hot weather that the wing of a butterfly grilled would be a sufficient meal, and there on a ricketty camp table is laid out a repast so terribly substantial as to throw one into a yet more profuse perspiration: a tough spatch-cock; curry made principally of the necks and shins of chickens, and in consequence scarcely satisfactory; a beef-steak of the most horrible description; some doubtful eggs; and a dishful of gigantic things, called "beef-chops," which look appallingly like mutton chops seen through the magnifying medium of a nightmare, and one of which would inevitably prove fatal to a boa-constrictor; such form the groundwork of our entertainments at a time when weary, hot, and appetiteless, our stomachs turn loathing from any but the lightest and most delicate food. During breakfast our coolies stand behind us with huge fans, and, as we are hard at work throwing ourselves into a profuse perspiration with hot tea, they are as busily engaged, though not so successfully, in endeavouring to keep us cool, till calling for a light for our cheroots, we return to our tents, there to lie down again panting on our beds. No books either to while away the time, or at least but a limited and well-thumbed supply—a *Shakspeare* and an old *Tom Jones* were my sole companions in the book line; the former was one of those horrible small print editions which ought to be forbidden by law, and which it is impossible to read for more than half an hour at a time; while for the latter, I had read it so often that there was not an action of the hero's, a piece of hypocrisy on the part of Master Blifil, or an oath of old Squire Western's, that I was not familiar with.

How shall I ever forget those long, hot mornings, when one's only amusement—if amusement it can be called—was watching the thermometer gradually working its way up to 114° or 116°, or gazing listlessly out at the quiet camp, where not a human being, except a sun-dried "nigger" perhaps, was to be seen, and over which swept the terrible furnace-wind of Hindostan, with its clouds of parched dust, pungent as dry snuff; while the great scorching sun beat down upon us with a heat which was almost past endurance, and all nature seemed the while to have fallen into a state of death-like lethargy.*

It is high noon now. The men in their tents are lying with nothing on but a shirt, or a pair of trousers, gasping for breath, prostrate and sickening beneath the fearful heat; the horses stand at their picket lines with drooping heads, and protruding under-lips, too lazy almost to whisk away the flies which buzz around and settle on them as if they were so much carrion; while hard by sit the syces fast asleep, having dropped in despair the piece of harness which they are

---

* On three occasions during this march the thermometer in our tents rose as high as 121°! and some notion may be formed of the heat from the fact that our drinking water which we had *cooled* in earthenware vessels, was 96°, or the temperature of a warm bath in England!

supposed to be cleaning, and given up as futile all attempts to appear busy. Under a neighbouring tope of trees are six elephants, equally lazy and sleepy, and goaded nearly to madness by insects (for strange as it may appear, that coarse black skin of theirs is not proof against that tiny tormentor, the mosquito); every now and then taking up a quantity of sand with their trunks, they throw it over their broad backs to drive away the flies, or by way of cooling themselves, squirt water over their bodies; anyhow, they are very restless and uncomfortable, now standing on three legs, now on four, swaying to and fro, flapping their great ragged ears, putting their trunks into their mouths and pulling them out again, or amusing themselves by picking up single straws at a time, by way of proving that their trunks have not forgotten their cunning, and regaling themselves on these straws deliberately, as a sort of hint to their keepers that they want their dinners; but this little *ruse* is lost on the keepers, for they are fast asleep too, and so very nearly is a pariah dog, who, with his tongue lolling out, and his eyes half shut, sits at a little distance, lazily watching the elephants, and looking as if he were making faces at them. There are some crows sitting on a tree, with their *beaks wide open, gasping for breath;*[*] and a flock of goats have made up their minds that it is much too hot to browse, and following the example of the herdsman, who is, or ought to be, tending them, have got beneath the shade of some trees, and gone to sleep; the native cooks, very

[*] Improbable and ridiculous as this may appear, it is, nevertheless, a fact.

salamanders, who are sleepily preparing the men's dinners, look as they sit beside the fires as if they would much rather be enjoying a *siesta*. There is a dead silence reigning throughout the camp, except when a " gay young deceiver" of a horse, taking advantage of the silence, or possibly concluding therefrom that it is night, walks off to pay his addresses to another horse of his acquaintance, who gives a squeal of disgust at having his nap disturbed, and kicks him for his pains; and a dozen syces wake up suddenly and begin rubbing their eyes, and the harness which they should be cleaning, very energetically, till one more zealous than the rest gets up and captures the horses, when they all go to sleep again.

Nothing seems to be moving, even the busy bazaar is still as death now, and its noisy buzz is hushed. The only things which have any activity in them seeming to be the hot wind, which is blowing higher, hotter, and more unmercifully than ever; the dust which is stalking about in tall cloudy pillars, like waterspouts of sand; and the sun which is blazing and scorching with a fury and intensity which has thus overpowered man and beast, beating down through our thin covering of canvas, and enshrouding in a dim mist of heat, like the haze of a mirage, the whole camp with its snow-white tents, green trees, horses, natives, elephants, all of which we see as if they were reflected in a glass which had been breathed upon.

Now at this intolerable time occurred to one in its full force and power, the signification of that curse which says :—*And the heaven that is over thy head shall be brass, and the earth that is under thee shall be iron, and the Lord shall make the rain of thy land powder and dust.**—(Deut. xxviii. v. 23, 24.) It seemed almost as if we, in our own selves, were doomed to realize the intense meaning which these nervous, glowing scripture words conveyed; and as we saw fresh victims daily laid in their graves beneath the shady mango trees hard by, and saw the strongest among us stretched helpless as children on the bed of sickness, we might perhaps be pardoned for thinking despondingly at times that even the concluding words of that curse—*from heaven shall it come down upon thee, until thou be destroyed*, were about to be worked out and accomplished.

But, let me not forget the flies! As one lies wearily tossing about on one's bed, so hot as to tempt one to doubt the possibility of ever getting cool again, these small evil spirits keep one in a continual paroxysm of rage; as the old lady in *Punch* says:—

"They settles on your noses, and they whizzes in your eyes,
And they buz-wuz-wuzzes in your ears; oh! drat them nasty flies,"

and you smother yourself by covering your face with a pocket-handkerchief in an attempt to escape them, and throw yourself into a yet more profuse perspiration by endeavouring to capture or kill them, it is needless to add, without the least success.

There is another evil also which must be borne, and "grinned at" if possible—I mean "prickly

---

* These pillars of dust are familiarly styled "Cawnpore devils."

heat"—a sort of rash which breaks out on you, and, as its name infers, prickly in its nature; I can only compare it to lying in a state of nudity on a horse-hair sofa, rather worn, and with the prickles of horse-hair very much exposed, and with other horse-hair sofas above you, and all round, tucking you in. Sitting on thorns would be agreeable by comparison, the infliction in that case being local; now, not a square inch of your body but is tingling and smarting with shooting pains, till you begin to imagine that in your youth you *must* have swallowed a packet of needles, which now oppressed by heat are endeavouring to make their escape from your interior, where they find themselves smothered this hot weather. We have read of such a thing in the newspapers, as a young lady or gentleman (I forget which), regaling themselves on a quantity of these extremely indigestible articles, and for ever after shooting them forth from all parts of their body, but I question whether we can ever have thoroughly sympathized with the unfortunate in question unless we have known what it is to suffer from "prickly heat" in *propriâ personâ*.

Occasionally, by way of a change, we had a dust storm, the meaning of which few but those who have resided in the north-west provinces of India can realize. The sun is, perhaps, shining high and bright, when suddenly the atmosphere becomes darkened, as though clouds had descended upon the earth, a light cool breeze is felt, it grows higher and stronger, while the air momentarily darkens, till at last black, dense, opaque clouds of dust come tearing down upon you, sweeping through the most tightly closed crevices, penetrating everywhere and everything, and for the nonce placing you in almost utter darkness, and leaving, as it passes over, a thick, gritty coating of dust upon every article in your room or tent, till even the sheets on your bed are brown, and you could easily write your name upon the pillow. The discomfort of the hot weather will perhaps be better appreciated when I state the fact that even these horrible dust storms are looked forward to and enjoyed as a temporary relief, cooling as they do the atmosphere for the time.

If you are a tiffin-eater, you generally find, about one o'clock, some viands of a coarse and heating description laid out for your repast, the *Khansamah* having carefully prepared, as at breakfast, the most substantial and least tempting food which he is acquainted with ; and after turning up your nose at everything on the table, you return to your tent and your cheroot, and again fall into that languid listless state against which there is no struggling.

About 4 P.M. as the shadows lengthen, matters assume a somewhat livelier aspect, the syces begin to wake up, and soldiers appear at the doors of their tents, yawning ; the dear old lazy elephants are led away to bathe in some neighbouring tank, and the pariah dogs get up and walk about with a show of activity, and the horses are taken " to water ;" while here and there among the tents flit the graceful figures of the " *doodh-wallees*" (women who sell milk) in their snow-white, almost classical, cotton garments, supporting on their heads with a pair of the most shapely arms in the world, bare and bronzed, and glittering with simple ornaments, the burnished brass pots which contain the milk, and which gleam brightly in the evening sun; while their soft cries of *"doodh-doodh,"* and their jingling anklets, make pleasant music in the camp. You are by no means sorry to be able to escape from the confinement of your tent, and in a costume which would do admirably for the character of "Zephyr," at a masquerade, you venture out, though it is still very hot. Even now you suffer from the same want of occupation; quoits, if you play at them, throw you into a fever, riding is a great exertion, you are probably rather ill already from over-smoking, and the hot wind, though it has considerably subsided, has still sufficient force to bring water into your eyes. Or you are "on duty," and obliged to attend "stables," and see the horses groomed, and hear the men talk gibberish to the syces: a British soldier having an idea that a native is bound to understand any remark of his, however lengthy, if a word of Hindostanee is thrown in here and there, making of the sentence neither "flesh, fowl, nor good red-herring," and it is not uncommon to hear such instructions as the following, given: "I say you syce, you just *puckrao* that *ghore's* head, and *saf karo* his legs;" or to a cook: "Now look'ee 'ere, you '*bobbachee*,'* if you don't let me have my *char*, at *char budger* another day, I'll break every bone in your body; I've told yer this more than once, don't let me have to tell yer again, that's *bus!*" which sentences being freely

---

* Properly *Bawurchee*, cook, but the soldier is not generally over particular about his pronunciation of the Hindostanee words.

rendered into English mean: "I say, syce, take hold of that horse's head and clean his legs;" and, "Look here, you cook, if I don't have my tea at four o'clock, I'll &c., &c."

Dinner-time comes at last, and with it a repetition of the horrors of the preceding meals, only exaggerated. A native imagines that quantity, not quality, constitutes a good repast; and nothing would convince our *Khansamah* that we by no means felt inclined to eat a whole leg of mutton each, or that we had the tastes of civilized beings, and not the appetites of cannibals, or wild beasts; the great and redeeming point of this meal however is beer, the beverage *par excellence* of Indian communities, and in which, astonishing to us "griffs," the old Anglo-Indians "hob and nob," and drink one another's healths. A cruel day it was when our supply of beer ran short; woe to the mess to whom this misfortune occurs! very few visitors will it see; and the guests who do present themselves, wax morose on discovering the fact, as men who have been decoyed by an unworthy artifice into a pitfall.

Night comes presently; night hot proportionally as the day, when enveloped in shirt, pyjamas, and perspiration, you toss sleepless for hours on your bed; night made hideous by yelling jackals and pariah dogs—now distressingly wide awake —by camels, with that diabolical noise of theirs which I have before described, between a groan and a gurgle; by *tom-toms;** by the droning

* A sort of native drum, whose excruciating sound bears about the same unpleasant proportion to that of an ordinary drum, that the pain of gout does to that of rheumatism.

chants of unfeeling and sleepless natives, who in spite of all sorts of sweeping edicts on the subject, *will* sing all night; by the squeals and kickings of loose horses; night, in fact, as unnatural from the presence of a variety of noises, as the day which preceded it was from the absence of the same; night, moreover, cut off in its prime of life, *i.e.* half-past three A.M., by a bugle, bidding us arise and don our harness, which we do with no great alacrity, feeling very much as if we had not been to bed at all, and lying on our backs, while our " bearer" pulls on our stockings, being much too sleepy to perform that office for ourselves.

All around is the tumult occasioned by the striking of tents, saddling of horses, loading of camels and elephants, and the subdued curses of men who, in every direction, are breaking their shins and the third commandment over unseen tent pegs; presently all is ready, the canvas city of an hour ago has disappeared; your own house, folded up like a " Patent Siphonia," is on the back of a camel; your goods and chattels ditto, or in the act of being kicked off again. Night is just struggling with day, and getting the worst of it, and through the gloom are visible dark masses of troops, moving quietly along, or elephants, or solitary horsemen, looking like phantoms; there is a dull rumbling of guns in motion, or the quick trampling and clinking of cavalry, and always an undercurrent of camel noises; and before you are sufficiently awake to distinguish the whole scene from a dream, you discover that you are on horseback yourself, moving away in your place with the rest of the column. Certainly marching

LAXITY IN DRESS.

in India is brought to a perfection which it seldom or never attains in Europe or other countries, and, barring the heat, it may be called " warfare made easy."

As regards the appearance of the troops on these occasions, the less said the better. Under any circumstances, the wicker helmet used by the men is by no means a becoming head-dress, giving an appearance to the wearer of being extinguished; but, when to this is added that the greater part of the troops marched, on account of the heat— hear this, ye lovers of stocks and belts and pipeclay! —actually in their shirt-sleeves, like a lot of insurrectionary haymakers, or that those who wore a coat at all, had one of faded *karkee*, in which dye and dirt were so incorporated, and mixed up together, as to produce a neutral tint, far from gorgeous; I think it will be admitted that our appearance must necessarily have been more remarkable for its novelty than its beauty. Alas! private John Smith, of H.M.'s—Regiment, how different a man art thou from the smart, red-coated soldier which thou appearedst when whispering "soft nothings" into the ears of blushing, buxom housemaids at home; very silly must be the housemaid with whom thy blandishments would prevail now, John Smith—scarcely worth the wooing would be the spinster who could listen to aught out of that wicker helmet; far and wide mightest thou go in that dust-stained *karkee* coat, I fear me much, before thou wouldest find a Sally to smile upon thee, my badly-dressed friend. It often occurred to me at this time how aptly we might have said with Henry the Fifth (only substituting in the third line some other word for "rainy"—say "dusty")—

> "We are but warriors for the working day,
>   Our gayness and our gilt are all be-smirch'd
> With *dusty* marching in the painful field;
> There's not a piece of feather in our host,
> (Good argument, I hope, we shall not fly,)
> And time hath worn us into slovenry:
>   But, by the mass! our hearts are in the trim!"

Aye! even the last line; for if at times our hearts sank within us, as we looked on our thinned ranks, and on the long line of doolies which followed in our rear, when fighting became the question, then, "by the mass!" were they "in trim," as Pandy found out to his cost on the 12th May, and as I shall shortly relate.

So passed away the time on the march, day succeeding day and bringing nothing new: a blazing sun, flies, hot winds, dust, prickly heat, and discomfort were our lot, and still no encounter with the enemy; it was a monotonous, wearying time, when one pined miserably for old England, and thought with many a sigh of the broad ocean which rolled between us and our home. The time had come when those things which by their novelty had hitherto helped to interest and support us, lost that charm, and with it that sustaining power; and a desperate loathing for India and everything belonging to it, amounting at times to a feeling of despair, came over us, while, enervated and ill from heat and exposure, we looked at everything with an intolerant and jaundiced eye; the natives and their peculiarities ceased to interest us; elephants palled upon us, and camels had long ago become an eyesore, I might add an ear-sore too; jackals we discovered to be nuisances; our familiarity with monkeys had generated contempt, and pariah dogs invariably inspired us with a longing to throw stones at them; bullocks we looked upon as bores; and even the wild pigs and peacocks of the jungle no longer afforded us amusement. In fact, the many strange scenes which India presented to the new comer, those scenes which Lord Macaulay in one of his admirable Essays has portrayed in a sketch, at once so graphic and suggestive, that I cannot refrain from inserting the passage:—" The burning sun, the strange vegetation of the palm and cocoa-tree, the ricefield, the tank, the huge trees, older than the Mogul Empire, under which the village crowd assemble, the thatched roof of the peasant's hut, the rich tracery of the mosque, where the imaun prays with his face to Mecca, the drums and banners and gaudy idols, the devotee swinging in the air, the graceful maiden with the pitcher on her head, descending the steps to the riverside, the black faces, the long beards, the yellow streaks of sect, the turbans and the flowing robes, the spears and the silver maces, the elephants with their canopies of state, the gorgeous palanquin of the prince, the close litter of the noble lady;" all these things were strange to us no longer, and we had tumbled " neck and crop" into the " Slough of Despond," whence the view we obtained of the glowing East, with all its bright and dazzling associations, seemed tinselly and unsatisfactory in the extreme.

We "griffins" were, perhaps, more sensible to this oppression of spirits and general languor than the old hands, who had a dormouse-like faculty of falling into a state of torpor, and after sweeping a spot tolerably clear to lie upon, and entwining the thorns which they found about them into a sort of quickset hedge of grievances, grumblings and disgust, sat within the charmed circle secure in its impenetrability, perspired, smoked, and drank beer stoically; while we, on the other hand, unused to handle the Axe of Philosophy, or ignorant as yet of the immense satisfaction to be obtained by grumbling systematically, threw ourselves in despair upon a prickly bed of misery, and vainly bemoaned our fate; while our Anglo-Bengalee comrades tried to console us, after the Indian fashion, by informing us that this was nothing to what we should have to endure in the way of heat, if we went up to the Punjaub!

CHAPTER XXV.

Doondiakera—Night March to Nugger—May 12th—Ravages of Sunstroke and Apoplexy—The Fight at Simaree—Serious Night Alarm and Panic.

THE morning of May 10th found us at Doondiakera (or Doondea-Kheyra) on the Ganges, a village notorious from the fact of one—and only one—of the boats full of Cawnpore fugitives having succeeded in getting thus far down the river in safety, when by order of one Ram Buksh Singh, talookdar or chief man of the district, they were attacked by hundreds of the natives who lined the banks.

According to the account given by Mr. Gubbins in his book on *The Mutinies in Oude* (he having heard it from the lips of one of the survivors), the affair seems to have been as follows : the boat grounded, and the wretched victims, fourteen in number, landed to endeavour to drive off their enemies. Overpowered by numbers, however, they were forced to take refuge in a small temple, close to the river, where they held out for a considerable time, till their foes contrived, by lighting a fire round the building, to force them to take refuge in flight, and, as a last resource, to charge through the dense crowd of assailants, sword in hand; it was a desperate chance, and only four, of the gallant little band escaped, these four, swimming the river, or floating down its stream for some distance, at last found refuge in the fort of the friendly Rajah of Moriarmow, whence after a stay of about a month, they proceeded to join Havelock's camp. These men were Lieutenant Delafosse, Lieutenant Thomson, an artilleryman, and a soldier of the 84th Regiment. I only regret that it is not in my power to detail the subsequent adventures of these four gallant men. Lieutenant Delafosse is, I believe, now no more; Lieutenant, now Captain, Thomson is in England, and about, I understand, to publish a narrative of his adventures, which, I doubt not, will prove intensely interesting; of the two private soldiers I know nothing.*

Such were the circumstances which gave a certain melancholy interest to this village of Doondea-Kheyra, and we were the first Englishmen who had visited the spot since the fatal day in question. How were the tables turned now! Where were now the hundreds of cowardly and insolent rebels who had massacred our wretched countrymen here, not a year ago? The bird had flown; not a sign of talookdar Ram Buksh Singh, with his gallant followers, except that we found a fort, some guns down a well, and the memorable temple with its sides pitted with

---

* Since these lines were written, I see, by advertisement, that Captain Thomson's book is on the point of publication. I doubt not that, on its appearance, it will be most eagerly sought after and read.

bullet-marks and blackened by fire; and, sad reminiscence of the tragedy here enacted, a human skull, lying, with a terrible significance, among the dust and rubbish of the deserted buildings. Destructive measures were immediately commenced, the fort and temple blown up, the village burnt, and Mr. Ram Buksh's property generally given to the dogs.

Two days sufficed for this, and on May 11th we received orders to be in readiness to march at midnight; where to, what for, was of course unknown to us. My recollections of this weary night march are, that nearly all the troops lost their way in the pitchy darkness; and that we wandered about in a state of much confusion and sleepiness, among gloomy jungle, and labyrinths of mango-trees, for several hours; that there was a succession of stoppages and delays, and a good deal of stumbling into ditches; that we became entangled, and, as it appeared for some time, inextricably, in a mud village, remarkable for nothing but its filthiness and a certain unsavoury effluvium; that the baggage, as seen through an obscure medium of darkness and drowsiness, presented an appearance of anarchy, the reverse of satisfactory; while the elephants and camels looked like the distorted shadows of people who were trying to go through a "Country Dance," without knowing the figure. At last, morning broke, and, judging from our fatigue, we imagined we must have travelled some fifteen or sixteen miles, when, behold! we had reached *Nugger*, a place only about eight miles from Doondea-Kheyra, and at which we had halted on May 9th, *en route* to the latter place. Here we made our camp, got our breakfasts, and resigned ourselves in our tents to another listless, idle day. In this expectation we were doomed to be disappointed; hardly was breakfast over, when an order came to strike our tents about noon, and have everything packed up and loaded on the camels, and the troops "fallen in," ready to march again, at 2 P.M. This was startling information, but when it became generally known that we were about to march out to attack the rebels, who were posted at a short distance from us, our spirits rose, and men who the moment before had been lying enervated, sick, and languid, on their beds, brightened up surprisingly, and then set to work "with a will," to do as much for their weapons, and prepare them for the fray. The orders were that the baggage and the sick should be removed to some neighbouring topes of trees, under the guard of a couple of guns, two or three companies of infantry and a few cavalry, and there remain until the return of the column, which was about, as I have before said, to move out to attack the enemy.

It unfortunately happened that this day, May 12th, was one of the very hottest during the whole of the summer, the thermometer standing in my tent at 117°, so that it was terrible work striking our tents at midday, and exposing ourselves to the full blaze and heat of an Indian noon; and the result was apparent almost immediately, several fatal cases of sunstroke occurring before the troops had fallen in!

The sick and baggage having found their way into the shade of the fine old trees in the neighbourhood, the rest of the column marched off, glad that at any cost they should at last have the opportunity of coming to close quarters with their slippery foes. Few who belonged to this column will ever forget that day —how the scorching rays of the sun beat through helmet, cap, and turban, and struck down by dozens the healthiest and strongest among us ; how, still cheered by the prospect of a fight, the men kept gallantly on, stepping out with a "pluck" and determination which cannot be too highly praised, scorning to murmur at the torture (for it was little else) which they were obliged to undergo. One after another, however, the doolies filled with wretched men in all the convulsions of sunstroke ; one after another, sergeants came up and reported some fresh victim. With some, the attack was only temporary; in a few hours, or days, or weeks, they recovered ; others lingered perhaps till evening, or the next morning, and then sank into their last long sleep ; but many fell, almost as if they had been shot, and in five or three minutes were no more. Never before had we seen sunstroke in all its horrors, and a more appalling spectacle it is difficult to imagine than beholding, not one, or two, but dozens of strong men lying speechless and insensible, gasping and jerking with a convulsive, tetanic action ; while *bhistees* standing over them, vainly strive, by saturating their heads with cold water, to arrest the sands of life that are running out so fast—to see the person with whom you are talking, suddenly turn pale and sick, and fall reeling to the earth, like a man in a fit, and to hear a quarter of an hour afterwards that he is no more. Who could have blamed our men if sights such as these had unnerved them, and daunted their spirits? But no! sanguine and big-hearted, fearing nothing for themselves, though there was not one among them whose turn might not have come next, but aching the while with grief, as they saw their comrades falling around, they kept on their way, and pressed gladly forward to the battle that was before them.

About 4 P.M. their exertions were rewarded, and they found themselves face to face with the enemy, at a place called Simeree. As regards the fight, much need not be said, as there was nothing remarkable about it. It was the old story of Europeans *versus* Asiatics : White *versus* Black; though outnumbering us four or five to one, they did not stand against us long; superiority of weapons, spirit and science, more than counterbalanced disparity of numbers, and the steady advance of our troops (for exhausted and sun-stricken as they were, they went up to the attack with light and buoyant steps), the pelting fire of our artillery, and its admirable precision, the quick rattling volleys of the Rifles, soon had their wonted effect. At about 6 P.M. Pandy fled in "admired disorder" from the field, leaving thereon between 300 and 400 dead,* and four guns; our loss being, I believe, two or three killed, and perhaps half-a-dozen wounded. Had we only had to combat a mortal foe, we might perhaps have found reason to congratulate ourselves on the result of the day's work, but

---

* The despatches, if I remember rightly, estimate the enemy's loss at more than this, but I have reason to believe the numbers I have stated are tolerably accurate.

alas! it was far otherwise, the sun had fought on the side of the enemy, a more potent ally than shot or steel, and before his deadly rays, above fifty British soldiers went down that day, to rise no more, and 160 (in all) were placed *hors de combat*. The 38th Regiment alone buried twenty men in twenty-four hours, and the other regiments and corps lost proportionately; our list of casualties was thus sadly swelled, and a gloom thrown over us, as the excitement wore off, which a dozen such victories as this one of Simeree would have failed to dispel; for it was a barren victory at the best; the action terminated too late to admit of pursuit, even supposing the men had not been too much exhausted, and General Grant being fearful lest the baggage should be attacked in his absence, was more inclined to return that night to our original camping ground at Nugger, than to follow up the enemy. It is difficult, in fact, to see what we gained by this victory: the slaughter of three or four hundred Sepoys, at the expense of between seventy and a hundred British soldiers, was an advantage too dearly purchased to be satisfactory, nor did the capture of four miserable guns, or the so-called " moral effect" (which with a people who look upon running away as the natural consequence of fighting, is hardly of much account), compensate us for the losses we sustained by sickness and sunstroke. However, it perhaps showed our foes that no circumstances of climate, however disadvantageous, could daunt English courage, and that even now, in the heart of the hot weather, we were actively scouring the country, and fighting battles, as eagerly as if the thermometer had been at 60°.

That night we bivouacked on the field of action, and a memorable night it will always be to those who were present, from a most extraordinary panic which occurred, and the particulars of which I will endeavour to relate. In the middle of the night, when the whole force, thoroughly wearied, was buried in sleep, a cry was raised that the enemy were upon us; several shots were fired, and people woke up wildly from their sleep, only to find all darkness, noise, and confusion. The discharge of fire-arms, throwing now and again flashes of lurid light over the scene; the press of men endeavouring in the darkness to find their places; the words of command, and orders to the men to fall in; the confused cries and shouts which always seemed to form themselves into the alarming words, " the enemy are upon us !" the whistling past of stray bullets; the feeling of uncertainty as to the direction from which the attack might be looked for; and, worst of all, the rush here and there of affrighted camp-followers, doolie-bearers, bullock-drivers, and other natives, who were mistaken in the dark for the enemy, and fired at accordingly, made the panic complete, and the men, half stupified with sleep, thus suddenly alarmed, lost for some little time all semblance of order and regularity, and became temporarily insane; at least if one may judge from the fact that, in some instances, they deliberately set to work to knock one another down with the butt-ends of their rifles, and even *to bayonet the comrades who were sleeping alongside them ! !*

For some time did this confusion and hubbub continue, until at last, by the exertions of the officers, and by a notion gradually dawning upon the minds of the men, as they became wider awake, that there was just a possibility of the whole being a false alarm, a hypothesis strengthened momentarily by the non-appearance of the enemy, who had been so strangely imagined to be among us, order was in some degree restored; and everybody, rather ashamed of themselves, dropped quietly into their proper places in the ranks, and the calm which proverbially succeeds the storm, ensued; many a head throbbing the while painfully from the intimate acquaintance which, in the *mêlée*, it had formed with the butt-end of a comrade's musket.

There were worse mishaps, however, than headaches, in the shape of bayonet wounds, for which the men had to thank one another; a shot wound or two similarly occasioned; and one, at least, serious accident with a revolver, an officer having unhappily (in an attempt to defend himself from a rampant soldier, who would insist on mistaking him for a Sepoy, and knocking him down accordingly,) shot himself through the leg; and last, but not least, a wretched native bullock-driver was killed, having been shot through the head with a pistol, by mistake.* Had it not been for these serious consequences, and the somewhat disgraceful nature of the whole affair, it would have been more laughable than anything else, some of the incidents having been of a most

---

* In the Rifle Brigade alone there were as many as seven casualties, scalp and bayonet wounds, caused during this panic, and inflicted by comrades; while, I believe, every regiment had similar specimens of misplaced animosity.

ludicrous description. Among others, it is related how a certain gallant colonel engaged in a desperate single combat with a private of the Sappers; luckily, however, having a tree between them, which prevented the engagement—in which, it is said, great valour was shown—from being sanguinary, the chief sufferer being the trunk of said tree. Again, an officer is said, on having been roused from his sleep by the noise, to have deliberately discharged the five barrels of his revolver all round him, without regard to persons, by way of clearing a space for himself, and as a preliminary to further operations; with many other legends of a like nature; none of them, however, being more amusing than the account which was given of the cause of the panic, but which, spite of its apparent improbability, is, I believe, the correct one. It is said that while the force were asleep as above described, a snake crawled over a soldier's face, who thereupon awoke, and not knowing, or thinking what he was doing, discharged his piece, thus waking up others, who, hearing a shot so near them, at once concluded that the enemy had got among us; and, in a state of semi-idiotcy from over-fatigue and sleepiness, began to yell, and give the alarm, which, spreading as fire does in tinder, soon communicated itself to the whole force. It is also easy to understand that with the excitement of the past day, the men's nerves should be in a state of extreme sensibility and tension; and in my opinion, we may find a further explanation of their conduct in the fact that the greater part, if not the whole of them, had felt most painfully the blazing sun of the preceding day as it beat down upon their heads, and that in consequence of this, and the excitement and other predisposing causes above mentioned, their overwrought brains might be said to be temporarily affected—an insanity thus brought on by the sun, instead of the moon.

So ended the 12th May, which will long be remembered by those who belonged to General Sir Hope Grant's column; memorable alike for the little skirmish of Simeree, the terrible ravages of sunstroke, and the tragi-comical panic which I have just described.

The following morning the column marched back to Nugger, and there rejoined the baggage and sick, who were by no means sorry to see them return, having during their absence been most perilously situated, constantly expected an attack, and debating the possibility of making any effective resistance in their crippled, and comparatively defenceless position.

CHAPTER XXVI.

Great Sickness—The Return March to Lucknow—Sick sent into Hospital at Lucknow—Brutal Conduct of some Sepoys—A Digression on a Subject which has been much discussed—Battle of Nawabgunge—Summary of the State of Affairs at the beginning of July, 1858.

WE rested at Nugger until May 15th, when it was found that the number of sick in our little force was so considerable, (one sixth part being *hors de combat*, and the daily occurrence of fresh cases further reducing our strength) that our proposed march to Roy Bareilly was necessarily given up, and a return to Lucknow directed, in order that there we might send in our sick, where they would obtain some few comforts, or at least shelter, and where we might receive fresh re-inforcements in their place. Doubtless also, another cause of this retrograde movement (which the enemy thought fit to call "running away," giving it out that they had beaten us at Simeree, and forced us to retreat,) was, that Sir Hope Grant had obtained information that the Begum was collecting a large body of troops at Nawabgunge (on the Fyzabad road), about eighteen miles from Lucknow (20,000 rebels, it was said, being under her standard,) and from this position was threatening the last-named city, our force at that place probably not exceeding as many hundreds as they had thousands. The presence therefore of our small column in the neighbourhood would prove a great additional protection; so it was proposed to encamp us under trees at the " old cantonments," on the left bank of the Goomtee, and by building straw roofs to the tents endeavour to make the temperature of these our canvas habitations more tolerable, and by digging drains, &c. &c. prepare for the coming rains.

Our march back to Lucknow was the same weary, hot, unhealthy business as our march thence had been; and the number of sick increased to such an extent that our doolies did not suffice to carry them all, and *hackeries* (or country carts) had to be employed for the purpose. Nothing eventful occurred to mark this time; we saw no more of the enemy, nor of their proud boast that having defeated us, they should pursue us hotly (they were careful to pursue at a very respectful distance!) and the only thing I recollect which broke the monotony, was another false night alarm, happily unattended with the serious consequences of the former. I have a dim recollection of being roused about midnight by a diabolical noise, and clattering of arms, and of a sentry rushing to my tent and vociferating in a voice husky with emotion, "The Sepoy cavalry are in the camp;" of jumping out of bed in a state of great mental aberration and excitement, and of hearing, the while, unceasing and hideous as ever, the horrible clatter and yelling which first awoke me,

> "As all the fiends from Heaven that fell
> Had peal'd the banner-cry of Hell."

of endeavouring to ignite a match, so as to throw some light upon the subject; and of failing so repeatedly that I at last gave it up in despair; of plunging legs foremost—but unluckily wrong side foremost—into a pair of pyjamas; of becoming terribly entangled in a pair of boots, and performing a sort of wild hornpipe on one leg, in consequence; of upsetting my table, and a few other articles of furniture; and of breaking more crockery than I imagined I possessed; of seizing a pistol and a sword, and trying in my confusion to cock the latter!—of tumbling over a tent rope in the endeavour to get out of my tent; of picking myself up in the full expectation of finding myself engaged hand-to-hand with a black gentleman, armed with big whiskers and a tulwar, and of a sort of shadowy presentiment that I should get the worst of it; of hearing people talking excitedly to one another, and men rushing to their places in the ranks; of all being for about five minutes noise and confusion; of waiting some time, and straining my eyes in an attempt to discover these phantom cavalry; of the tumult subsiding as suddenly as it had commenced; of the whole thing being at an end and proving a false alarm. We then returned to our beds more leisurely and in a serener state of mind than when we left them, while we enjoyed a hearty laugh the following morning at the whole affair, which this time had been caused by a pack of jackals rushing through the camp uttering their unearthly yells and shrieks: so originated the alarm in question. It is really wonderful how little will suffice, more especially at night, to cause a panic.

MOVEMENTS OF GRANT'S COLUMN. 291

May 21st found us back at Lucknow, or rather encamped on the banks of the Goomtee, in the neighbourhood of the Martinière; and arrangements were immediately made for sending our numerous sick to the general hospital at Lucknow, some fresh troops taking their place in the column.

I was so unfortunate at this time as to be invalided, the exposure and fearful heat of our last march having completely knocked me over; and as we found that instead of encamping quietly for the remainder of the summer, as we had expected, the column was to march off again somewhere immediately, fresh information of the presence of the rebels having been received, I was advised to return into Lucknow, and there endeavour, by rest and quiet, to recruit my health. These arrangements were hardly completed, and the sick disposed of, when the indefatigable General Grant and what remained of his column, again started off, much in the same direction that we had marched before; among other places they revisited a little village called Poorwah, where we had halted for a day or two during our last trip, and where, last time we were there, several men had died of sunstroke, among them a company-sergeant of artillery, who, with some comrades, had been buried under a tope of trees in the neighbourhood, a tin plate having been affixed to one of the trees, with a simple inscription upon it, to mark the spot. When the column paid this second visit to the place, it was discovered that during our absence the enemy had opened the graves, defiled them in a most disgusting manner, torn up the bodies, and after scattering the bones all round the place, had carried off the heads for trophies! This little anecdote speaks volumes for the *animus* of our vile, barbarous foes, and yet all the while pseudo-philanthropists at home were crying out for mercy for the poor Sepoy, and trying with that *laudable* spirit of perseverance and benevolence which would seek to wash the Ethiopian white, to palliate, almost to vindicate his deeds of cruelty and mutiny.

With no little astonishment, as we read speeches and leading articles, did we behold the respective positions of Sepoy and Englishman reversed, the former being the martyrs now, the latter the persecutors. Misguided officers and soldiers who had been inwardly congratulating themselves that they had established a sort of claim upon the gratitude of their country, by their services in India—and by this had been cheered up all along, through heat, sickness, and hardships—suddenly discovered, on reading the record of proceedings at Exeter Hall, and elsewhere, that it was all a mistake; and that they were, by certain sets in England, looked upon, individually, as something between a cannibal and a grand inquisitor. One unfortunate who, not anticipating this revulsion of public feeling, and who, when the cry of "no quarter" was echoing far and wide through England, had written a little letter home, stating with much satisfaction that he had killed several Sepoys, was astonished to find by return of mail that he was a monster, and not the least bit of a hero. In fact, we were told that "Jack Pandy" was not half so bad a fellow after all, and we really had been a *leetle* too hard on him, and we should for the future take more into consideration the provocation he had received —the dread the poor fellow so naturally had of having his caste destroyed, the— Pshaw! why repeat these canting sophistries, which really are quite sickening.

It is not, perhaps, so difficult to understand how this feeling has arisen in England; the reaction of the first overpowering excitement had taken place, and from one extreme people fell into the other; but those who had taken part in this war —who had witnessed the devastation and misery caused by these mutineers—who had heard over and over again the terrible tales of the early days of the outbreak, from the lips of eye-witnesses— who had seen their comrades stricken down by the rebel steel, or by the yet more fatal sickness —who looked daily upon the pale inmates of the hospital, and to whom came, day after day, tidings of some loved friend's death—who had seen the dead bodies of their companions cruelly and horribly mutilated—who had witnessed in nearly every village which they marched through fresh evidences of Sepoy brutality, in maimed and disfigured natives whose only crime was their loyalty —who heard one day of a "dâk-runner" being *burnt to death*, the next of a comrade's grave being defiled, and always by these black-hearted foes; those, I say, who had these reminders constantly present before their eyes, were little inclined to elevate their foes to martyrs, or to smother their feelings of deep and lasting animosity.

Nor did familiarity with the general character of the Asiatic particularly incline us to mercy; and though I by no means agree with those who would make this a war of extermination, I am strongly of opinion that the time for showing leniency had not yet arrived. Cruelty is ever odious, but justice surely is not only politic but right; and those who know the Indian character best, who have been brought up, and lived among them, will tell you that punishment, summary, decisive, and even severe, is the native's ideal of justice; that mercy, with an Asiatic, is only considered as such when placed in relief against a dark background of punishment; and that the mercy which precedes the show of might is as a pearl thrown before swine.

I am afraid I have digressed somewhat, but my excuse is, that it was impossible to pass over in silence a subject which was for some time a universal topic of conversation throughout the army in India.

On June 11th, after a short trip, Sir Hope Grant returned to Lucknow, but only to start off again, without resting for more than a day, in the direction of Nawab-gunge, on the Fyzabad road,* picking up *en route* a considerable reinforcement of cavalry, infantry, and artillery.

Marching from Chinhut, on the night of June 12th, he made a forced march, and at daybreak on the 13th, came upon the centre of the rebel force, which was strongly posted at Nawab-gunge, on ground made difficult by ravines which ran across it here and there. It seems not

* There are two villages called Nawab-gunge in the neighbourhood of Lucknow, one on the Cawnpore road, the other on the Fyzabad road; the one to which I now refer is the latter.

improbable that the guide who served us on this
occasion was doing, or willing to do, a good turn
to the Sepoys also, and kill two birds with one
stone—for he led our column straight up to the
centre of the enemy's position, to the very
point where they were best prepared to receive
us, and exactly where, supposing him to have
been in collusion with . them, he would be likely
to lead us, thinking thereby to place us in their
hands, or at least at a disadvantage. But, as usual,
Pandy "caught a Tartar," and in spite of every
preparation was unable to hold his ground;
He disputed the field, however, more stubbornly
than was his wont, and the fight was a sharp
one. At one time our small force was completely
surrounded by our numerous foes, and the fight
was raging in every direction : a series of determined conflicts taking place in various parts of
the field, the most serious of which was one with
a body of desperate fanatics, who planted the
sacred Green Flag in the ground, and hundreds
whose courage had begun to waver, and whose backs
were already turned upon the field, gained fresh
heart as they saw this emblem of the Moslem
faith waving in the air, and gathered round it
prepared to die beneath its sacred folds ; but with
a wild cheer a battalion of the Rifle brigade threw
themselves upon them, and for some few minutes
a sharp and deadly strife was waged round the
Green Banner: flashing bayonets and keen
tulwars glimmering about the confused mass of
combatants, while quick shots and cries of anguish,
or, at times, a ringing cheer as the little Riflemen
steadily fought their way on, and found their foes

gradually giving way before them, were the sights and sounds which caught the ears of the spectators, till at last discipline and courage prevailed, the sacred standard and its defenders went down before the nervous arms of our soldiers. Fanaticism, faith, paradise and its dark-eyed houris, with their waving green scarfs were all forgotten, and broken and dispirited the survivors fled, followed by showers of hissing rifle bullets, which their conquerors poured in upon them.

The 7th Hussars too, in a glorious charge, dulled the edge, and dimmed the brightness of many a sabre, as they rode gallantly through the affrighted enemy; and elsewhere the artillery by keeping up a searching fire, which no native troops, much less mutineers, could stand against, completed their discomfiture. It would however be unfair to praise one part of the force more highly than another, for all did their duty well on this day, as may be seen by the result; viz., the total defeat of the enemy, with the loss to them of 600 or 700 killed, and seven guns which we captured —and to us of about half-a-dozen killed, and perhaps twenty or thirty wounded. As usual, however, we had to mourn several cases of sun-stroke, though not nearly so many as on the day of Simeree; we lost also a few camp-followers and grass-cutters, who, with a portion of baggage, having mistaken their road, fell into the enemy's hands and were cut up.*

* We had here an opportunity of noticing how much more rapidly wounds heal in a native than in an Englishman; the blow that would prove fatal to the one, closes up in a week or so when received by the former, as we saw in the case of one of

BATTLE OF NAWAB-GUNGE. 297

Such was the little battle of Nawab-gunge, a most successful affair from the fact that the Sepoys, trusting in their great superiority of numbers and position, had been so confident of victory that they almost courted the attack, and their total defeat hence came upon them as a sad blow. Their visions of recapturing Lucknow, to which I doubt not this battle, had victory fallen to the other side, was intended to have been a preliminary, faded away once more, and a general gloom was thrown over their force by the issue of this day; whilst it is said—I believe with some truth—that this, our victory, small and meagre as the results may at first sight appear to be, did in reality more to discourage and damp the little remaining ardour of the enemy than any repulse which they had sustained since Delhi fell. At all events there is no doubt that it had a much greater moral effect than was to have been expected; and any little hope which the Sepoys up to this time may have entertained, seems to have died away in their breasts, as they received this fresh proof of how impossible, with every circumstance of numerical superiority and of position in their favour, it was for

our grass-cutters, who, cut up by the enemy, but not killed, had managed to crawl into camp covered with the most ghastly wounds. I recollect going to see this man, and never did I behold a more pitiable object; he had one slight cut on the arm, another of a more serious nature down the left shoulder blade, a third, a terrible stroke, diagonally across his stomach from near his left hip to his right breast, and, worst of all, a blow on the back of his neck which had nearly severed the head from the body. A month after he had received these injuries, he was able to walk about! Of course the simple way of life of the Hindoo, his abstinence from meat, and the consequent purity of his blood, are the chief causes of this.

them to cope with our troops. The effect of their defeat was at once made evident to the Civil authorities, by the rapid submission of certain districts, and the more peaceable disposition of the Oude people generally which ensued, as if they now saw beyond a doubt which was the winning side, and had determined, in true Asiatic style, to play their cards accordingly.

At other places in India, too, our arms had been triumphant; Shahjehanpore and Bareilly had for some time been in our hands, and Rohilcund was overrun by our troops; in the Southeast corner of Oude, Sir Edward Lugard was steadily accomplishing his difficult task of clearing the dense jungles of Jugdespore of the enemy, and a few days after the victory of Nawab-gunge, we received news of Sir Hugh Rose having brought to a glorious conclusion his long and admirably conducted march across half India, (which had throughout been a succession of hard fights, brilliant triumphs, and dashing pursuits,) by the capture of Jhansi and Gwalior, and the subjugation of Bundelcund. To our great satisfaction, we heard that the Ranee of Jhansi—that fiend in a woman's form, to whose instrumentality so many of our poor countrywomen owed their deaths—had been killed in the former engagement at the head of her troops; and as if fortune had determined to act not only up to the spirit, but the letter of the proverb which says, "It never rains but it pours," and to shower all her long withheld favours upon us at once, we also heard about this time of the death of the Moulvie of Lucknow, one of our bitterest opponents, and, from the fact of his presence with the troops imparting, from the sacred nature of his office, a sort of religious character to the struggle, also one of the most influential.

Such is a rough outline of the state of affairs throughout the disturbed districts of India, at the beginning of July, 1858. How different to what it had been in the July of the year preceding; then mutiny and rebellion stalked in bloody triumph across the land, and anarchy reigned supreme; very feeble apparently was our tenure of India then, as the storm-rack scudded blustering overhead carrying all before it. Here and there, however, even in that sad day, were bits of blue sky to be seen peeping through the dark clouds, as at the Residency at Lucknow; at Delhi, round which the toils were surely though slowly closing; with Havelock's gallant little band, as it fought its desperate way through a network of foes, setting at nought the terrors of climate and sickness, laughing at shot and steel; such were the bright specks on which the eye rested—oh! how gladly! But these were few and far between, and so small that it seemed as though the huge bank of black clouds, looming on the horizon, must inevitably obscure them before long, and plunge all into hopeless, dreadful darkness, while dismal tales of the tragedies of Cawnpore, Bareilly, Jhansi, Futteygurh and a score more places were in all men's mouths; and solitary Englishmen, disguised by suffering, were wandering outcasts about unhealthy jungles, dependent for their very existence on the doubtful hospitality of a few loyal natives. From Calcutta to the Punjaub hardly a stronghold which we could call our own; our treasuries, magazines, supplies, all in the hands of our foes; with the unhealthy wet season just commenced, with all gloomy and dark before us, not knowing what a day would bring forth, or how much further the plague-spot of mutiny might not extend; such had a year ago been our position in India. But, where was now that brave rebel host, twelvemonths ago so flushed and mad with triumph, reeking and drunk with the blood of helpless women and children, like uncaged tigers in their cruelty and wrath? Scattered to the winds; with the curse of Cain upon their foreheads,—hunted from Oude to Rohilcund, from Rohilcund to Central India; driven from village to town, from town to jungle, from district to district, nor finding resting-place in any,—broken up into small bands of wearied fugitives, who knew no home, and who must long ago have lost all hope. Men who had sown the wind, and who now the harvest time had come were reaping the whirlwind; Tantia Topee, Bainee Madhoo, the Begum, and some few other leaders, it is true, still held unfurled the standard of revolt, feebly and vainly attempting to stem the tide of defeat, disaster, and retribution which had set in, an overwhelming torrent, upon them. But on every stronghold floated the English flag, and wherever the eye turned it fell upon the glittering bayonets of English troops, who, side by side with their Sikh comrades, were scouring the country in all its length and breadth; mud forts, loopholed villages, guns, arms, and position after position falling with scarce a struggle into their victorious hands. Such was the picture which the summer of 1858 presented. The Tiger was brought to bay at last, he was down now, and with teeth and claws broken or wrenched out, he lay struggling weakly in the grasp of the avenging Lion; scratch and bite as he would now, he could do but little harm, feeble and innocuous fell his blows—the day of his bloody triumph had gone by, and retribution had come at last.

CHAPTER XXVII.

Commencement of the Rains—The Camp at Nawab-gunge—
Away to Fyzabad—The History of Rajah Maun Singh of
Shahgunge.

ABOUT the middle of June, the first drops of rain which had fallen for months came down in a cooling, delicious shower.

Never shall I forget the sensation of relief one experienced as it came pouring down. I hardly know what to compare it to; the first sniff of the sea-side after a stifling season in London; the first bottle of soda-water in the morning which succeeds a night, which—which—what shall I say? well, which had concluded about 3 A.M. with devilled bones and anchovy toast; the first glimpse of England's white cliffs after a long absence from home, or after a long sea-voyage; extract the essence of delight from all these together, and the result will, perhaps, give you a faint idea of the delightful sensation of the first shower of rain after the hot season in India.

The heat had previously become terrible; even at night the thermometer in the open air stood at 100°, and all nature was dusty, parched, and worn-out with the dry scorching temperature—the very air indeed seemed discoloured with heat; imagine then our delight when the clouds which had been collecting for some days, began slowly to yield a few large, heavy drops, thunder rumbled portentously, and at last, down it came, cool, refreshing, and invigorating: at once everything became animated and endowed with fresh life, horses neighed, goats ba-a-a-hed, men hurried briskly to and fro, and once more every one breathed freely, as a pleasant breeze, smelling freshly of rain and earth, blew in, lowering the thermometer 8° in as many minutes!

It was night when this occurred; and in a very thin shirt I went out to welcome it, and revel in nature's shower-bath as it came pouring down upon me, while I invoked blessings on the rain, the breeze, the thunder, and everything connected with this glorious down-pour, feeling as though a cord which bound me, and the tension of which had been fast increasing to an unendurable pitch, had at last been loosened.

Such are my recollections of the commencement of the rains in India; I think, by comparison, the most enjoyable moment of my whole existence.

After this first shower we were some days without having more rain; but at last, about the commencement of July, the wet season fairly set in, and it was soon after this that, having recovered my health, I went out to Nawab-gunge, to rejoin Sir Hope Grant's force, which had remained encamped there since the action of June 13th.

Great preparations for protecting the men from the bad effect of the rains were in progress: raised platforms of earth were being constructed for the tents to stand upon, and the latter were moreover to be covered with roofs of grass and straw; an extensive system of draining was also being carried out, while the officers were, for the most part, busy in building small mud houses, with thatched roofs, for their own use, and our prospects on the whole looked as cheerful as could have been expected under the circumstances. The fact of a little repose after our labours was sufficient to make any quarters agreeable, and though there was every probability of the whole camp being continually under water, and of our living in a sea of mud and an atmosphere of damp, with chronic colds in our heads, we regarded these as minor evils, to be laughed at so long as we remained stationary for a few months.

By a wise order of the Commander-in-chief, the men were encouraged in every sort of sport and amusement, to prevent the time hanging heavy on their hands; and races, jumping, tilting with spears at tent-pegs, running in sacks, &c. &c. were "got up" in the column, and beguiled a few days pleasantly enough. It was difficult, however, at this time to find either ground or weather suitable for races, as the dampness of the latter kept the former almost constantly in a state of mud; of course there were several days when no rain fell, and then the sun, as hot as ever, always improved the occasion by at once sucking up all moisture, and doing his best, in these short intervals, to reduce nature once more to that "baked brick" state which it had attained before the rains. Once or twice we had terrible downfalls of rain—for a day and a night, perhaps, would it come pelting down, without cessation, laying the whole surrounding country under water, swamping tents, and bringing out whole armies of frogs, who, with the voices of stentors suffering from bad colds, croaked for whole hours with a determined ferocity and gruffness which I never before saw equalled, at least by frogs. In addition to these gentlemen we were honoured with the society of locusts, grasshoppers, white-ants, snakes of various descriptions (but generally harmless), and scorpions. The latter animals were, I think, the most objectionable of our visitants, and I one evening had the extreme satisfaction of discovering a large brown one serenely seated on my pillow, just as I was about to get into bed. Their sting is most painful, and a wound in the finger will cause the whole arm to swell up to an enormous size.

Such was the state of affairs at Nawab-gunge on July 16th, and we were as comfortable in our huts or roofed tents as circumstances would permit, or as people living continually either in a warm shower-bath, or, between the showers, in a vapour-bath, could be, when, to our intense astonishment (scarcely equalled by our delight), an order came for us to be in readiness to march in a few days to Fyzabad, there to relieve our doubtful ally, Maun Singh, who informed us that he was besieged in his own fort, at Shah-gunge, by a large body of rebels, and that, unless we went immediately to his assistance, he should be unable to hold out.

Farewell then to our comfortable huts—what palaces they seemed now we were about to leave them! farewell to repose and quiet, and once more to arms! Dim visions, in which the leading feature was mud, flitted before our eyes. Long, weary marches, wet, miserable tents, encampments on ground two inches deep in water, sickness, dysentery, and, looming indistinct and vague through this damp and foggy future, a shadowy figure of Glory, wringing the wet out of her clothes, and beckoning us towards her, with about as earnest and tempting hospitality as Mr. Pecksniff exhibited when he invited his friend to "make merry" on a couple of hard biscuits. But poor as might be the fare wherewith Glory now strove to tempt us, and disinclined as we might be to sit down to so meagrely furnished a table, there was another host, who, by appending his name to the invitation, clinched the matter, and put declining with thanks out of the question. This host's name was Necessity; so, *nolens volens*, we must e'en pack up our portmanteaus, and buckle on our swords, and be ready on June 22nd to commence our march to the relief of Rajah Maun Singh, talookdar of Shah-gunge.

A few words respecting this gentleman may, perhaps, not be out of place.* He belongs to a Brahmin family, originally living in the Arrah district; but his grandfather had migrated to a village near Shah-gunge, with his family, and there taken up his abode. Durshun Singh (father of Maun Singh) and Buktawur Singh (brother of Durshun Singh) served under the King of Oude with distinction; the latter in the military branch,

* For the substance of this account of Maun Singh I am chiefly indebted to Mr. Gubbins, who, in his *Mutinies in Oude*, gives much information concerning him.

receiving, as a reward for his services in the same, the title of Rajah; and the former in a civil capacity, in which, as Governor of Sultanpore, he at one time "held the government of more than one half the province of Oude." "Both brothers," says Mr. Gubbins, "amassed much wealth, and acquired several talooquahs, containing many villages, in the usual way; but Buktawur Singh having no son, and Durshun Singh possessing three, the landed property became merged into one, and the sons of Durshun Singh succeeded to it." These three sons were Ramadeen Singh, Rugburdyal Singh, and Maun Singh. Rugburdyal Singh appears to have turned out a failure, and to have obtained an unpleasant notoriety for rapacity &c. &c.; and with this character he retired from the scene, and went to live at Fureedabad, in the Jounpoor district, and we hear no more of him, the family possessions in Oude devolving in consequence on the two brothers, Ramadeen and Maun Singh. The former being the elder, was of course the rightful heir, "but" (I quote here from Mr. Gubbins) "Maun Singh's superior energy and talent led him to be acknowledged as the head of the family; and the fort at Shah-gunge" (which, by the way, had been built by Durshun Singh his father) "was held by him, Ramadeen residing much at Benares." Maun Singh now figures rather discreditably in the various intrigues and disturbances which, from time to time, convulsed Oude, and in which he in the capacity of head of the Hindoo party, and representative of the interests of the sacred Brahmin city of Ajoodhea, found himself opposed to the Mussulman government at Lucknow, the former city being the Hindoo capital of Oude, as Lucknow, on the other hand, was the Mahomedan; and he appears at one time (but for the British interposition) to have been on the point of marching upon Lucknow, "for the purpose of destroying the Mahomedan dynasty, and establishing a Hindoo government in its place." Such is the earlier history of this man, specked and spotted here and there (like the skin of the cruel, cunning leopard) by black tales of the treacherous deeds which he has done—the murder of Hurpaul Singh, to wit, as related in Colonel Sleeman's work on Oude— and characterized throughout by treacherous cunning, coupled with great personal courage and determination.

The part he has taken during this rebellion has fully sustained his former character. It has been a careful system of "hedging" throughout; an evident leaning on all occasions to what may have appeared at the time the stronger side, and yet so playing his cards, that with neither party did he *irretrievably* compromise himself.*

It appears that a short time before the outbreak of the mutiny in Oude, he had been arrested by the English authorities—doubtless on very good grounds—and placed in confinement in his own fort at Shah-gunge; but that about the

* This sketch of Maun Singh's character might be applied more or less to the *genus* Rajah generally, though of course there are many exceptions. But I have dwelt upon it at some length, considering that it gives not a bad notion of the principal features of the Asiatic character.

beginning of June (1857) he wrote to Colonel Goldney, Chief Commissioner of the Fyzabad District, warning him of the intended rising of the troops at this station, and promising, if released, to aid the English and protect them in his fort i upon this he was released, when he immediately set about preparing his fort for defence, and raising levies. At last the mutiny broke out at Fyzabad—it is a long and bloody tale, which has been told over and over again—and among those who were brutally murdered was the gallant Colonel Goldney, while a few fugitives who, trusting in Maun Singh, had taken refuge in his fort, were by him protected.

However, it did not suit his plans to keep them very long under his protection, for he was playing a double and a difficult game, the game of "fast and loose;" he had done sufficient to produce as evidence of his loyalty to our cause in case it should be advisable, while he had not done enough to compromise himself with the Sepoys, should they prove triumphant; so, pretending that he could no longer protect the fugitives from the fury of the mutineers, he launched them in boats upon the Gograh, and dropping down the river, accompanied by some of Maun Singh's levies, they at last—more lucky than many of their countrymen similarly situated—reached in safety the station of Dinapore.

From the position which he held in the country, and from the valuable assistance which it was probable he could afford to us, the most liberal offers were made to him, in case of his remaining faithful to our cause. What were his answers? "Generally," says Mr. Gubbins, "evasive; promising generally well, but complaining that he now neither possessed followers nor guns with which he could assist us." But, though he had no followers and guns wherewith to assist *us*, this treacherous ally discovered in September, 1857 (after General Havelock, failing in his first attempt to relieve Lucknow, had been obliged to fall back across the Ganges, and our cause, in consequence, appeared more hopeless than ever), that it was his policy to take a turn on the Pandy side; and the matchlock-men, who had not been forthcoming at our request, now appeared to swell the ranks of the insurgents then besieging the Residency at Lucknow; and Maun Singh with his followers, when they made their appearance in the city, were received by the rebels with a salute, and other demonstrations of delight! How often after this he changed sides I do not know; but the summer of 1858 (after our capture of Lucknow, be it remarked, and when the star of England, as the shortest sight might discern, was in the ascendant) found this worthy Rajah once more our ally, and—as I have before said—sending messages requesting us to hasten to his relief at Shah-gunge, where he was besieged by the rebels. And thus, in the midst of the rains, with the whole country under water or a sea of mud, we found ourselves dragged from our huts, and sent trudging away towards Fyzabad, to rescue him from a fate which policy, perhaps, but certainly neither justice nor his previous conduct or misconduct, demanded we should shield him from; and I question if there were many among us who would not gladly have heard of the capture of Shah-gunge, and the death, at the hands of his countrymen, of that Prince of Double-dealers, the Rajah Maun Singh.

CHAPTER XXVIII.

The March to Fyzabad—The Kupoorthulla Rajah's Troops—
Sketches on the March—Derriabad—Outskirts of Fyzabad
—We encamp—Maun Singh's Visit to Sir Hope Grant—
Maun Singh's Breakfast, and a few Words about the
Siege of Shah-gunge—Operations of Brigadier Horsford's
Column, and Fight at Sultanpore—Conclusion of Summer
Campaign.

DURING our march to Fyzabad we were luckily favoured with better weather than could have been expected, and though, of course, there were several heavy downfalls of rain, and the country was in consequence rather too soft and muddy to be pleasant, and the so-called road bore a close resemblance to a ploughed field, still, on the whole, we must consider ourselves to have been extremely lucky.

The appearance of the country was lovely: thanks to the influence of the rains, green herbage and bright-hued flowers were appearing through the—until quite lately—hard, barren ground. Our little force was swelled by some native troops under the command of the loyal Rajah of Kupoorthulla, who was to accompany us half way, and there be left for the purpose of keeping open the communication between Fyzabad and Nawab-gunge. The gay colours of these men's turbans, shawls, and dresses, with something indescribably picturesque and warlike in their swarthy, handsome faces, general appearance, and bearing, as they careered about on their horses, spear in hand, or galloped forward in little groups of five and six, scouring the country, enlivened the scene considerably, and added much to its beauty.

The first morning of our march, as I looked upon the surrounding country, I thought that it was, perhaps, better to be enjoying this lovely scenery, with, at any time, the chance of a skirmish, than remaining idle and inactive in our mud-huts. The feathery foliage of the tamarind trees—the dark groves of mangoes—the beautiful date-palms—the dense hedges of the prickly pear—the tangled jungle and brushwood—those charmingly picturesque mud villages, half fortified, and o'ershaded by stately old trees, with generally a pond in front of them, wherein flocks of bullocks, camels, and elephants are drinking or bathing—the fine old gateways, dilapidated relics of bygone times, more unsettled even than these, which stood in many cases at the entrances of these same little village fortresses—the wide-spreading fertile plains, with the green corn just bursting into life—the mass of camp followers, baggage, elephants, waggons, syces leading spare horses, bheestees collecting round a well to fill their *mussocks*, "grass-cutters" riding along on their hardy little ponies, Sikh Irregular Cavalry, and the Kupoorthulla Rajah's followers above mentioned, in red turbans and flowing white robes, be-tulwared, be-pistolled, and be-shielded " up to the eyes"—the karkee-clad English troops tramping along sturdily, the black belts of the Rifle Brigade, the blue cap-covers of the Madras Fusileers, the dust-coloured clothing of the Punjaubee Infantry, contrasting effectively with one another—the rumble of the heavy siege guns, as the elephants dragged them along, the jingle of the harness chains of the field artillery, and the clatter of the steel scabbards of the cavalry—the native police turning out at their different stations to do us homage, with the matches of their rude matchlocks lighted ready for service—the people of the villages lining the streets as we passed through, or salaaming to us outwardly, while they cursed us in their hearts—the neighing of horses, and the shrill trumpeting of the elephants,—made up a scene at once animated and charming, a scene which gleamed gaily in the refulgent sunlight of early morning, which seemed to spread over it like a delicate golden veil—a scene which was distinguished pleasantly from a similar panorama that I described during our march in the scorching, parched, and rainless month of May, by a total absence of dust and hot winds, and by the fresh, green appearance of the country generally.

All, however, was not *couleur de rose;* there were dull, cloudy mornings, when the rain poured down unceasingly, and when our march was far from pleasant, wading through heavy mud and deep puddles, or, in places, swollen streams, encamping on wet ground, in wet clothes, and feeling very miserable; but when are not the bitters mingled with the sweets in this world? what is there which has not its alloy? so, though it might be wet to-day, we looked forward hopefully to a bright to-morrow, and, on the whole, enjoyed our march exceedingly.

During the march a troop of Royal Horse Artillery, 200 English Cavalry, 200 Irregular Cavalry, and a like number of Punjaub Infantry, were detached from the column, to make a *détour*, and, by executing a flank movement, endeavour to drive the enemy into Derriabad, a village two marches ahead, and where our column, coming upon them unawares, might " give a good account of them." However, the movement proved unsuccessful: the cavalry were absent two days, during which time they were able to do very little. The 7th Hussars cut up a few Pandies, and the artillery fired one or two shots at the enemy, or at some bullocks, they were not quite sure which, but inclined to think the latter, from the fact of a wretched bullock being subsequently discovered with a horn shot off!

On the 24th of July we arrived at Derriabad, where we had fondly hoped to come upon the enemy, but we were doomed to be disappointed; and as we rode through the streets of the large village, almost a town, we found them deserted, except by an old woman, shrill of voice and fiery of eye, who stood resolutely over her hearth and home, prepared to defend it, and who amused us considerably by the energetic way in which she strove to protect two horses, in which she appeared to have a proprietary interest, from " being looted," running first to one, and then to the other, as she saw a British soldier, or a Sikh, on plunder intent, approaching either. Besides this aged dame, there was an old fakir, with matted hair, and a naked body not remarkable for cleanliness, who was squatting by the roadside, and appeared to be amusing himself by uttering anathemas and invoking curses upon our devoted heads, ably seconded in his performance by a howling dog, while the embers of fires still smoking showed how recently the place had been deserted by its inhabitants. And so, with an old scold abusing us, a fakir cursing us, and a dog howling at us, and with one or two dark faces lowering at us from house tops and from behind walls, and with the whole place looking strangely deserted and quiet, we passed through the village, and under the high mud walls of its fort, and encamped, after a long, hot march, at the old cantonments beyond it.

Before the mutiny Derriabad had been a station of some little importance, boasting a treasury, a collector, and one or two other civil officers, with a regiment of native infantry as a guard; but it shared the same fate as all the other stations throughout the country; and long rows of roofless huts, and a few burnt bungalows, were all that now remained to mark the old Sepoy lines and the quarters of the English officers who had lived here. At the time of the outbreak the 5th Oude Irregular Infantry had been quartered in these lines, and for some little time it was hoped they would remain loyal; but, on the commanding officer endeavouring, as a precautionary measure, to remove the treasure (about three lacs of rupees), the mutiny broke out, and the Europeans had to flee, all, happily, escaping into Lucknow.

In spite of some pressing messages which Maun Singh sent, informing us that he had only " quarter rations for four more days," and begging

APPROACH TO FYZABAD.

us to hasten on to his relief, we remained two days at Derriabad, not continuing our march till June 26th, and leaving the Kupoorthulla Rajah's followers in garrison at this place. As we approached Fyzabad reports reached us continually of the flight of the Pandies, who, thinking we were getting too near to be pleasant, had already begun to raise the siege.

On the morning of July 29th we found ourselves in the beautiful park-like scenery and among the long avenues of magnificent tamarind trees, with foliage feathery and soft as ostrich plumes, which skirt Fyzabad. Some picturesque old walls, mossy and decayed, and some half-ruined Hindoo temples, with a straggling village or two, stood by the road-side, while crowds of chattering monkeys skipped about the branches of the trees over our heads, or made faces at us as we passed. Here, about two miles short of Fyzabad, we halted and encamped; the cavalry and horse artillery, however, being detached for the purpose of clearing out the town, and following up the enemy, some of whom were still about the neighbourhood; they passed through Fyzabad, an insignificant, dirty Mussulman town, and galloped on down to Ajoodhee, the sacred Hindoo city I have before referred to, and there found a few of the enemy trying to escape across the river (Gograh) in boats. A round or two from our guns quickened their movements considerably, and I believe did some little damage; but they were soon well away, and, as there was nothing left to be done, the cavalry, &c., returned to camp; and thus the siege of Shah-gunge was raised, and Fyzabad, without bloodshed, fell into our hands; while so, to our intense disgust, died away our last fond hopes of a fight and its attendant excitement, the prospect of which had cheered us up continually since we had left our quarters at Nawab-gunge.

It now became evident that a considerable portion of the force must remain at Fyzabad during the rains; and large gangs of coolies were employed in erecting raised platforms of earth for the tents to stand upon, in digging drains, making apologies for roads, and otherwise preparing the ground hard by the old Native Infantry lines—now, of course, together with all the bungalows in the vicinity, mined and destroyed—for our reception. And on the 9th August, all being ready, we moved our camp, and took up our quarters on the ground prepared for us. On the same day a small column, consisting of a troop of horse-artillery, a few cavalry, and the Madras Fusileers, the whole under the command of Brigadier Horsford, marched for Sultanpore, about thirty or forty miles off, in a south-easterly direction. This column was to have marched several days previous to this, but incessant rains had postponed their departure, and even at the time they left, the weather was far from favourable.

I should have mentioned that, two days after our arrival at Fyzabad, Maun Singh came to the camp to pay his respects to General Grant, accompanied by his elder brother Ramadeen Singh, and a few excessively dirty and ferocious-looking followers. He rode up, and with many salaams and bows entered, with stockinged feet, the tent of Sir Hope Grant, who, with Mr. Tucker, the

Civil Commissioner, received him cordially enough; more so, it struck us all, than there was any necessity for, considering Mr. Maun Singh's past conduct.

The elder brother, Ramadeen, is a fat, babooish, good-natured, oily, commonplace-looking man; just the person, judging from his appearance, who would be too lazy and inactive to dispute anything his younger brother chose to advance or claim— an indolent Esau, glad enough to part with his birthright in exchange for repose and quiet. A far different-looking man is Maun Singh; short of stature, spare and wiry, very dark even for a native, short black hair, small but thick black moustache, no whiskers, and with those thin sharp features so expressive of determination and cunning, and not unfrequently of cruelty, which, being pitted with smallpox, made up altogether about as villanous a countenance as one would wish to see: and never, I thought, had I seen a person whose face was a more faithful reflex of his character. After an interview of about half-an-hour he retired with his suite, and a few days later Sir Hope Grant, accompanied by several officers, rode out to Shahgunge to pay a return visit. My health would not permit me to join this party, but I heard from those who went how they fared, which was badly, as the breakfast set before them, being composed chiefly of nasty dishes saturated with *ghee*,* proved no very agreeable repast after a six or eight miles' ride. In fact, Maun Singh's hospitality does not appear to have been overpoweringly great, and

* Bad butter clarified.

several old Indian officers conversant with the ceremonies usually observed in like cases, but neglected or slurred over in this, were inclined to consider the whole affair more in the light of a covert insult than anything else. Possibly this may have arisen from spleen engendered by the bad breakfast; and one must admit that few things would so tend to make men look on things with a jaundiced eye as a hot, eight-mile ride, with nothing but ghee at the end of it.

However this may be, most of Maun Singh's guests returned with a worse opinion of their host than they held before, which is saying a good deal; and they further stated their conviction that the whole siege, from beginning to end, had been a hoax got up by Maun Singh himself, in order to give us a high opinion of his loyalty, as measured by the hardships which he wished to make it appear he had undergone in our cause.

The grounds upon which they formed this opinion were certainly tolerably plausible; the fort presented no appearance of having been besieged, hardly a shot-mark upon its walls; the guns did not look as if they had been fired; there were no corpses to be seen; and when they as'·ed to see the sick and wounded, they were informed that they had all been "sent away to their homes;" and, as some one very justly argued, is it not probable, if there had been any wounded, that Maun Singh would carefully have kept them till we arrived, and shown them to us with a sort of pride, as evidence of the sharpness of the struggle and the obstinacy of the defence? Moreover, would there not of a surety have been some cases of a serious nature, which it would have been impossible to remove within the short time—four or five days—which had elapsed between the raising of the siege and our visit to the place, and who *must* have lain in Shah-gunge till their wounds were sufficiently healed to admit of their returning to their homes, as we were informed they had done? All this looks suspicious, it must be admitted, and I am inclined to think that, at any rate, Maun Singh had very much exaggerated the whole affair, and indeed several of his men admitted that they had never once been on reduced rations; whereas I have before stated that Maun Singh had sent out to us at Derriabad, stating that they were reduced to quarter rations, which proves at least that one piece of deception had been resorted to, to give a high colouring to the affair. When we, in addition to all this, consider the tenor of Maun Singh's past conduct, his shifting from side to side; the necessity there was for him to give us (now that we had the upper hand) some signal proof of his loyalty, to counterbalance his former repeated treacheries, and reinstate him completely in our favour; the very opportune juncture (all things considered) at which this *soi-disant* siege took place; the admirable way in which a deception of this sort would suit his purpose; the man's character, such as we know it to be, which would render a scheme like this, at once bold and cunning, peculiarly congenial, it is impossible to set totally aside suspicion of Maun Singh's conduct in this business.

However, enough of this precious ally, for ally he is at present, and seems likely to remain, as long as it suits his interests, and let us turn to pleasanter subjects, the movements of the Sultanpore column, of which we obtained tidings a few days after it had started, General Grant receiving a despatch from Brigadier Horsford detailing a successful affair in which they had been engaged with the rebels, on his arrival at Sultanpore, on the 13th August, the result of which was that the enemy, who had been posted in large numbers about the village, were driven, with some loss, across the river (Goomtee), but from want of boats, bridges, or material for the manufacture of the same, we were unable to follow them. Feeling very secure with a river between them and us, and proportionally courageous, the Pandies stationed themselves in great force on the right bank, and beat drums, and bugled, and fired guns, and otherwise showed a great deal of spirit, while our troops occupied the village of Sultanpore, situated in a horseshoe bend which the river makes at this point, unable, however, to reply effectively with their light six-pounders to the heavier metal of the enemy; affairs being thus at a standstill, General Grant detached two nine-pounder guns, with a battalion of the Rifle Brigade, as a reinforcement. This detachment marched on the 16th August, and on the 19th, a further reinforcement, consisting of a company of Royal Artillery (Talbot's) with heavy guns, all the remaining 7th Hussars, and a wing of the 53rd regiment (which had arrived at Fyzabad the previous day) and some Madras Sappers, the whole under General Grant himself, started off to Sultanpore; thus leaving Fyzabad almost entirely denuded of troops, there being left in garrison there only a few of the "Bays," some Irregular Cavalry, six field-guns, half an English regiment, and the Ferozepore Sikhs.

I shall not attempt to follow the movements of the Sultanpore column further, but content myself with saying that when the heavy guns, after a toilsome march through the mud and wet, arrived at Sultanpore, and opened fire on the enemy, away they went; the first few rounds were enough for them, and they broke off abruptly their bugling and their drumming, and broke away themselves with much alacrity; upon which General Grant, by means of some rude rafts, pushed over his troops in pursuit, and obtained possession, one after another, of the forts, villages, and strongholds on the right bank. A detailed account of these subsequent operations, consisting chiefly of a series of pursuits and skirmishes of an intricate nature, it is impossible for me to give, not having been with the column; moreover, this is perhaps the most fit point at which to conclude the narrative of my military adventures in India, for it was the stage at which the summer campaign may be said to have concluded, and the winter campaign (in which my health would not permit me to take part) commenced.

Any one who will take the trouble to look at the map, will see, at a glance, what was the state of affairs in Oude at this juncture; the enemy's force consisted of two large bodies, one under the Begum, which occupied the Beraytch district, *i.e.* the portion of Oude north-east of the Gograh; the other, under the celebrated Bainee Madhoo, holding Roy Bareilly and the neighbouring country. This latter force, against which it was intended the first operations of the ensuing campaign should be directed, was, it will be seen, completely encircled by our troops, the cordon passing through Allahabad, Futtehpore, Cawnpore, Lucknow, Nawab-gunge, Derriabad, Fyzabad, Sultanpore, Pertubghur, and back to Allahabad, thus forming a complete chain, which was kept intact by certain small intermediate stations being occupied by detachments of English regiments, and by strong patrols constantly moving between these places. Within this circle, as I have before shown, was Bainee Madhoo, with his followers, holding still some few places, such as Ameatie, Roy Bareilly, and a few other forts, which though tolerably strong were of no real consequence; and this may be said fairly to represent the position of the two forces before the commencement of the winter campaign. I have taken no account of a few other disturbed districts, out of Oude, for though we had several columns employed in scouring Rohilcund, some in hunting down the ubiquitous Tantia Topee, and others down in the Azimgurh district and elsewhere, their operations were of no great importance: partly from their having assumed the character of a desultory guerilla warfare, but chiefly from the fact of its having become evident that Oude was the stage upon which the last scene of this bloody drama would be fought.

CHAPTER XXIX.

How we spent the Time at Fyzabad—A Day in Camp during the Rains—A Dreary Picture—I start on Sick Leave to the Hills—Horse-carriage Dâk—Cawnpore to Delhi—Visit Futteygurh *en route.*

OUR little force which had been left behind at Fyzabad, amused themselves as best they could, killing snakes, catching turtles and alligators in the river hard by, riding about under the beau-- tiful tamarind trees, or by the little mosques scattered picturesquely along the Gagra's banks, or making pilgrimages to Ajoodhea to inspect the many curious and wealthy temples of this sacred Hindoo city : the most celebrated of these being that erected to " Hunooman," the monkey god, whose shrine glistened with jewels, and whose grotesque image received all the homage and adoration which fanaticism could bestow. Ajoodhea certainly was an interesting city, its ancient streets filled with painted Brahmins, of the highest and proudest castes, or with filthy fakirs, who not unfrequently paraded through the streets, without a rag of clothing on their dirty bodies, while their thick, dusty hair hung in matted confusion over their shoulders, giving them the appearance rather of devils than men. Revolting as this was, there were even worse instances, too revolting to describe, of the all-powerful influence of fanaticism, which, when under the guise of religion, can deaden the soul to all sense of decency and morality, permitting its disciples to witness without a blush scenes so hideous as scarcely to be credible.

It was dull enough work in camp now: dull, rainy, miserable days which seemed interminable, or bright mornings almost as miserable, when the sun, sucking the vapours from the drenched ground, generated a close, stifling heat which was almost unbearable. The health of the troops, which for the last month or so, under the influence of change and excitement, had been very tolerable, now began to fail again, and dysentery, that terrible "scourge of armies," set in, carrying off, sometimes in a few hours, many a poor fellow, whose frame was already worn and weakened by the suffocating and unnatural heat, and the fatigues he had gone through. The time slipped wearily by, so there was nothing to do but to wait patiently for the cold weather—oh! pleasant time to look forward to—nothing but a repetition of monotonous, idle days, during which our poor men sickened fast, and lay hovering between life and death in the hospitals, or were borne down by sorrowing comrades to their rude graves. Day after day, with nothing to interest or amuse one, with no event to mark one week from another, with no books, no change, no news, the cheerless time "dragged its slow length along."

Few people who have not passed the rainy season in India under canvas, can appreciate the utter dis-

A WET DAY IN CAMP. 327

comfort of a wet day in camp, the state of hopeless despondency one gets into, the . . . But, let me take a page out of my journal on the subject; I sketched a day in camp in the hot weather, why not one in the rains?

Le voilà: Rain, rain, rain, pouring, pelting, pitiless rain! the whole country converted into a lake, and the scene out of my tent-door dreary and desolate in the extreme; the small dry spot which my native servants, by dint of an old carpet overhead, and banks and ditches all round, have contrived to secure, and on which very damp, cold, uncomfortable and crowded, they are squatting with their brass pots, and bundles of clothes, and cooking utensils, situated as it is in the middle of a waste of waters, bears a strong resemblance to a raft, on which a party of shipwrecked mariners are wandering about the broad Atlantic, or some equally wet place.

It is not pleasant to find the shirt you are about to put on furry with mildew, or that you can wring the wet out of your coat, nevertheless such is, at the present time, unhappily the case. The state of rust and damp everything gets into is perfectly miraculous, while as for some little brass images of Hindoo gods and goddesses, which stand on my table, they are rapidly becoming "jolly green," in the most literal acceptation of the term, and much more so than is seemly or natural for divinities. There are great deep ditches, more like canals than drains, round my tent, full to overflowing, and a frog has lately engaged one of them to give an unsolicited concert in, and is croaking out a husky solo, much more to his heart's content than mine; and for want of something better to think of, I begin to speculate as to whether it is not possible that the huskiness of voice which characterizes the frog species generally, is attributable to their always inhabiting damp places.

The smells of rising vapours are at this moment more various than pleasing, a few horses near my tent, whose bodies are surrounded by a halo, like angels, only it is steam and not glory, have a very strong odour, and the same may be said of some damp natives, the shipwrecked mariners aforesaid, who are making matters worse by smoking the most disagreeable tobacco, the clouds of smoke from which hang heavy and nauseous in the damp air. Every article in my tent has an individual and peculiar smell of its own: some old newspapers, limp and redolent of fresh ink, seem to have just come from the printer's hands, my blankets smell as moist blankets only can, my boots, saddlery, coats (especially the waterproof ones, which "come out very strong" on these occasions), towels, sponge, the very tent itself, all have their own little aroma; while to this must be added a dreadfully earthy smell, the overpowering smell of damp nature, which though not disagreeable in a quiet way, becomes objectionable when carried to this pitch. A wary eye must moreover be kept for scorpions, water-snakes, and the like. I have already been made miserable by the appearance of several small crawling insects, like embryo crocodiles, on the floor of my tent.

The very flies this morning are damp, and

"demnition" cold and unpleasant (as Mr. Mantalini would say), and their liveliness being of a forced and ghastly nature is painful to witness. Such is the state of affairs in-doors, but it is as bad, if not worse without; one or two muddy mortals, strolling about between the draggled, muddy tents, a constant drip, drip, drip, to which all nature bows its head: trees droop, horses, animals, men do the same, and seem to vie with one another as to which shall look the most thoroughly wet through and miserable. Sometimes a horse drawing the picket-posts to which he is fastened out of the soft ground, proceeds by way of amusing himself to (literally) "run a muck," slush! slush! slush! with a huge peg suspended to a rope hanging from his head, and with another from his heels, away across the "lake," over tent-ropes, and through mud,—paying but small respect to those charmed circles, the niggers' cooking places, which it is pollution for the shadow of man or beast to fall upon—till he finally entangles himself inextricably with a picket-line, and is captured; or challenging another horse to single combat, by neigh, and sniff, and kick, and bite, receives a kick for his pains, which disables him, and he is caught, and led back limping through the mud to his proper place, and there made fast again.

But stay!—even as I write the rain has ceased, and the blazing sun come out—ugh!—this is worse than ever. A sensation of sitting over a boiler with the lid off. Prickly heat too breaks out more violently than before, and, although the thermometer perhaps does not stand higher than 94° or

96°, perspiration is more profuse than in the hottest days of May, till one is nearly driven mad by this accumulation of miseries. Such is a day in camp in the rains—does any artist want a gloomy subject, let him illustrate this.

It was at this time that my health, which had been very bad for some time, was such as to oblige me to go on sick leave to the Hills; accordingly I bade farewell to Fyzabad, and, escorted by some of Hodson's Horse, travelled in a doolie to Lucknow, and succeeded, by dint of having a large number of bearers to relieve one another, in arriving at Lucknow in four days, whence having passed a Medical Board, I set out for Simla, in the Himalayas.

I would willingly have given a detailed account of my travels, but space will not permit me to do so, and I must pass over this, the concluding portion of my sojourn in India as rapidly as possible, merely glancing at such objects *en route* as I think may be likely to prove of interest.

From Lucknow to Cawnpore I travelled by " Horse-carriage dâk," as it is called, a mode of conveyance which requires some little explanation. At the time appointed for starting, having previously ordered a "gharree" (or carriage) from one of the dâk-agents, you find said gharree at your door. Its appearance is something between that of a large palanquin on wheels and a green coffin with wooden windows, and on the roof of this extraordinary machine you place your baggage. The interior is much like that of an ordinary carriage, *minus* its comforts and cushions; while at night-time, by placing a board over the "well," formed by the space between the back and front seats, and by laying down a mattress over all, you convert it into a sort of couch, on which you sleep as best you may. The gharree is drawn by an animal called by courtesy a horse, virtually a sort of raw-boned pony, rather above the average height of Newfoundland dogs or donkeys; this wretched animal, the most travel-worn, uncared-for, unhappy-looking brute imaginable, who looks as if his rations consisted of a straw a day, while his groom cheated him out of that, is generally covered with galls and sores, and it is some little time before one can reconcile oneself to allowing so miserable a brute to perform a task to which he is, apparently, physically unequal. But hearts harden in India generally, and in dâk-gharrees particularly very quickly.

All is ready; you enter the vehicle, your servant mounts on to the roof, your Jehu on to the seat, but this latter is, as you very soon discover, merely a matter of form. You shake hands with your friends, shout to the driver to go on, throw yourself back in the gharree, and fondly imagine that the pangs of parting are o'er. Deluded mortal! the smart cracks of a whip are heard, and a good deal of shouting, with other attempts to urge on the good steed whose duty it is to drag you—but the result is *nil;* more cracks of the whip, more shouting—the same result; your driver dismounts from his seat, calls out for assistance to "spoke the wheels," and the "whole strength of the establishment" is put into requisition to overcome *inertia ;* the machine is pushed on a little, and the good steed is pushed with it, at last he begins to exert himself—joyous moment—alas!—his strength is applied to push the gharree backwards, instead of pulling it forward, and by a retrograde movement you find yourself once more opposite the door, with your temper scarcely as good as it was ten minutes ago.

Again the wheels are spoked by some dozen shouting natives, the "galled jade" begins to wince as he feels the pressure of the collar on his old sores, he kicks and plunges frantically, you go sideways into a ditch, backwards against a gatepost, every way but forward, till at last, when you least expect it, and are about to give up the thing as hopeless, it suddenly seems to flash across the horse's mind that it is no use struggling against destiny, or a dâk-gharree, and " like an arrow from a bow"—if I may be allowed to use a poetical metaphor—he dashes forward, the shouting natives shout still louder, the coachman, obliged to run alongside for a short distance, cracks his whip and yells, and finally scrambles up into his seat, and away you whirl at the rate of a dozen miles an hour, with the rickety "trap" shaking, trembling, and swaying from side to side, and behold you are away! Such is about the fashion of it.

After about half a mile at a great pace the horse suddenly stops, and the scene, as I have described it, is re-enacted, till after four or five such stoppages, the miserable nag gets into a sort of monotonous pace between a gallop and a trot, at which he continues till the end of the stage, usually six or eight miles from the starting-place.

Here another horse, woe-begone, raw-boned, and jaded as the first, is led out and harnessed in, and, as if obstinacy at starting were a point of honour to be observed by dâk-horses, he goes through the same evolutions as his predecessor, before he is kind enough to start, which of course he does eventually.

At last sleep overpowers you, and you compose yourself in your jolting bed, your dreams haunted by spectral horses, raw-boned and sore, who are jibbing obstinately, and the next morning, when you awake, behold you have reached the Ganges at Cawnpore. Swollen and turbid with the rains, the river is difficult to cross; but, with the assistance of bullocks and natives, you succeed, after about an hour and a half, in getting over, when you drive to the Hotel, a dirty place, kept by a native, yclept Noor Mahommed, but which affording somewhat better accommodation than a dâk-bungalow is patronized in preference.

There is nothing particular to notice between Cawnpore and Delhi, a magnificent road—the "Grand Trunk"—and a country level as a bowling-green; you pass temples, tanks and fountains, villages, old forts, and pleasant shady topes of trees; over bleak uncultivated wastes, by broken ravines now filled with muddy rain water; you pass swollen streams, or inundated fields, patches of dâl and tobacco and rice, green and flourishing; you sometimes pass——but hold! I am but repeating my description of the scenery which we beheld as we travelled up by bullock train between Raneegunge and Cawnpore, *plus* the effect of the rains, and in truth the description which has answered for the one may do well enough for the other. There is a monotony about the scenery on the Grand Trunk Road, from Calcutta to Umballa, which makes it like a revolving, but never changing panorama: the ingredients of the picture are the same all along; here perhaps a temple may stand alongside a village, there it is alongside a tank; here a fountain may be o'ershaded by mango-trees, there it is overhung by palms, but that is all; and the artist taking a sketch of any portion of the Road, and then having a number of copies struck off and stitched together, would have produced nearly as faithful a picture as he who might have laboured up its whole length, and drawn, with pre-Raphaelite precision, spot after spot *en route.**

I went a little out of my way to visit Futteygurh, where I stayed a few days; it is a pretty station, with a large fort, (immortalized by Mr. Thackeray, in his "Tremendous Adventures of Major Gahagan,") situated on the green banks of the Ganges. The gun carriage factory of the Bengal Artillery is situated within this Fort. Here too is the palace of Dhuleep Singh, now used as barracks for our troops; and I was shown, among other objects of interest, the spot where some unfortunate English at the time of the outbreak had been placed against a wall, hard by the fort, and shot down with grape: the marks still remain.

A great number of fugitives, it will be remembered, had escaped from this place, and dropped down the river in boats, only, however, to fall into the hands of the butchers of Cawnpore, who took

---

* Of course I except from this general charge of monotony the portion of the road which I have mentioned in a previous chapter, as passing through the Rajmahal hill, near Shergotty, and the bit which winds round the base of Parasnath, about sixty or seventy miles from Ranee-gunge. With these exceptions, however, there is hardly a rise along the whole extent of eleven hundred miles.

CAWNPORE TO DELHI. 335

them out of the boats at that place, and massacred them. Others more lucky, were taken care of by a friendly Rajah, and escaped with their lives.

Among other places that one passes through *en route* to Delhi is Alligurh, recalling to one's recollection the old wars of Lord Lake, and the terribly murderous assault which our troops made on the strong Fort at this place, the old walls of which are still in existence.

CHAPTER XXX.

I arrive at Delhi—The "City of the Great Mogul"—The "Delhi Hotel"—Scene in the "Chandney Choke"—The "Jumma Musjid"—A Bird's-eye View of Delhi—The Palace—The "Cashmere Gate"—Scene of the Assault.

ON the morning of the 11th September, on waking in my gharree, I found we were approaching the celebrated city of Delhi, winding over a broad plain, dotted here and there with trees, bungalows, and villages, and at this season with a large portion of it under water, till at last, on our left, came into view the red granite walls, the green parapets, the batteries, and formidable looking fortifications which constitute the defences of Delhi, and within this the minarets and palaces, and the dark groups of cypresses, which constitute a prominent feature in that indefinable Orientalism which all these Indian towns possess, but none more markedly than this one. The first view of Delhi is indeed most imposing; apart from the consideration that less than a year from the time at which I saw it, it had been the spot on which the eyes of all the world had been riveted with mingled hope and anxiety; that but twelve months back its traitorous guns were vomiting forth their iron showers upon that small

band of English soldiers whose white tents had
glistened on the now bare, brown ridge, away
there to the right—the ridge at whose base couch
pleasant clusters of bungalows, dark trees, and
fruitful orchards, smiling peacefully, and looking
from this distance as if they had never known war,
nor had been spectators of (and indeed, we may add,
sufferers from) the deadly strife then raging around
them. Independently of these associations, the
coup d'œil is such as at once to command one's
attention and admiration; and, indeed, were I
asked, Paris-like, to which of the two towns,
Lucknow or Delhi, the golden apple of Discord
should be awarded, I would unhesitatingly name
the latter.

The river Jumna, now broad and rapid,
swollen with rain and melting snows from the
hills, and hastening to discharge its turbid waters
into the Ganges, and so into the sea, flows
under the high red walls and forms an effective
foreground to the scene. Enormous adjutants—
not military men, but birds—were stalking about
the marshes, or collecting round some dainty bit
of offal, with that grave air which is peculiar
to them; fine times these birds, with the jackals,
vultures, and others of the obscene genus, must
have had a year ago about this city! Bullocks, as
is their wont, were bathing with their spines and
with only the tips of their black noses and rough
horns visible above the water, looking supremely
indolent and happy. The hot sun streamed down
with terrible force over minaret and dome, palace,
temple, and fort: its rays sparkling back in
dancing showers of light from the waters of the

Jumna, and giving one some idea of what a warm berth this same Delhi must have been in the months of May and June; and what a penalty existence must have been, on that bare unsheltered ridge, when the waters were in and dust reigned in their stead; and when the hot wind tore over the parched and withered plain, bearing its clouds of dry, heated sand towards that little band of heroes, who, with only a thin sheet of canvas between them and the "copper sky" and blazing sun, had undauntedly kept watch and ward over the doomed city, till the time came for them to bring their patient labours to a glorious and successful termination.

Such was my first view of Delhi, such the reflections which it suggested to me.

We cross the Jumna by a bridge of boats, and winding along under the high parapets, and past old massive gateways, guarded by the English soldiers whose bayonets had picked their locks a twelvemonth back—by the red walls of the palace, which look almost too new (so well have they worn) to have been the production of the Moguls, but too fantastical to have been the handiwork of anyone else—by trees, and bungalows, and gardens, curiously mixed up with the fortifications—till we reach a splendid street, the broadest and finest I ever saw in an eastern town, with a stone aqueduct or canal, and a fine row of trees planted down its centre, and on either side shops glittering with the jewellery, scarfs, coloured silks, shawls, and the other manufactures for which Delhi is celebrated.

Having heard there was an hotel, I determined to go there; and my gharree accordingly pulled up opposite the dirtiest, narrowest, and most unpleasant little lane I ever saw, while the driver, dismounting, informed me that up here stood the hotel. Thinking there must be some mistake, I hesitated about getting out; but a free-and-easy and rather dirty Englishman, who made his appearance at this critical moment, assured me that this was the place. Glad to find any one who could speak English, I followed him. I have been in several remarkable establishments calling themselves hotels, but never had I entered one so utterly unworthy of the name as this. It was situated in a filthy courtyard filled with broken-down carriages and buggies, and with piles of *débris* of the most mixed, but uniformly dirty description, while the house itself had the air of a marine-store dealer's shop in a bad way. The room which—carrying out the fiction of calling this place an hotel — acted as "Coffee-room," presented a dingy appearance of chaos, more singular than pleasing. Furniture, new and old, and not a small quantity ante-diluvian; potted meats and treatises on astronomy; faded neck-ties and bloater-paste; preserved soup and books without backs; glass lamp-shades and rusty knives; rakish old chairs on three legs, making love to young bookcases with no books in them; dust also clinging lovingly to walls and windows, doors and chairs, and the articles aforesaid, in a shameless and barefaced manner. In the middle of this a round table, half of which was covered with dust, and the other half with a dirty tablecloth, with, beside it, a dirty khitmudgar, making salaams and requesting you to partake of "all the delicacies of the season," which, when produced, you find consist of bad eggs, fish with a fine musty flavour, butter with a rancid relish, buffalo milk, which (if I may be permitted a Hibernicism) tasted unpleasantly strong of the smell of a *cow-house*, and altogether so exceedingly uninviting a display of *eatables*, that though I had had nothing but a dry biscuit for sixteen hours, I was hardly able to touch anything. Such was "Lewis's Hotel" at Delhi. I hope, ere these pages are printed, it may have been improved; for, until such improvement is made, it is impossible conscientiously to recommend it to the traveller. Finding, on inspection, the remainder of the accommodation equally inferior, dirty and disgusting, I moved to the dâk-bungalow, which is a large native house situated in the main street, and but one degree superior to the hotel. However, I secured a room looking out into the street, which was an advantage; and, sitting at the window, I amused myself by looking at the passers-by.

This street—the "Chandney Choke"—is most striking, with the gay crowds passing up and down it, a motley collection: fat natives ambling placidly along on equally fat ponies, droves of snow-white, big-humped bullocks; a palanquin or two; now an elephant with handsome crimson howdah, now a camel with a string of bells round his neck, which make pleasant music as he trots along; now a Sikh horseman; now a detachment of soldiers; now a party of Nautch girls, with big rings in their noses, and tinselly gewgaws about their persons, tinkling the bracelets on their bare, finely-shaped arms, singing and pirouetting with a sad sort of mocking *abandon*, in hopes of attracting attention; now a knot of little naked boys, rolling one another over in the dust, and playing blithely; or a beggar, deformed and loathsome, crying out in cracked, discordant tones for alms; and always a mass of natives in the rose-coloured turbans which seem peculiar to Delhi, and which add to the gayness of the scene; while the bright, glittering appearance of the shops, which I have before noticed, gives a pretty finish to the whole.

It is pleasant, when the sun has gone down, to stroll along this the Regent-street of Delhi, and mingle with this busy crowd, stopping now and again to bargain for an embroidered scarf, or a piece of jewellery, or pressing on through the crush towards the palace-gates. In walking along one's eye is attracted by a peculiar piece of woodwork, rearing its head ostentatiously in the very centre and most busy part of the street. It is a very simple, rough-looking affair—two upright pieces of wood and a bar across them, a swinging board rather more than the distance of an average-sized man's height from the upper bar, and capable of being let fall abruptly at pleasure, a few steps leading up to it, and that is all. It is the gallows! Here, in the heart of the rebel city, did many a Sepoy expiate his crimes and cruelties, and, let us hope, by his death, struck terror into the hearts of the beholders; here, in this very street, delicate English ladies had been led up and down, as we read, in cruel triumph, exposed to the taunts of the merciless fiends, who sought thus to refine and prolong their agony and shame ere they consummated that last terrible act of indignity, which made even death welcome; here, close to the spot where the brains of children had been dashed out upon the stones, and English officers had been shot down by the men they had led, and lived among; yes—here! on the very ground where the Sepoy had flaunted in all the insolence and bloodthirstiness of his temporary triumph, retribution o'ertook him; and with what terrible force must thoughts and recollections such as these have occurred to the guilty wretches as they stood upon the fatal plank, and looked their last up the fair broad street down which the joyous morning sun glinted bright and clear, seeming to laugh and sparkle in cruel mockery at the scene which he thus illumined.

Leaving this spot, so fraught with interest, I turned towards the "Jumma Musjid," or principal mosque of Delhi—a noble building, approached by a magnificent flight of broad stone steps—when, passing through a handsome gateway, you find yourself in a wide paved court, on one side of which stands the mosque. It is built of a red sandstone, and surmounted by three enormous, white marble domes, narrowly streaked at intervals with black, and the whole finished off by two gigantic red minarets similarly streaked with white, the general effect being grand and imposing in the extreme. This once sacred spot, which not long since it was sacrilege for the foot of a Christian or "unbeliever" to enter, is now occupied by Sikh troops; one of whom volunteered, for a consideration, to show me over it. I

THE JUMMA MUSJID.

determined not to lose the opportunity, and so toiled, and gasped, and panted up to the top of one of the minarets, where such a view burst upon me as repaid me triplefold for my pains. I should fail signally were I to attempt to convey to my reader an idea of the scene which lay spread out like a map beneath me, confusedly grand; the mass of buildings and temples; the vast courts and halls of the palace, the massive belt of fortifications; the glittering river Jumna, winding far away in the distance; the busy throng flocking up the "Chandney Choke;" the labyrinth of narrow crowded streets; the bright cupolas and domes; the dark clusters of trees; the fine old red walls, contrasting effectively with the snowy-white buildings which they enclose—till, with dazzled, weary eyes, one turns for relief to the broad peaceful plain, which stretches out all round, covered with the mouldering ruins of "Old Delhi"—ancient tombs, villages, fine old forts, clumps of shady trees, and miles of fair green meadows, covered here and there with the waters; away and away in the distance, far as the eye can reach—away beyond Delhi, and its extremest outskirts—away beyond the silvery Jumna, and the old palace, and the red walls does the misty view extend, exciting you to expressions of delight and admiration, which lead your Sikh conductor to conclude that you are a raving maniac, who has ascended the minaret for the sole purpose of committing suicide.

As you turn round, your eyes light upon the ridge which our troops occupied during the siege, and your wandering thoughts are recalled thereby to the deadly strife which had raged here. Only last year, and cannon were thundering forth from palace, mosque, and ridge; only last year, and musketry flashed from loopholed houses and loopholed walls, and men fell never to rise again, while others remained maimed and crippled, but heroes for ever; and Nicholson, Home, Salkeld, and many others made for themselves such names as shall ever be proudly and gratefully remembered;—only a year ago all this! and on this very spot; and death was rife within and without these walls, and corpses lay festering in these streets; and now—see how quiet it all is! Can this be Delhi—can this be the city over which the red tide of war rolled so lately? surely not!—and yet that deep dent in the walls of that house hard by looks suspicious, and that rugged round hole through the gable end, which we can see to our left, is not unlike the handiwork of an 18-pounder; and why are those walls pitted as with the smallpox? Can bullets have had anything to do with it? It is not impossible. I descend the winding staircase of the minaret, the exertion of which, together with the panegyric I have mentally been indulging in, leaves me but little breath to describe the palace; indeed, being anxious to give to my reader a correct and tolerably vivid notion of the general appearance of Delhi, rather than to weary him with tedious details, I shall condense my description of the palace as much as possible.

It consists of a series of large courts and halls, in some respects like those in the Kaiserbagh at Lucknow, and among these is conspicuous the noble hall called the "Dewan Khas," which originally contained the celebrated "Peacock Throne," and where the old, oft-quoted inscription,

> "Oh, if there be a Paradise on earth,
> It is this, it is this,—"*

is still to be found.

In this "Elysium," which sparkles with porphyry and cornelian, let into the ceiling and walls, and in the surrounding "Bowers of Delight" (to apply an Eastern metaphor), which are similarly fantastically decorated, now dwell British soldiers; and you may see them smoking their pipes, and whistling irreverently "Pop goes the Weasel," or such-like airs, in the throne-room of Shah Jehan and his illustrious successors. What a short step is it from the sublime to the ridiculous! Private Patrick Murphy now sits and pipeclays his belts where Arungzebe, in all the pomp of majesty and greatness, had spoken forth his edicts in days gone by; while the vast palace of the Great Moguls rings with the hearty jokes and echoing laughter of English infidels; the royal gardens, hallowed by romance, and within the shadow of which Lalla Rookh, as we are told in that exquisite poem, had passed her young days, are desecrated now by stalwart sergeants and privates, who stroll at eventide about the broad stone walks and among the shady trees, "fighting their battles o'er again;" and all the while a puppet king, the last feeble representative of the once all-powerful Moguls, lies a miserable captive within the walls, sick and

* See *Lalla Rookh*.

aged, but with his withered hands dyed with crime, and cruelty, and English blood, forsaken by all except a few of the inmates of his harem, who remain upon compulsion rather than from choice. So is thy glory departed, oh, mighty dynasty of old!—so are thy halls, and palaces, and mosques, even thy own royal persons, in the power of the "accursed Feringhees." *Sic transit gloria mundi!*

I paid a visit to the celebrated Cashmere Gate, and, engaging a soldier who had served through the siege as cicerone, examined the different points at which the assault was made. Here was the ridge before us which had been our position; here our batteries had been posted; there were "Ludlow Castle," and "Hindoo Rao's House," names "familiar in our mouths as household words;" there, away to the right, was the "Water Bastion," breached by our cannon; here, under our feet, was the half-repaired breach which we had made in the "Cashmere Bastion;" while a third crumbling heap of *débris*, away to the left, marked the "Moira Bastion," where the third breach had been made. Every inch of the surrounding scene was fraught with interest and glorious associations. This winding sally-port up to the Cashmere Gate was the spot at which Home and Salkeld had immortalized themselves; the powder magazine, which stands at some distance behind us, was the scene of young Willoughby's noble devotion; and there to the left, behind the long line of wall, fell the gallant Nicholson, mortally wounded; across these broken walls, and among those orchards and ruined villages, had our troops swept on to the assault, over the ditch and up the breach, some through the gateway, and others as best they might, did they come pouring in. "It was terrible hot work, and we lost a many men, just here, sir," quoth my guide hoarsely, and I hoped he was going to wax communicative, but recollections of his lost comrades seemed to crowd thick and fast upon him as he spoke; perhaps the shadowy outlines of the "old familiar faces" dimmed his eyes; at any rate, he rubbed them, and as he did so I felt that he was telling me the story of the assault with a simple eloquence surpassing that of words or rounded phrases, and I seemed to see the ditch beneath me filled with bleeding forms, and to hear the cannon thundering out, with feverish mouths, their harsh and never-varying song; to see the crowded mass of camp-followers, flocking in the footsteps of our victorious troops; to see, pressing on, fighting yet, the shattered, but undaunted column, its track marked with blood and corpses; to see the struggle, sharp and murderous, round the magazine, the winning, step by step, and inch by inch, of the desperate way; the pelting bullets falling in quick showers from the surrounding houses; the rich plunder, as it was borne away by half-maddened soldiers; the six days' fierce fighting about the palace and in the crowded city, and narrow stifling streets; the isolated and desperate conflicts with knots of fanatics, and, lastly, the wild excitement and confusion of victory, the mad joy, so seasoned, though, with sorrow;—all this, vivid and life-like, seemed to be passing before my eyes as I stood upon the bastion hard by the Cashmere Gate.

So, in visiting the most interesting spots in Delhi, I passed two days pleasantly enough, filling up the spare moments by holding a sort of little levies of jewellers, shawl merchants, and others who flock to the dâk-bungalow like vultures round a dead body, enticing travellers, whom they generally find very easy prey, to invest in studs, brooches, and rings, or "Cashmere shawls," made in Manchester.

CHAPTER XXXI.

Delhi to Umballa—Kalka—Travelling by "Jampan"—The Himalayas—Hurreepore—Scenery by the way—Simla—How time is passed there—I leave Simla to return to England—Cessation of the Company's rule in India—The Queen's proclamation—Farewell to India, and to the Reader.

ON again along the Grand Trunk Road, as level and monotonous as ever, through Kurnaul, once our frontier station, to Umballa,* where you change the jolting gharree for a palanquin, and so travel on to Kalka. This little village lies at the foot of the hills; and here again your mode of conveyance is changed, and you enter a "jampan :" a barbarous machine, which looks like a four-post bedstead, curtains and all, which has been condemned to do penance as a sedan-chair, and which is carried by four men. In this you are unable to lie down, or to sit with the slightest degree of comfort, being constantly in dread of tilting over; so that it may be compared somewhat to the sensation of being in an "out-rigger" on a breezy day, though scarcely as comfortable!

* Having referred, in depreciatory terms, to the hotel at Delhi, let me here, as a sort of set-off, mention that the one at Umballa, kept by Mr. Parker, is exceedingly good, being by far the best I had entered since leaving Calcutta.

But all discomfort is forgotten when you get among the magnificent scenery of the Himalayas; perhaps, after a residence on the parched plains, one of the most enjoyable moments of one's life. The ascent, at first, is tolerably easy, winding round and round mountains, on the sides of which the road is cut in the most serpentine manner. It was before sunrise when I left Kalka, and as we ascended, and day broke, the scene was most lovely; and very soon I was sensible of a delightful change in the atmosphere. A cool, almost cold wind, which seemed to breathe fresh life and health into one, came sighing down towards me; and I inhaled every breath of it with a relish only to be appreciated by those who have known what it is to pant and swelter for months beneath the burning sun of India, sucking it in as the wretch who is dying of thirst does the cup of cold water which the hand of charity holds out to him; while it wafted with it the most delicious fresh smell as of new-mown hay, and flowers, and clover, seeming, with Epicurean delight, to extract the sweetest of the fragrance from the rich foliage which clothes the mountain sides, as it swept and whistled down them; the dear country smell, reminding one of old England, and its pleasant shady lanes, and fragrant, sunny hay-fields. More and more lovely grew the scenery; high, magnificent hills crowding in confused beauty together, their tips gilded by the rising sun, their sides still wrapped in shadow, and with the dew yet lingering and glistening on the leaves; well-wooded, too, and with high grass and bushes, and flowers which waved over one's winding path; and now

THE HIMALAYAS. 351

and again a glimpse of the parched plains below, over which the almost sulphurous heat is now rising like a misty cloud. Here, on one's right, an abrupt rise of some 400 or 500 feet, covered with tangled brushwood; there, to one's left, a steep descent of the same distance, with, at the bottom, a narrow gully, through which pours impetuously a mountain torrent, sparkling and bubbling, prancing and dancing along over the stones and rugged bits of fallen rock, and hurrying (oh, foolish little stream!) away towards the sultry plains below.

The villages are few and far between, on narrow ledges on the mountain side, or wherever they can find a level bit of ground to establish themselves upon; which it is difficult to do, for it is a peculiarity, indeed, a fault, in the Himalayas, that these mighty hills do not enclose any widespreading, fertile valleys, but are all crowded together in such a way, that their bases, connecting with one another, form only narrow, rocky passages, or pathways for the mountain stream such as I have just mentioned, much of their grandeur being necessarily lost by this want of contrast. It is all hill, and looks, as one surveys it from some favourable spot, like a rough, boisterous sea, composed of mountain-tops and steep green banks, hill-sides and precipices; a sea in which, far as the eye can reach, away to the dim, purple hill-tops, which form the broken horizon, you can distinguish no calm, no repose; all is tempestuous, and huge billows of mountains come rolling majestically one over the other, each hill seeming, as it were, to grow out of the side of its neighbour.

For this reason it has been difficult for the natives to discover spots to cultivate, and they have been forced to level a series of terraces on the hill slopes, and sow their little crops on these; so that in places you see rows of gardens, or steps, covered with waving vegetation, rising in ridges one above the other, in the most charming manner imaginable, embosomed in the midst of the rugged scenery of the surrounding hills, like a ray of sunshine peeping out from behind a bank of clouds, or a pretty face smiling from beneath a hood.

I made a two-days' journey of it from Kalka to Simla, travelling the first day as far as the dâk-bungalow of Hurreepore, about twenty-six miles from Kalka; and thence on. Between Kalka and Hurreepore lies the little station of Kussowlie, prettily situated on the top of an exceedingly high hill, and surrounded by woods. A church, some few bungalows in the Swiss-cottage style, some buildings for invalids, a dâk-bungalow, and a small native village, compose the station; while a few rosy English children taking "constitutionals," a mounted English officer or two similarly employed, some ladies sniffing the fresh cool morning air with a keen relish, and one or two philosophical natives smoking their "hubble-bubbles," seemed to compose the population.

After leaving Kussowlie, we descend for some distance; then ascend again, and wind and twirl about miraculously, through scenery more lovely than ever, and over the rivers Khutwar and Gumber: shallow bubbling streams, flowing down the prettiest little gullies in the world, and effecting their junction beneath the shadow of some grandly precipitous rocks, 800, or 1000 feet in height.

> "It seemed some mountain, rent and riven,
> A channel for the stream had given,
> So high the cliffs of limestone grey,
> Hung beetling o'er the torrent's way.
> Yielding along their rugged base,
> A flinty footpath's niggard space."

If the Khitmutgar at the dâk bungalow at Hurreepore had been told that I was an invalid, he would probably have given vent to his astonishment by exclaiming "There is but one God, and Mahomet is his prophet!" for the glorious mountain air gave me such an appetite that I felt positively ashamed of myself; while the general exhilaration of spirits, the revival of all one's dormant energies, the glad coursing of the blood through the veins, and the "healthful music" which the pulse once more made, placed me in the seventh heaven of delight. It is impossible for those who have not experienced it themselves, to realize the sensation of the invalid who, languishing and worn out with the sickening heat of the plains, finds himself once more breathing the pure fresh air; once more sniffing in the dewy fragrance of flowers, once more revelling in a temperature cool and delicious as that of an English spring.

Two things are noticeable after leaving Hurreepore: viz., that the hills become grander and more majestic, but, at the same time exhibit a more barren look, being clad principally with the dark clumps of pine trees peculiar to great elevations, while the grey rocks and stones peep out through the scanty brushwood more frequently than heretofore. With these exceptions however, the scenery is much the same, massive, and stupendous as ever; the same winding, twisting road, up and down, round and round, till it seems interminable; the same sheer cliffs of some thousands of feet, above and below one; the same little headstrong torrents pouring down the hill sides, the same simple villages, and pretty terraced gardens. Perhaps, if anything, the road is more broken and rocky, in places running along the stony bed of a half dried up stream, at others deeply rutted and seamed by a watercourse which the melting snows and the rains when they are out come tearing down; here you are travelling down a steep hill whereon your bearers can scarcely keep their feet; there toiling wearily up a slope of 45°, or resting on its summit to gaze upon the lovely scene around; now you are pressing on across a little sparkling river, or along a level, but ever winding bit of road, or halting beside some welcome well, and refreshing yourself with a draught of its clear, icy water, till at last, forty miles from Kalka, you come in sight of Simla.

This charming station, the summer resort of invalids, wearied Governors-General, and Commanders-in-Chief; the spot whither ladies, whose husbands are detained by their duties in the plains, flee for shelter from the furnace-winds and blazing suns of May and June; where *coups de soleil* are not, and punkahs and tatties are unknown; where enlarged and refractory livers, yielding at last to the potency of blue pill, assume once more their ordinary dimensions;

where forage caps may be worn with impunity, *vice* helmets discarded as unnecessary; where, in short, Indian life at last ceases to be a burden. This charming station then, I say, is situated near the summit of Mount Jacko, 7000 feet above the level of the sea, the side of the hill being terraced out, and covered with houses; a large and proportionally dirty native village, a little watering-place-looking English town, with its library and Racket-court; a few larger buildings, the *ci-devant* club (now hotel) to wit, and the Assembly Rooms; a pretty homely church; a quantity of delightful little bungalows in the Swiss cottage style, dotted here and there about the hills and among the trees, with numerous roads cut in the hill side, and carefully railed in, watered and looked after: such is Simla, and a delightful appearance of civilization and comfort does it present.

The view too herefrom is most lovely; in addition to the surrounding scenery which I have described as characterizing the Himalayas generally, there are visible in the distance the white, glistening summits of the "Snowy Range," forming a worthy background to this magnificent picture; while in another direction, on a clear day, one can see the broad hot plains stretching away, dim and boundless, below. But, what is still more pleasant is the blue smoke to be seen curling lazily upwards from a hundred chimney-tops, suggestive of crackling fires within, and snug evenings spent over them, as at home; and oh! glorious moment, when you once more sit over a blazing hearth, burning the skin off your legs in the height of your excitement, and exhibiting a reckless prodigality of fuel, which becomes appreciable only when you receive your bill!

The days here pass monotonously enough, paying visits, galloping, or walking on the "Mall," picnics, private theatricals, love-making and scandal are, after seaside fashion, the principal amusements; but, for the first week or so, one scarcely wants occupation, the pure cold air, the fireside, the magnificent scenery, the pleasant walks, the sensation of returning health and strength, these will suffice for some time, and when they begin to pall on you, I should suggest a shooting expedition into the interior. I had already planned one, and, in anticipation, had slaughtered a large number of fat bears, when my old complaint, which had been smothered temporarily by this bracing climate, but not extinguished, returned with more violence than ever; after some weeks of dosing and blistering, a medical board decided that it would be necessary for me to return to England for the complete restoration of my health, and accordingly, as soon as I was sufficiently well to enter a doolie, I bade adieu to Simla.

Here also, reader, I will bid adieu to you, for I have little more to add: a description of my return journey, *per* jampan, palanquin, and dâk-carriage, to Calcutta would scarcely prove interesting, while of the movements of the troops, now entering upon their winter campaign, I could not speak with sufficient precision to justify me in attempting an account of them. Suffice it to say, that the proclamation which placed Her Most Gracious Majesty Queen Victoria at the head of her

Indian possessions and rung the knell of "John Company," was promulgated, shortly before I left, throughout the land; and was immediately followed by the submission of several of the rebel chiefs, and the surrender of some large forts, *Ameatie*, for example, with a number of repentant Sepoys. It thus seemed probable not only that this campaign would be the last scene of the great drama of the Sepoy Mutiny, but that it would be a very tame affair, less characterized by blue fire, and cold steel, and of a far less bloody nature than the last scenes of tragedies ordinarily are; and indeed it appeared that, with the exceptions perhaps of a few isolated engagements, and of a good deal of marching about of columns of troops, the work still remaining to be done would devolve more on the civil, than on the military powers.*

At Calcutta attempts were made to celebrate the auspicious event of her Majesty's assuming the Government of India, by a display of fireworks, and thirty thousand rupees were expended in Roman candles, squibs, and rockets. Everything was done to ensure this display being successful, and the officers into whose hands the management of the affair was entrusted, laboured like drayhorses to make things go off as befitted the occasion; but, alas! the results of their efforts were not commensurate with their zeal. An unexpected

---

* These lines, which were penned on board ship, have, I find, since my return to England, been completely verified: the first news that greeted me on my return being Lord Clyde's welcome notification that rebellion no longer existed, and that the war was at an end.

explosion during the performance, the eccentric behaviour of fifteen thousand headstrong rockets, that suddenly went off "sky-larking" in every direction on their own account, before they had received any orders to do so; the obstinacy of some "Catherine wheels" which steadily refused to revolve when required, or, to use an old pun of Thomas Hood's, which were not "whizzable;" the misconduct of some other extraordinary fireworks, called in the programme "serpents and cornucopias," which devoted themselves to fizzing imbecilely, looking the while more unlike serpents than anything else in the world—except cornucopias; the unfortunate destruction of an immense wooden edifice erected for the occasion, and intended to represent Mount Vesuvius, which was intended to irrupt after the manner of its namesake, and had for the purpose been stuffed with combustibles, which, taking fire before their time, converted Mount Vesuvius unexpectedly into a bonfire, instead of a volcano, and destroyed it utterly; and last but not least, the fact that a transparency intended to represent "her Majesty on horseback," met with a similar fate, and the Queen was, thus to speak, burnt in effigy, to the no small delight of some disloyal natives who shouted "Wah! Wah!" and seemed to see herein an omen not wholly disagreeable to them. These with a few other *contretemps*, made the Calcutta fireworks rather a failure, and scarcely a cheap three thousand pounds' worth; so with fire and smoke, and booming guns, squibs and crackers, was "John Company" buried, and Queen Victoria

FAREWELL. 359

proclaimed in his stead; so ended the long and unparalleled career of the Merchant Company, which had conquered in its day a mighty empire, and now laid the "brightest jewel in the English Crown" at the foot of England's Queen.

H.E.I.C. where art thou now?—a thing of the past—matter for History! mentioned only as "the deceased," by some few perhaps as the "dear departed;" thy race run, thy Raj over, thy territories and possessions passed to the hands of another! Well! it is the way of the world, John; we must all die some day, the most powerful as the most insignificant—so peace be with thy ashes! Thou hast had a worthy burial, and "God save the Queen" we have chanted as thy dirge. "*Le roi est mort; Vive le roi!*"

Simultaneously with "John Company's" departure from India, I took mine, returning to England in a sailing ship, *viâ* the Cape of Good Hope, and so ended my year's sojourn in Hindostan, which I have roughly sketched out in the course of these pages.

It is impossible for me to shut my eyes to the many shortcomings of this narrative, and, as I can hardly expect my reader to be less discerning than myself, I only hope that he will be sufficiently good-natured to accept, as my excuse, the admission that the greater part of it has been written during a period when ill-health and prostration prevented my giving it that attention which I should have wished, or when duties of an imperative nature allowed me but little spare time for the due revision of these lucubrations.

A temperature of from 90° to 120°, it will I think be generally allowed, is by no means favourable to literary pursuits, however light; and I feel compelled to avow that these Adventures of a Feringhee "among the Pandies," have suffered nearly as much from the overpowering heat as the "Feringhee" himself.

THE END.

www.ingramcontent.com/pod-product-compliance
Lightning Source LLC
Chambersburg PA
CBHW021959160426
43197CB00007B/193